We Are Not Refugees

We Are Not Refugees

True Stories of the Displaced

Agus Morales

TRANSLATED BY CHARLOTTE WHITTLE

imagine!

2019 First US Edition
Translation copyright © 2019 by Charlotte Whittle.
All rights reserved, including the right of reproduction in whole or in part
in any form. Charlesbridge and colophon are registered trademarks of
Charlesbridge Publishing, Inc.

An Imagine Book
Published by Charlesbridge
85 Main Street
Watertown, MA 02472
(617) 926-0329
www.imaginebooks.net

Originally published as *No Somos Refugiados* by Círculo de Tiza
Copyright © Círculo de Tiza (Derecho y Revés, S. L.), 2016, Madrid
www.circulodetiza.es
Text copyright © 2016 by Agus Morales
Published by special arrangement with Agus Morales in conjunction with
their duly appointed agent The Ella Sher Literary Agency and the co-agent
2 Seas Literary Agency.

Cover photo copyright © Rubberball/Duston Todd/Getty Images

Library of Congress Cataloging-in-Publication Data available upon request.
ISBN 978-1-62354-532-1

Printed in the United States of America
10 9 8 7 6 5 4 3 2 1

Contents

Before We Begin

I MET KHALID in an Istanbul apartment in spring 2013. He had fled the violence in Iraq. He was suffering from hypertension, diabetes, asthma . . . he was taking pills of every color under the sun and couldn't stop complaining about his illnesses, even though he'd just received the news of a lifetime: he'd been granted asylum by the United States. At my assurance that an ideal future awaited him, Khalid finally allowed himself to be carried away by euphoria—he lifted his hands as if turning a steering wheel, and then he waved and bestowed a haughty glance on an imaginary crowd. I'll buy myself a great set of wheels in Detroit, he seemed to be thinking.

This is an image that President Donald Trump would like to suppress. With Trump's rise to power in the United States, the construction of the refugee as an enemy—a criminal, a terrorist, a threat to U.S. safety—has reached its peak. The fact that most people seeking asylum in the United States and Europe are like Khalid—ordinary people trying to escape violence—is a reality that Trump and his supporters deny. Refugees, then, become objects of fear; the human dimensions of their stories are erased and replaced by a caricature promoting the agenda of a president for whom fear is politically expedient.

The truth is that the story of Khalid's asylum is an exception. He is part of a minority. Millions of people flee violence every year, but most will never attain official refugee status, whether in the United States or anywhere else. Their requests are likely to be denied because asylum systems, even where they exist, are not prepared to deal with millions of applications. In the case of the United States, new restrictions banning citizens of predominantly Muslim countries (which were challenged in court after they were issued) paint an even more dreadful picture. But most important, many in need of asylum will never even reach the point of being able to apply. The vast majority of those fleeing violence remain in their own countries or in neighboring ones, experiencing scenarios very different from that of Khalid, and many do not identify with the label *refugee*—because they haven't obtained asylum, because they don't want to become refugees, or simply because they don't want to be labeled at all.

Although there is no single, universal refugee experience, most of the people whose stories appear in this book share a struggle to escape conditions of brutality and privation that most of us can only imagine. The paradox is that we tend to focus precisely on these moments of crisis, and fail to understand what happens before or after they flee. We think of them not as human beings, but as either victims or objects of suspicion, depending on our ideology. We tend to define these people exclusively by their wounds.

Before We Begin

But to come closer to understanding their situation, we must listen to them speak not only of hardship, but of hope; not only of moments of crisis and escape, but also the tedium of waiting, and of uncertainty. Only then can we engage in the cultural battle to define who these people are. And maybe the answer is much simpler than we thought.

Over the past decade, I've spoken with hundreds of refugees and nonrefugees. Some of them were unwilling to speak publicly due to fear of reprisal, even death, at the hands of security forces and militias. But many were eager to talk, to give voice to the experience of millions of others like them whose stories will never be heard. Why risk speaking to a journalist, a foreigner and stranger, after you've fled air strikes in Aleppo or gangs in Honduras? I wouldn't have done it myself had I been in their shoes. And yet many of them did. These are their stories.

Barcelona, January 2019

For Anna, travel and life companion, for making me a better journalist, and above all a better person.

For Magdalena and Antonio, migrants.

And grant me my second
starless inscrutable hour

SAMUEL BECKETT,
Whoroscope

"We Are Not Refugees"

H IS LAST ACT OF FREEDOM was to gaze at the Mediterranean.

Ulet was a fifteen-year-old Somali boy who'd been enslaved in a Libyan detention center. He boarded the rescue boat wearing a yellow tank top, with black bruises on his tailbone that were revealed when the doctors lifted his shirt. He couldn't walk unassisted: he was like an ungainly bird with broken wings. The nurses took him into the clinic, and at first, he seemed to be responding to the treatment they administered for dehydration. "Mom" and "Coca-Cola" were the only words he could utter.

Ulet was alone, a child with no known friends or family. The Somalis traveling with him said that he'd been tortured and had done forced labor in the detention center, without anything to eat or drink. According to the medical team on board the boat, he was also suffering from a chronic illness, though we'll never know which one.

It was incredible that he'd made it so far in that condition, to the crossroads of Europe and Africa; to the coordinates where every life begins to matter, if only a little; to the territory where death is explained and becomes news. The symbolic hinge between the North and the South: a haphazard line, in the middle of the sea, that marks the difference between the lives that matter and those that don't; between European land and African limbo.

A few nautical miles, but a world apart.

When Ulet arrived on the boat, he could only stammer, sputter, murmur his wishes. Wearing an oxygen mask, and with the marks of violence on his back, he struggled to survive, clinging on to his life. There wasn't a single familiar face there to encourage him.

After the rescue, the boat sailed on for hours toward Italy. Ulet began to feel better, and asked the nurse to take him out on deck. From there, he watched the rhythmic movement of the waves, felt the Mediterranean breeze on his face. Far from Libya, the inferno of war and torture that had determined the course of his life, he lost consciousness.

They tried to resuscitate him for half an hour, but he died of pulmonary edema, according to his death certificate.

If Ulet had died in Libya, no one would ever have known.

I WANTED TO WRITE a book about people who, like Ulet, are fleeing war, political persecution, and torture. I wanted to write a book that followed the paths of their lives, that didn't end with the traumatic moment of war or with the joy of finding refuge. I wanted to write an endless book, full of stories that went on forever. I wanted to write a book about the people that both official and unofficial sectors in the West are trying to turn into the enemy of the twenty-first century.

I wanted to write a book about refugees.

I had almost finished it when I thought of Ulet. And I realized he wasn't a refugee.

I thought of Ronyo, a teacher from South Sudan, who was still in his own country. And I realized he wasn't a refugee.

I thought of Julienne, a Congolese woman who'd been raped by the Interahamwe militia. And I realized she wasn't a refugee either.

Then I thought of those who were, at least in theory: Sonam, a Tibetan librarian in India; Akram, a businessman from Aleppo in the Greek port of Lesbos; Salah, a young Syrian who was granted asylum in Norway. And I realized they didn't identify as refugees.

The librarian was born in exile in India, and he identified only as Tibetan: he didn't feel like he had anything in common with Syrians or Afghans fleeing from war.

The businessman from Aleppo had plenty of money before the war, and he said he had nothing in common with the refugees who were fleeing northward.

The young Syrian granted asylum in Norway had become part of a global minority that enjoys relative freedom of movement. He knew he no longer had anything in common with those risking their lives at sea.

Seventeen countries and around two hundred interviews later, I realized that the word *refugee* is used mostly in the countries that host them. For the displaced people whose voices we hear in this book, the word *refugee* acquires its meaning when they attempt to defend their rights and seek international protection, but it is rarely one they use to refer to themselves. Perhaps the word *refugee,* so often repeated by Western media, is meant mainly for a Western audience.

According to the Convention Relating to the Status of Refugees—the famous Geneva Convention of 1951—a refugee is someone "who, as a result of events occurred before January 1 1951 and owing to well-founded fears of persecution on the basis of race, religion, nationality, belonging to a given social group, or for political opinions, finds themselves outside their country of nationality."

Here, the word *events* refers to World War II. The Geneva Convention and the UN High Commissioner for Refugees (UNHCR) were established, in the beginning, to serve Europeans. Many refugees were illustrious figures: writers, painters, scientists. In these instances, the refugee carried an aura of prestige and was seen as deserving, persecuted, and fleeing brutality.

Now, war is located elsewhere, and (non) refugees are, too. Some 84 percent of refugees come from developing countries. Three of those countries—Syria, Afghanistan, and Somalia—contribute over half of the total. Today, refugees are largely non-European, and they are seen as persecuted and fleeing brutality—but undeserving.

These refugees make up almost 1 percent of the world's population. More than sixty-eight million people. Barely a third of them are in fact refugees who have crossed international borders, and almost all the others are internally displaced people, also known as *IDPs*: this isn't just a refugee crisis. Almost nine out of ten live in developing countries: this isn't just an American or a European crisis.

Is almost 1 percent of the world's population an accurate figure? The official figures from the United Nations (UN) do not include, for example, the Central Americans fleeing from gangs and trying to cross Mexico to reach the United States because such people are considered by the United Nations to be migrants, not refugees. Often they face death if they dare to return home to countries like Honduras, where the daily murder rate is higher than that of Iraq.

There have never been as many refugees as there are now.

There have never been as many refugees in poor countries as there are now.

There have never been so many people fleeing war zones and other crises, vulnerable people for whom we have no collective name. This book is about both refugees and nonrefugees. About those who have arrived, and those who never will. About people in Hamburg, Oslo, and Barcelona, but also—and especially—in Bangui, Dharamsala, Tapachula, and Zaatari. Because those are the scenes of populations in motion, forced to flee from violence: Africa, Asia, the Americas, the Middle East. And also Europe.

There's no portrait of refugees as the invading enemy in this book, of the kind that certain sectors of the right want to construct: there's no Islamophobia, no racism, no defense of borders.

There's no portrait of the vulnerable friend in this book, of the kind that certain sectors of the left want to construct: there are no angelic figures, no pious lies, no defense of open borders.

But there's no false sense of impartiality in this book, either: there are people who struggle, who cry, who get angry, who refuse to give up; who try again, and again, and again.

And there is also injustice. Because sometimes the world is a terrible place.

AFTER ARRIVING in the Italian port of Vibo Valentia, the body of Ulet, the fifteen-year-old Somali boy rescued on the high seas, was removed in a wooden coffin.

The Italian police said they were looking for somewhere to bury him, which was no easy task because Vibo Valentia was a small city, with no room in any of the local cemeteries for this Somali who crossed the Horn of Africa to reach Libya, who was enslaved in a detention center, who was beaten and humiliated, who managed to board a small migrant boat and cross the Mediterranean, and whose harrowing story is similar to that of so many others; for this Somali who had the crazy dream of making it to Europe by sea when he was on the verge of death, with nothing but a yellow tank top for protection, and who died fleeing from slavery, at the very moment when he was about to achieve his goal.

For this Somali who was never a refugee.

PART I

Origins
Why Are They Fleeing?

Violence increasingly affects marginalized groups.

GILLES LIPOVETSKY,
The Age of Emptiness: Essays on
Contemporary Individualism

W HY DO WE KILL EACH OTHER? What kind of reason would drive you to kill? Would you take up arms for your country? For your values? For a flag? For your family? Have you ever killed anyone? Would it be easy for you to kill? Do you think the full force of the law would be brought against you? Do you have weapons in your home? And what if you did? What are your limits? Would you kill if everyone around you were doing it? Do you think your neighbor could kill you? Or any of your loved ones?

Have you ever been threatened? Have you ever considered fleeing your home? How long could you endure a situation of extreme violence? What's your red line—for bombs to fall on your house, for a gang to extort money from you, for an army to surround your neighborhood, for a terrorist group to take control of your city? Would you leave your children behind? Would you stay? What if your daughter didn't want to flee? Would you know where to go? How would you plan your escape? What are you waiting for? Would you feel you had the right to request asylum? To have a roof over your head? To eat?

Who would you turn to? Would you kill those who forced you to flee? Why not? And what if those who forced you to flee had also killed your childhood friend? And what if they'd raped your niece? And if you did kill them, would you tell that to those you turned to for help? How much would you be willing to forgive? Would your friends and family accept that forgiveness? How much energy would you dedicate to revenge? How far does your solidarity go? If you managed to escape, would you help those fleeing like you? What price would you be willing to pay? Would you share shelter with another family? What if there were no room for your children? What if the family belonged to the other side?

Have you ever felt persecuted? Do you belong to a minority? Have you ever extorted money from anyone? Have your people ever been attacked? Would you lie about what happened to you in order to obtain asylum? Have you ever been attacked because of your race? If so, did you turn the other cheek? Can you allow yourself to do so?

Is your country at war? Surely it must have been once. Are your parents immigrants? Did they escape from poverty or violence? Or from both? Are you an immigrant? How have you been received? Do you speak the language of the country where you sought refuge? Does anyone speak yours? Would you take a Muslim into your home?

Do you believe walls are necessary? What about borders? What should be done about population influxes? Do you think they should be controlled? Do you feel threatened by those seeking refuge? Would you risk your life and those of your children by boarding a migrant boat, even if you didn't know how to swim?

Do you know what's happening now in Kabul? Or in San Pedro Sula? Aleppo? Calais? Bangui? Peshawar? Dadaab? What do you think of refugee camps? Does indifference mean violence?

Are you a refugee? Can you be sure you never will be?

Origins

"WHY ARE YOU HERE?"

"Here" is the largest Syrian refugee camp in the world. "Here" is the Zaatari refugee camp in Jordan. "Here" is one of those caravans that line the streets and avenues of this refugee camp, named after places like "Downing Street" and "Champs-Elysées": one never knows whether for romantic or ironic reasons. "Here" is the home in exile of a Syrian family that fled from the bombing.

"Why are you here?"

"Here" is a mat on the floor: a father seated next to me smiles, watching over his four-year-old daughter, and prepares his perfect answer.

"Tell him. Explain to this man why we're here," the father says with a hint of irony.

"Sawareekh."

"Missiles," the little girl says in Arabic. She doesn't even look up from her toys as the word emerges sweetly from her lips: sawareekh.

ASKING A REFUGEE what they are doing outside their country is an insult. They've left because they are fleeing from war.

In every civilization, in every era, collective violence has been relentlessly expressed through war. Despite historical changes, despite the most radical social transformations, war has maintained its social legitimacy; it exists and is part of human nature, even if we only see it on a screen. Sometimes we even tell ourselves it's necessary. War has consequences, we tell ourselves, and refugees are just one of them. But then, suddenly, we are troubled by an image: a little boy dead on a Turkish beach, huddled masses of people crossing Macedonia by train, a fishing boat sinking in the Mediterranean. We are moved by compassion. We think—at the same time—that Europe is being invaded by these hordes of people fleeing from war. Millions of people on the move. Diaspora, flight, exodus. That same suffering that we used to view as sterile and distant—that of the wars of others—begins to make its presence known in our own world.

And then we begin to ask questions, some of them selfish.

Why now? Is this the most violent moment in history? Are other countries, about which we know nothing, now living through their own World War II? What can be done to make them stop coming? How can those wars be ended? (Not to prevent deaths, but to make these people stop coming.)

And then, when we emerge from our self-absorption, from the cage of our circular reasoning, we want to get to the root of the matter. Why are they fleeing? And then the question seems to make sense. Origins.

Things have erupted in slow motion. In the twenty-first century, displaced populations are growing because exoduses caused by new wars such as Syria have been added to the constant trickle of people fleeing from deeply embedded conflicts, such as Afghanistan or Somalia, whose roots go back to the Cold War, or to the early years of the new world order. More than a world where war has triumphed, this is a world where peace has failed. Afghanistan, which for thirty years—thirty years—was the country with the highest number of refugees spread throughout the world, is one of the forgotten scenes that best explain why we are where we are: foreign interventions, geostrategic interests, short-term solutions, second and third generations of refugees in exile without any prospects, and, above all, failed peace processes. In Afghanistan, people long ago lost any hope of an end to the violence through dialogue. No one even has any idea who should sit down at the negotiating table.

The anatomy of war has changed. The great conflicts between the wealthy nation-states of the twentieth century are now a thing of the past. So too are the conflicts typical of the Cold War, among countries supported by either the capitalist or communist bloc. The twenty-first century is an era of foreign military interventions (Afghanistan, Iraq), of civil wars (Syria, South Sudan), and of militarized states versus insurgent groups (Pakistan). Deals, networks, alliances. Militias, warlords, paramilitaries: the number and inequality of armed actors compound the uncertainty. A single conflict might involve American drones, guerrilla forces fighting both against a regime and among themselves, mercenaries waging war on the government, and to top it all off, factions demanding the presence of UN peacekeepers. Today, there are dozens of armed conflicts in the world, the majority in Africa and the Middle East. If, like Syria, they are unusually violent, some of these wars can cause massive population movements, but both these and other, undeclared conflicts almost always cause smaller tides of refugees that gradually accumulate over time.

THE JOURNALIST Thomas L. Friedman once claimed that there had never been a war between two countries with a McDonald's. This is known as the Golden Arches Theory, born of the euphoria for globalization during the 1990s. Numerous conflicts since have debunked this theory, but the significant part remains: it's not that capitalist democracies are peaceful, but rather, in truth, that war has been displaced and distanced from the West. So far, Western Europe in the twenty-first century has been the safest place in the history of humanity, with an annual murder rate of 1 per 100,000. From this place of refuge, we have constructed a new, exotic image of war, which in Europe used to be so familiar. Through glamorized depictions in film and on television, we have shrouded war in an undeservedly mystical aura. And we have come to imagine it — arbitrary, meaningless, without purpose — in an African or Muslim setting.

War is an objective, historical fact, which occurs in faraway, non-Western places.

There are two extremes. One: according to scholars such as Steven Pinker, light is triumphing over darkness, and we live in the most peaceful moment in history. The other: according to the UN High Commissioner for Refugees (UNHCR), more people have left their homes due to violence now than at any other moment in history; according to international aid organizations, there have never been so many humanitarian crises all at once.

Why should one reality or another change our perspective on the world? How much are we willing to tolerate? What kind of cosmic cataclysm would it take to awaken our solidarity, or at least our curiosity?

Perhaps none.

This chapter, on origins, tells three stories about war: Afghanistan (and Pakistan), the first war of the twenty-first century; Syria, the bloodiest war of this century; and South Sudan, a war concerning the youngest country in the world.

These aren't just stories of war.

They're stories of our time.

Bin Laden, Refugee

Afghanistan and Pakistan

> September 11 came at the right moment to justify
> America's aggressive military expansionism: now
> that we are also victims, we can defend ourselves
> and strike back.
>
> SLAVOJ ŽIŽEK

MAY 2, 2011. I receive a call first thing in the morning about a story I need to cover for Agencia EFE, the Spanish news agency I work for. It's a warm summer morning in Pakistan, and the sun's first rays are shining brightly into my east-facing office. Outside there are no cries, helicopters, or military vehicles. There's no sound in the streets, or anything to suggest that the history of this part of the world has just changed forever.

The news is of the killing of the world's most wanted terrorist, Osama bin Laden. The earliest leaks say the attack took place "in the outskirts" of Islamabad, where I work as a correspondent. Still sleepy and in pajamas, unable to believe my ears, I delve into my memory of the weekend, in case I happened to attend some party in the area surrounding the Pakistani capital and the scoop had been staring me in the face. The strangest ideas can pass through your mind at moments like this.

Soon, President Barack Obama makes an appearance to confirm the killing of Bin Laden in Abbottabad, a city populated by retired military personnel, about two hours from Islamabad by car. I turn up the volume on the television. Twenty-three Navy SEALs in two Black Hawk helicopters have just carried out a bold operation to kill the leader of Al Qaeda, who was hiding out in a three-story house just a stone's throw from Pakistan's principal military academy, according to the official story. They entered in the wee hours on a night with a new moon, pumped him full of bullets, and threw his body into the Arabian Sea.

Elite American troops. Black Hawks. Osama bin Laden's refuge. Roll the dice.

They had destroyed the West's symbol of evil—the fanatic whose crimes had justified a decade of invasions and exoduses, the man responsible for the deaths of thousands of people and for planning terrorist attacks all over the world.

I get dressed and get my camera ready. While my Pakistani colleague and interpreter, Waqas Khan, is on his way, I call the number of every contact I have—every single one—who might know something. The only one to answer is the spokesman of Pakistan's main Islamist party, Jamat-e-Islami.

"Osama bin Laden is the leader of a way of thinking. He isn't alone. He's the leader of the greatest regime in the world."

I call some intelligence sources to find out if the Pakistani army has set up roadblocks, which is more than plausible—the United States has violated the territorial sovereignty of a country in possession of nuclear weapons, governed from the shadows by the military. A country that rejected the West's accusations that it was harboring terrorists, and that had now seen a team of Navy

Bin Laden, Refugee

SEALs kill the leader of Al Qaeda not in the hostile Afghan borderlands, but in a city full of its own soldiers.

As I'm about to leave the house and get in the car with Waqas, my roommate gets up and, still disheveled, starts making breakfast.

"Looks like they've killed Bin Laden," she yawns. "It's going to be a busy day for you, right?"

IT ALL BEGAN on the other side of the border, in Afghanistan. In October 2001, as the Twin Towers still smoldered, some forty thousand American soldiers and four hundred military planes invaded Afghanistan to topple the Taliban regime and dismantle Al Qaeda, the terrorist network it was hosting. The major television channels broadcast live coverage of the dreamlike pursuit of the perpetrator of the 9/11 attacks, the Saudi Osama bin Laden, who managed to escape across the mountainous border between Afghanistan and Pakistan, the Durand Line, perhaps by motorcycle or on horseback. Like thousands of other jihadists, Bin Laden established his new base of operations in Pakistan. It's impossible to separate the history of these two countries: AfPak is the revealing acronym coined by American diplomats to refer to the region. For Washington, D.C., this is a joint theater of operations: AfPak.

But despite its being the setting of the first major war of the twenty-first century, the media never shone a light on the suffering of the millions of refugees roaming throughout the region, even when they began to arrive in the West. When American boots set foot on the soil of this corner of the world, it was hardly a blank page. There were already millions of Afghan refugees in Pakistan and 1.4 million in Iran, the result of over two decades of war and instability. And at the dawn of the new century, a new exodus was about to spill over.

We Are Not Refugees

This part of the globe has always represented a nightmare for foreign armies. Similar in size to Texas, Afghanistan has a population of some 34.6 million. With no coastal access, and divided between north and south by the Hindu Kush and the Pamir Mountains, the country has survived despite being surrounded by three great civilizations and the empires that were founded there: Persia to the east, Central Asia to the north, and the Indian subcontinent to the southeast. Historians have resorted to epic language to describe the famed military defeats that have occurred there: "The Graveyard of Empires." "The Heart of Asia." "The Great Crossroads."

Civilians have paid dearly for this strategic position. The Afghan writer Saboor Siasang tells the story of a man who, despite hating politics (or so he said), would systematically display in his home the gold-framed portrait of whoever happened to be the Afghan leader at the time. His wife disliked the practice, to which he clung increasingly in the face of the volatile political situation, and the country's successive wars. One day, he accepted his son's suggestion that he replace the portrait with a map of Afghanistan. Not long after he did so, their house was riddled with bullets.

One day, I felt as if I'd met that man who always knew which portrait to hang in his house.

Since the beginning of the U.S. invasion, one of the Taliban's favorite places to plant explosive devices had been the road connecting the city of Kabul to the airport. Yellow taxis, children crossing the street without looking, NATO convoys with soldiers taking aim from the turrets, dilapidated cars, Afghans riding bikes in turbans, all-terrain vehicles from humanitarian organizations: a parade of the contradictions of war, waste, and poverty, divided by a thin median.

It was July 2010. Black goats sniffed at trash blooming by the side of the road, as if the highway were a river with life growing up around it. Military checkpoints, birds taking flight, noise, dust, street vendors, downcast faces.

"My son lost his life in an attack on this road," a street vendor told me, staring off into the traffic. "Anything I said about what's going on here would dishonor his memory."

From the road that so hypnotized the street vendor sprung alleyways where the noise died down: a neighborhood with a history of pain in every step, with deserted pathways and blue metal doors. Behind one of these lived Muhammad Khan, a retired employee of the Afghan Ministry of Transport.

On August 15, 2009, five days before a presidential election tainted by fraud, Muhammad was on his way to the Ministry to collect his pension. A suicide bomber at the wheel of an all-terrain vehicle loaded with explosives detonated his bombs near the NATO headquarters and the U.S. embassy, in the unprotected heart of Kabul. Seven people were killed and ninety-one injured.

Muhammad was among them.

"A vehicle arrived suddenly, and exploded. I was seriously injured. I spent four months in the hospital. I had three surgeries—on my stomach, on my liver, on . . ."

The old man paused. He lifted his ochre tunic to reveal a swollen abdomen, a map of infected scars. The surgery cost him forty thousand afghanis (over six hundred U.S. dollars). In Afghanistan, the average income per capita is less than that.

"I can't support my family," he said, stroking his granddaughter's hair.

"Do you think things in Afghanistan are worse than ever?" I asked.

"Can't you see? Anyone can see," the old man answered, somewhat annoyed by my ridiculous question. "Not that I can judge anymore, since I spend all day in bed."

We Are Not Refugees

Muhammad bowed his head. His pride was wounded. Suddenly, he raised his cane and declared himself a "revolutionary," a seeker of change, a dreamer. What did he mean by "revolutionary"? The old man clarified that the word had nothing to do with communism, nothing to do with the regimes that the Soviet Union installed in Kabul during the Cold War. He didn't support the Russians. Nor did he support the Americans who had invaded his country at the beginning of the new century. Nor did he support the Taliban, who were now threatening to return to power. He was a revolutionary because, even though he was retired, he hadn't lost hope that the Afghan people would one day rise up.

Muhammad didn't belong to anyone. At sixty-five, he didn't need anyone to explain the story of the portrait of the leader and the map to him.

"I have no opinion about the peace process between the Afghan government and the Taliban," he said at the end of our conversation, sitting with his cane in his hand. "We have to support this government, because it's the government we have right now."

I HEAD TOWARD Islamabad by car, in the direction of Bin Laden's final residence in Abbottabad, a town flanked by hills that rise before the traveler as the legendary Karakorum Highway, one of the highest in the world, begins to steepen. There are two possible routes. To avoid the checkpoints, or perhaps because I'm entranced by the mountains, I choose the less direct, more scenic route, which meanders along by the Karakorum Highway, passing through peaceful Pashtun villages, among them Murree, a tourist enclave often visited by the upper classes on weekends. There is nobody here: the way is open. There's no sign to suggest that this operation of global dimensions has really taken place. At the wheel, my fellow traveler, Waqas, speeds ahead of those crazed Pakistani buses, an eastern homage to *horror vacui*: an orgy of color, mirrors, lines in Urdu, woodcarvings, religious motifs. We pass a man climbing the road on horseback, clothed in a cream-colored tunic and a pair of wide-legged trousers, the traditional *shalwar kamiz.*

Journalists were aware that Osama bin Laden had taken refuge in this impenetrable part of the world, but the end of his fluid biography seemed, once again, a fiction. There was something about the trajectory of his life and the script of his death—a mask, an exaggeration—that revealed the spirit of the new era. The castle of conspiracies and paranoia, of taboos and fears surrounding terrorism and Islamism in AfPak, seemed to be teetering on the verge of collapse.

I arrive in Abbottabad.

"Bin Laden's house?"

"That way," a Pakistani resident of Abbottabad tells me with a mischievous smile, not hesitating to offer me some tea. It doesn't seem like a good moment to stop.

The soldiers halt me as I'm about to reach the finish line. This haven of peace is Bin Laden's neighborhood, Bilal Town, now cordoned off by security forces. I can't see the house, which stands in a clearing of over 1,000 square feet, near the police cordon. I talk to a few neighbors to see if they can access the compound and take a picture of the house with a cell phone, but they ask for too many rupees in return, and Agencia EFE doesn't have the budget for that kind of extravagance. When I try to get through the checkpoint by force, a soldier stops me by putting his hand on my chest.

"Some things should remain secret," he says with absurd haughtiness.

While the journalists threaten to riot, the only person wandering around with a smile on his face, with the satisfaction of a mission accomplished, is the ABC news reporter Nick Schifrin, who has managed to obtain some exclusive images from inside the house—bloodied sheets, medications, chaos—most likely thanks to the first officials who inspected the dwelling.

The neighbors can't believe it.

"It's just a show put on by Obama to get his troops out of Afghanistan," says Faisal Ilyas, a government employee from Abbottabad who lives just a few miles from the house of the sheikh.

Disbelief, skepticism, cynicism.

"It isn't true, the U.S. is lying," says everyone I speak to.

Only the fresh eyes of the neighbors, somewhere between fearful and indifferent, excited and cautious, betray that Osama bin Laden is dead, and they don't know what to do: the hum of ubiquitous, attentively watched televisions in stores, small businesses, and ground-floor apartments provides the soundtrack to their bewilderment.

What story can be told from there? All you can do is speak to the neighbors and see, touch, sense the end of an era; watch as the region once again disappears down the drain of history, losing what little interest the world had in it. And most of all, doubt. The most-often-recalled image of that operation against Bin Laden is not of Pakistan, where it took place, but rather the team overseeing the operation in the White House Situation Room, with a grim-looking Obama, and Hilary Clinton covering her mouth with her hand.

These are the times we live in.

IN 2007, I took one of the best vacations of my life, not far from where Bin Laden was killed, when I visited the idyllic Swat Valley with a friend. It was known as the "Switzerland of Pakistan." We stayed in a semiabandoned luxury hotel, traveled the roads of Swat with a Pashtun who acted as our guide and driver, and who played music at full blast on a cassette player while we stuck our heads out of the hole in the car's broken roof, as if we were riding in a convertible, shouting about who knows what. Swat: only the babble of a river and its splashing against the rocks, cable cars dangling from tattered cables, bare-bones gas stations, bends in the road where breezes blew but time stood still, stands where you could buy meat stew.

Only a month later, the Taliban took control of Swat Valley and established sharia law. There, the radical group was headed by the Mullah Fazlullah, more widely known as Mullah FM for the tirades he broadcast to the valley's inhabitants via radio exhorting them to take up arms, who rode throughout the region on a white horse.

This tourist enclave transformed into a battleground was the unknown scenario of one of the largest exoduses in the entire region. Two million people fled the conflict in the valley. These people are the internally displaced, the IDPs, those who do not count as refugees, those unable to leave their countries and receive international protection. Two million is a tremendous figure that passes unnoticed amid terrorism, jihad, the destabilization of the country, questions of national security, and all those words gilded with threats that represent only the shell of a much harsher, more painful reality: that of people dying and fleeing from bombs.

Swat leapt into the international headlines when the Taliban, after a series of battles, managed to position itself around sixty miles south of Islamabad, and speculation intensified about what the militant Islamist group would do if it got hold of a nuclear weapon. The furor drove the army to launch a military operation to oust the Taliban from the valley. This was the setting in which Malala Yousafzai, the Pakistani student who wrote a blog for the BBC about life under the yoke of the Taliban, came close to being murdered. Convinced of her cause as a promotor of girls' education, Malala challenged the radicals, spoke in defense of the rights of women, and ended up becoming, at only seventeen, the youngest-ever winner of the Nobel Peace Prize.

Amid that infernal situation, in an area of the valley reconquered by the Pakistani authorities, the army launched a remarkable pilot program to convince journalists that it was reintegrating members of the Taliban into society. The idea was to set up two reeducation centers to reform militants and potential "terrorists." The Taliban recruited from among broken families of lower socioeconomic categories, but although the cliché goes that terrorism emerges from poverty, the exploitation of grievances is a much more effective strategy: the son of a Pakistani killed in a military attack made an ideal recruit for the Taliban.

The soldiers gave us brochures detailing how 40 percent of the students joined these programs "voluntarily," and another 40 percent consisted of militants who'd been arrested by the authorities and obliged to attend this kind of reeducation camp. Detox centers. Religious and social rehab clinics.

"Why did you come here? Were you forced, or did you come voluntarily?"

"I chose it myself. I decided to come. I want to be an electrician," answered one student, twenty-two years old. They had been well indoctrinated to give appropriate answers to the press.

In the adult education center, it was moving to see militants who had given up their rifles absorbed in electrical and engine repair, carpentry, and even sewing and jewelry-making: a group of men were threading colorful beads onto cords to make bracelets that would be a sensation among hipsters everywhere.

Throughout the visit, I couldn't get the soldiers to leave me alone. The army was using security as an excuse to be able to control the press. On paper, journalists weren't allowed to venture outside the major Pakistani cities of Islamabad, Karachi, and Lahore without a permit. We did so all the same, since the permit often never arrived. But we had so much contact with the military that, for better or worse, a strange and dangerous kind of camaraderie and mutual understanding was established between us.

At the beginning of that visit to the rehab centers of Swat, the soldier accompanying us day and night took me aside at one of the numerous military checkpoints and told me that we couldn't go on, that I had to go back to Islamabad since I didn't have the necessary permits to go to Swat. "You know how strict they are about that," he told me. It was a cruel joke. How could I not have permission, if I was part of his convoy? He had a good laugh at my expense. That was how life went in Pakistan—between the certainty that straying into some places could put your life at risk and the feeling that at least part of that surrealist montage was a hoax.

WITHIN TWENTY-FOUR HOURS of the arrival of the press in Bin Laden's neighborhood, the Pakistani authorities decide to open the barrier and allow the journalists in. We enter in a stampede, like shoppers during sale season. We're able to verify that the property is at the center of a plot of arable land, a stone's throw from the Military Academy of Kakul, the West Point of Pakistan and the cradle of its army. A place supposedly under constant surveillance, where the soldiers of Pakistan were trained.

Sheikh Osama had been living at the same compound for at least five years. American sources valued it at a million dollars, which was evidently an exaggeration, though with a lick of paint and a few fixes, it might have sold for a good price. When we approach the house—they won't let us inside—we see the remnants of a fire in the garden adjacent to the main building. This is where the Navy SEALs landed and then went up to the third floor to kill Bin Laden. Everything happened just as Hollywood would have planned it. "Geronimo E.K.I.A. [enemy killed in action]," the commando who killed the leader of Al Qaeda said over the radio. Geronimo—Bin Laden's code name—killed in action. Only one mistake was made during the operation: one of the helicopters suffered a malfunction and crashed. The soldiers blew it to pieces to get rid of it, but the tail was still left behind in that garden. "It's a way of marking their territory, of proving that they were there," a Western intelligence source tells me.

I walk around the house. A drab cushion hangs from the barbed wire protecting the property, which is surrounded by cameras and reporters doing live broadcasts. A poor farmer reprimands people for trampling his crops that grow rampantly a few feet from the home of the most wanted terrorist on the planet, along with some wild marijuana. On the door, a dilapidated Commax doorbell with something illegible painted on it— the number of the house?—is waiting to be pressed, but the Pakistani soldiers guarding the entrance prevent us from doing so. I meet a fifteen-year-old kid who says that he lives about 1,200 feet from the mansion.

"Did you see Bin Laden around?"

"No. There were six or seven children under twelve in the house, who spoke Pashtun and Urdu, but they never played with us."

There are kids everywhere. They play in the fields around the compound. They squeal "Taliban! Taliban!" as if trying to simultaneously lure and taunt the journalists eager for information about the most iconic terrorist of recent decades. Spectators begin searching for pieces of shrapnel that might have come from the crashed helicopter. Journalists jostle one another, trying to broadcast from the terrace closest to the building. People take photos of each other. The Abbottabad compound has become a terrorism theme park.

Bin Laden, Refugee

Days go by. The Pentagon and U.S. Central Intelligence Agency (CIA) revel in leaking information. The past is examined. A silent video is released in which an aged Bin Laden, wearing a woolen hat and stroking his beard, changes the channel every time Obama appears on screen. American sources claim to have found porn films on hard drives at the house (did this make the figure of Bin Laden seem ridiculous, or did it humanize him?). The circus nears its conclusion. The Pakistani army closes the perimeter of the compound off to the press. Nine months later, on February 26, 2012, when Bin Laden's death has been forgotten and all eyes are trained on the Arab Spring, his house is bulldozed so that no trace of that strange refuge remains.

A Doctor Is More Dangerous Than a Fighter

Syria

> If the only one bearing witness to the human is
> the one whose humanity has been wholly destroyed,
> this means that the identity between human and
> inhuman is never perfect, and that it is not truly
> possible to destroy the human, that something
> always remains. The witness is that remnant.
>
> GIORGIO AGAMBEN, *Remnants of Auschwitz*

March 15, 2011. The Syrian revolution begins.

The best account I have read of the war in Syria, the one that best tells the story of the millions of civilians fleeing the bombs, is not by a journalist or a historian, but by a sixteen-year-old Syrian girl called Nermin, who kept a diary of her flight on a few sheets of school notepaper. The title is chilling: *Things That Have Happened to Us Since the Beginning of the Revolution in Syria*. Neat handwriting, with red and black letters, a precise and direct language that doesn't dwell on feelings: a journey through the gradual transformation, from the first protests against the regime of Bashar al-Assad in 2011, imbued with the spirit of the Arab Spring, to the bloodiest armed conflict of the century thus far.

August 5, 2011, the protests and the revolution begin in Azaz.

Azaz: a place like any other, fated to suffer through war. Azaz: a rural area with thirty thousand inhabitants in the north of Syria, near the Turkish border, surrounded by olive trees, dust, and rocks. Azaz: a strategic location on the outskirts of Aleppo, a city that was once the economic and industrial capital of Syria but now has been destroyed by bombs and battles. Azaz: one more town to which the protests came, a town that soon fell into the hands of the opposition, a town that's witnessed an endless river of civilians fleeing toward the border, a town that's been viciously bombed over and over by Assad's regime, a town that was occupied by the Islamic State, by the Syrian rebels, and by the Syrian branch of Al Qaeda.

February 25, 2012. Syrian Armed Forces enter Azaz.
February 28, 2012. Syrian helicopters arrive in Azaz.

Nermin writes of clouds. The whole town looks up at the sky as if it were a battlefield, the oracle of war. The whole town is hoping for clouds, storm clouds, rain, because if the sky is clear, a bombing is more likely; the sun means death, destruction, chaos. The regime wasted no time in its response to territorial gains by the opposition: from the beginning, it attacked schools and hospitals, roads and traffic circles, houses and parks. Or it just sent planes to fly over the most densely populated areas, without dropping any bombs. *Tayarat, tayarat, tayarat.* Planes, planes, planes. Everyone cried the same word. That's how you terrorize people from the clouds.

**February 29, 2012. We flee our house in Azaz, and go to
my aunt's house in the town of Ihtemlat. We stay there
for three days.**

Nermin flees with her diary, her seven brothers and sisters, and
her parents. She writes down whatever seems important to her
wherever she can—on scraps of paper, or in a notebook that's
falling apart—then copies it out neatly onto her spotless pages.
For the internally displaced persons (IDPs), for those refugees
whom nobody calls refugees, for those civilians who can't or don't
want to leave their country, the first support network they turn to
isn't the authorities in power or a humanitarian organization, but
their family. Abandoned buildings harbor cousins, distant relatives, friends. Short-term solutions. Improvised shelters that have
often already collapsed.

**March 6. We go to my grandfather Ahmed's house, in Aleppo.
March 27, 2012. We rent a house in Aleppo.**

The family, accustomed to living in the countryside, moves to
the regional capital. To the city where the decisive battle is being
waged. Aleppo: the symbol of a war, destroyed schools and mosques
and highways, hospitals reduced to rubble time and again, that
fall down and are rebuilt—selfless doctors, ambulance drivers
who risk their lives on a daily basis—shifting front lines that leave
entire neighborhoods under siege, without supplies or medical
attention. The conflict in Aleppo forced Nermin's family, like so
many others, to flee. Again: to escape in circles, return, escape,
return, not knowing where to return to.

A Doctor Is More Dangerous Than a Fighter

July 29, 2012. We leave Aleppo and return to our house in Azaz.

August 18, 2012. Bombings. 105 dead and many wounded. We leave Azaz once again, hide out in my aunt's house, and then for four hours among the olive trees.

Among the dozens and dozens of Syrians who have chosen to share their story with me, only one desire is repeated: the desire to go home. They look for reasons to hope, a glimmer of light—a cease-fire, a reprieve from the attacks, a few days without bombings—they tell themselves that things will get better, that they can't get any worse. They don't just say that they want to return; some of them actually do. When Nermin and her family returned to Azaz, local businesses had reopened their shutters, there was food to be bought, the town was coming back to life, and its people were stocking up on provisions in preparation for Eid, the last day of the holy month of Ramadan.

And then suddenly, boom. When the bombing began again, Nermin's father was riding his bike. He fell to the ground, saw several flattened houses, realized one of them might be his own, and went in search of his family. A bus passed as they hid among the olive trees. Are you coming? Yes, we're coming. They went to a camp for displaced persons on the Turkish border. They had breakfast and stayed a while, but then they returned to Azaz. They always returned to Azaz; they always returned.

September 19, 2012. My sister Ramin is engaged to a young man with a house. It was empty, so we stayed here from September 19 until ...

This is where Nermin's diary stops. For the last few weeks, the family has been living in a ramshackle house on the outskirts of Azaz, in the middle of a stretch of wasteland. Sitting on the carpet in the cold living room, Nermin's father rereads some fragments of the diary, turns the pages, checks the dates, digs through his memory in search of more details, reliving the bombs they've left behind. It's November 2012. I ask for their phone number and tell them I'd like to follow their story for a few weeks, a few months. They give it to me.

Six months later, on my second trip to the area, the number I dial is out of service, out of service, out of service. The interpreter traveling with us says the family has fled to Turkey. That's what he says. But he can't be sure.

NEAR NERMIN'S HOUSE and that abandoned wasteland in the north of Syria lies the town of Al Salama, still in Syria, near the Turkish border. The streets are deserted: just a few kids kicking a ball around, women walking hurriedly back home, a silence that swallows the hours. The *mukhtar*, or village leader, says that eight thousand people live there, but it's hard to tell.

The photographer Anna Surinyach and I accept the *mukhtar*'s invitation to his house, even though he keeps refusing to tell us his given name or let us record him. At this point, the town is in the hands of the Free Syrian Army, the armed opposition. Tomorrow, who knows? According to my calculations, approximately half the town's inhabitants must be here, in the courtyard of the *mukhtar*'s house, following the interview and observing the foreigners.

"People are coming here from towns in the north, fleeing the conflict. Tal Rifaat, Marea . . . every ten days, five hundred people come to the border by bus. The war continues because the international community supports the regime. The Free Syrian Army has no weapons, and the regime uses artillery. The people who came here thought the fighting would only last twenty days and that they could stay here and rent, but now the attacks are continuing. When there's a bombing, you don't know where your family is, whether they're being attacked, whether they're in the hospital, whether they escaped . . . the regime is responding very violently: it's using missiles, bombs, chemical weapons."

The most painful thing about the *mukhtar*'s speech is that he made it in May 2013: before the arrival of the Islamic State, before barrel bombs dropped from planes and helicopters became widespread, before the largest exodus of recent decades arrived in Europe.

A young man interrupts the conversation. He knows that we want to interview families who've been displaced by violence, and he invites us to his house, a five-minute walk away. While some people are wary of strangers asking questions and are unwilling to speak, others are eager to share their experiences. We ask the *mukhtar* to excuse us and go with twenty-one-year-old Ahmed to his home. We're invited to sit down again in the tea room. Twenty-three people live in this house. There are many children.

"We came here because of the bombings," says Ahmed, wearing a worn-out Adidas jacket that he keeps on despite the heat. "Life in Tabqa [about ninety miles away] was terrible. The rebels tried to occupy the area, and the regime attacked all the neighborhoods from the air. The war brought everything to a standstill: schools closed, there were no stores to buy food, there was no work. It took us a whole day to get here, moving from town to town, renting cars, dodging military checkpoints, taking the most difficult roads."

The young man looks to his left and sees his mother, Asma, in the living room, preparing vegetables for tabbouleh: parsley, lettuce, tomatoes, bulgur, herbs, a few slices of lemon. We invite her to join the conversation. We go out into the courtyard, which is full of children singing and playing.

"The war began in Tabqa, the area was bombed by fighter jets, and people began to leave. We were afraid, especially for the children. We came here with only the clothes we were wearing, we could hardly bring anything with us. It's easier to die than to go through all this."

The hum of an airplane drowns out Asma's voice. The children raise their hands to their foreheads to shield their eyes from the light, and try to catch a glimpse of the plane. Today, no one seems afraid.

"Before, we would run when we heard the fighter planes. We didn't know where to go, but we would run," says Asma's cousin Fatya, upon seeing our concerned expressions. "But when you hear it day after day, you get used to it. We're not as afraid as we were before. Where are we going to go? There are airstrikes everywhere. Everywhere's the same. There's no solution. There are airstrikes in Aleppo, there are airstrikes in Azaz, there are airstrikes in Tabqa."

We follow the family into the living room, not because of the hum of the planes, but because the meal is ready. A huge group seated around a large dish of tabbouleh. Laughter, games, quarrels. The children are the first to finish eating and go back out to the courtyard. There, they begin to sing the songs of the revolution; the family supports the rebels and is opposed to President Assad's regime, which has been at war with several opposition groups since 2011. The adults continue with their tasks. Only every now and then, among the anti-Assad slogans, a children's rhyme slips in, though it's almost impossible to tell the difference.

THE CENTER OF GRAVITY of the town of Al Salama, overflowing with the displaced, is the hospital set up by Doctors Without Borders. Two buildings: in the first, sixteen beds—separated by gender—an emergency room, a delivery room, an operating room, and, outside, a few tents providing space for outpatient care; in the second, the pharmacy, the storeroom, and an upper floor where the staff smoke and gaze up at the sky.

A Doctor Is More Dangerous Than a Fighter

Doctors Without Borders set the hospital up in a school. Drugs in the classrooms. A rebel flag painted on the walls. Enormous sandbags to protect the facility from artillery fire and shrapnel. A bunker. Sand, lots of sand. And, most of all, patients.

In the women's ward, an elderly woman who has been shot twice in the stomach shows me her wounds.

"I was in Aleppo, in the street, there was fighting, and they shot me. It was some soldiers from the regime."

She can barely speak. Beside her, a young woman exposes her feet, which are covered in burns. It looks like she's escaped from a fire.

"It happened two months ago, at five in the morning, " says Nora. "They launched some missiles against our house and destroyed it. They killed my three sons and one of my daughters. My husband and I were injured, and one of my daughters survived. Now she's living with her grandparents. There's nothing left of my house. They attack all civilians, calling us rebels. It isn't true. I don't want to go back to Aleppo. Ever. I'll stay at my parents' house, or somewhere else."

Some patients enter a phase of resignation and despondency, but Nora is indignant. She wants us to know. She wants to tell her story. That's why, as I was talking to the elderly woman beside her, she uncovered her feet, almost in protest. A sign, an appeal. Most patients avert their gaze and don't want to talk about what's happened to them, but Nora looks straight into my eyes with determination. She has a bitter need to tell her story. I ask her if I can film the interview. She thinks about it and then says no, that we can only take pictures of her wounds. Her desire to denounce an attack by the regime—which is also a need to express and exorcise her pain, to put her thoughts in order—collides with her fear of being identified. In that burning gaze, there is now a strange sense of powerlessness. Denounce an attack, yet another injustice, that would just drown in a sea of information about other wars and attacks, or stay silent and not risk your life to say something that won't change anything in Syria.

The law of silence.

Many, such as Muhammad Abyad, a young Syrian surgeon with full lips, do not respect that law. Muhammad exudes charisma, constantly greeting patients and colleagues as he walks around the hospital. It's impossible to stop him for even a second; you have to follow the trail left by his green lab coat. He cracks jokes, criticizes the regime and the jihadists, and isn't afraid of the black jihadist flags now flying on the outskirts of the town. Syrian doctors are a target in this war, and many have gone into hiding, but when I finally catch up with Muhammad, he immediately accepts the invitation to be interviewed.

"Doctors are facing a lot of problems, they work in a dangerous setting," says Muhammad. "The regime is attacking all of Aleppo's hospitals; some of them have been attacked four times in a row. The security forces are pursuing doctors they think belong to the opposition, and many civilians, too. It's hard to get drugs into cities like Aleppo. Civilians there aren't getting the medical care they need, not even aspirin, or treatment for diabetes. People can't go to the mosque or the hospital because of the attacks and the snipers. Medical supplies are dwindling, and doctors too." During our interview, I learn that Muhammad works in this hospital from Monday to Friday, and at another clinic in the province of Aleppo on weekends. He never rests: he's a machine in the service of the war's victims.

"My work here is mostly to treat those injured in the war, victims of bombings and explosions, but I also treat civilians who need surgery or have other kinds of problems. Many of the injuries I treat are those of victims who were wounded a few days or weeks ago and didn't get the necessary treatment at that time, then they show up here needing surgery."

Of course, there are also fighters among the wounded. In this area, they tend to be rebels or members of Islamist groups.

"A patient is a patient, whether they're a soldier or a civilian," says Muhammad.

A few weeks earlier, a bearded guerrilla fighter had undergone surgery on his hand. According to the medical team, the patient's greatest concern wasn't to be able to write, or eat with a fork, but to have the necessary range of motion to be able to pull a trigger.

Muhammad treated these patients out of obligation, but he never concealed his militant atheism. As the black flags gained ground in Syria, his friends begged him to keep quiet—he was risking his life, they would come for him.

"I'm not going to sacrifice freedom for safety," he said. Some of his colleagues thought his attitude was a provocation. And they kept watch on his movements.

Muhammad invites me to attend a surgery in the afternoon, so in the meantime, I have a few free hours to keep looking for stories in the hospital and in town. I meet one of the anesthetists, Nidal, who tells me that a pregnant woman who arrived at seven this morning has lost her baby.

"She was bleeding a lot. We did a C-section, but we couldn't save the baby. We've decided to send her to a hospital in Turkey, on the other side of the border, as soon as she's stable enough."

Turkey has closed the border, but emergency cases are allowed through. This has given rise to pregnant women arriving at the border as they're about to give birth, so they can leave the country. Or to people paying to flee Syria by hiding in ambulances. Paying, not to cross Europe or board a precarious boat to Greece, but to escape the inferno in which they live.

As I wander around the center of town, I see an old man I know: Ahmed, a local commandant in the Free Syrian Army. The last time I spoke to him was in his office, six months ago, to let him know that I would be conducting interviews and taking photos in the town. He seems somewhat surprised that I haven't gone to pay my respects this time around. He invites me to a cup of tea I can't turn down. He wants me to go back to his office. Not right now, I tell him, I'm waiting to go into the operating room with a surgeon, so I can interview him. Come, let's talk for a moment.

We sit down at a stand selling tea and coffee at the entrance to the hospital. He asks me to give a message to Doctors Without Borders. But I'm not the right person for this. Should I be worried? Is it serious? He says it's important. He asks me if we can record a message. All right, I say. Here? "No, office," he says in English. I insist that I can't right now. Can we do it here? "No, office." I can't. In the end, we decide he'll write the message down on paper. Before we go our separate ways, he tells me out of the blue that he's a supporter of Bayern Munich, a soccer team in Germany. What do you mean, you're a Bayern supporter? Are you trying to provoke me because Bayern just beat Barcelona 4–0?

In the end, he doesn't give me any message.

The woman who lost her baby is evacuated to Turkey. These are the indirect victims of war, those suffering from the collapse of the health-care system. Bullets aren't the only things that kill. In Syria, where, unlike other countries with fewer resources, women were accustomed to receiving obstetric care, the displacement and lack of doctors are leaving pregnant women without the care they need. The list doesn't end there: diabetics who suffer amputations because of lack of access to medications, other chronic illnesses that go untreated, ordinary accidents that become tragedies because there are no doctors left, the spread of cases of cutaneous leishmaniasis (also known as kala azar). Illnesses that were practically nonexistent in Syria, like measles, or which had been eradicated for fifteen years, like polio, have suddenly reappeared as epidemics due to the interruption in vaccinations.

"As far as the government is concerned, a doctor is more dangerous than a fighter. I don't know why," says one of the doctors.

The sun sets, and I go into the operating room with Muhammad. The patient is a bearded man who seems to have no objection to his image being circulated on the Internet, since he's given his permission for the photographer, Anna Surinyach, to be there for the surgery. It's a simple operation on his legs, which are riddled with shrapnel. Muhammad had already operated on him: now he just needs to stitch up the wounds once he's made sure they aren't infected. As Muhammad speaks, calmly imparting harsh criticism of the regime, lamenting the devastation of his country, and expressing frustration at the hijacking of the revolution by Islamic extremists, he skillfully sews up the lesions. Everything is clean, hygienic, green, and quiet. Surgical masks, a hospital bed, the faint sound of the machine tracking the patient's pulse. It's extraordinary that an operating room like this exists in Syria.

That was the last time I saw Muhammad. A few months later, on September 3, 2013, his body was found in the province of Aleppo. He was one day away from turning twenty-eight. A group of armed men attacked the house where the aid workers were living near the hospital and took away only Muhammad, the handsome volunteer doctor who wasn't afraid of anything, who worked seven days a week to ease his people's suffering, who spoke out in person and online against radical Islamism, and who refused to be quiet; the doctor killed for his atheism, who stitched up war wounds with skill and a confident smile; the doctor who refused to become a refugee.

———

We Are Not Refugees

"I DON'T UNDERSTAND why this war isn't being covered."

We're in the Bab al-Salam refugee camp on the Syrian-Turkish border, just a few miles from the hospital where Muhammad worked. Over ten thousand people are waiting in tents to cross into Turkey and leave the horror behind forever.

They are not refugees.

In this camp, there are hair salons and barbers, schools, grocery stores, and stands run by nongovernmental organizations (NGOs) handing out food. There's a wall around the camp's perimeter, which is in fact the old customs barrier. The Turkish NGO İnsan Hak ve Hürriyetleri İnsani Yardım Vakfı (IHH), the American organization International Medical Corps (IMC), and the Syrian Arab Red Crescent all work here. A few tents stand out, larger than the rest, almost at the edge of the road. These are the schools where the children go to learn math, history, Arabic . . .

RIGHT AT THE ENTRANCE to the camp stands the press office of the political wing of the Free Syrian Army. A little farther south is the mosque. There's a shortage of tents, so many families seek shelter inside the temple. I enter the complex and am greeted by the imam, who is teaching children to read the Koran. In this place, I don't sense the suffocating religious atmosphere of other Koranic schools I've visited in places like Pakistan. The Islamic State still hasn't arrived here. A kid in a Barcelona T-shirt starts questioning me. His father comes over to see if he can help us understand each other any better, but the result is even more chaotic. Finally, I realize he's asking me about the latest soccer match, and I manage to explain that we lost 4–0 to Bayern yesterday, which plunges him into a depression which at first seems serious, but he manages to recover in just a few seconds. We leave the mosque, and his father says: "Are you going to Aleppo? Don't go to Aleppo, it's very dangerous."

A Doctor Is More Dangerous Than a Fighter

I approach the camp, where an improvised game of soccer has been organized next to the tents reserved for recent arrivals. Perfect white lines have been drawn on the ground. The bibs are distributed (where do the bibs come from?): there's a red team and a yellow team. The red team plays much better and soon scores a goal. Suddenly, an ambulance passes on the road behind us. Someone watching the game says: "This is a reminder . . ."

That the war goes on.

I walk around the camp. I don't find the kind of consensus I was expecting: yes, many people want to get out, but others are biding their time, waiting for the bombs to fall silent so that they can return to their homes in Syria. Jalid Abu-Muhammad tells me, "I don't want to be a refugee, I don't want to leave my country. I'd rather stay."

I wander around. Children bring their yellow jerricans to the water points set up throughout the camp. They begin to follow me around. I try to detach myself, but they'll be a nuisance to the end. They're the only ones pleased to see a journalist around here. In general, families don't want to talk, don't want their faces to be recognized, for fear of reprisals from the Syrian army or from the rebels. I run into several women having an argument, and the spontaneity of the encounter allows me to get a little closer. They decry the camp's conditions, point at the ground, hold their noses from the smell of sewage. I keep walking. I stop and talk to Saleha, a forty-four-year-old Kurdish woman. She's a widow: her husband died of a heart attack. She's alone with her four-year-old son. They have a pot of rice, which she's heating on a portable stove.

"We came here because of the bombings and the helicopter attacks. And because I'm a widow. I'll go to Turkey, if that's what my relatives want."

It's almost impossible to conduct an interview because the

children have launched a violent shouting campaign. At times, it seems as if the tent is about to collapse.

The children run after me. It doesn't matter how annoyed I get. I'm about to give up. I notice an unassuming tent and decide to knock on the plastic. Muhammad, a forty-eight-year-old, olive-skinned construction worker with gray stubble, a booming voice, and trenchant words, lives here. He invites me in to talk. He lives in this tent with his wife and five children. They're from Aleppo, from the Sheikh Saeed neighborhood, one of those most severely affected by the conflict. Two schools near their house were destroyed by bombs, so they decided to flee.

"The story of what's happening in Aleppo needs to be told more often," Muhammad says as he takes a sip from a cup of coffee in his store. "For the regime, a camera is more dangerous than a rebel. They'd sooner kill a journalist than a rebel. I don't understand why this war isn't being covered."

DOCTORS AND JOURNALISTS.

Doctors: from the beginning of the conflict, humanitarian aid was restricted in the area controlled by the regime—only those with a green light from Assad were allowed in, and this excluded most international organizations. In areas controlled by the opposition, organizations had to negotiate from town to town—with the Syrian Free Army, with the Islamic State, with Al Qaeda—exposing themselves not only to the risk of bombs, but also to the risk of being kidnapped by the same Islamist groups that had accepted the presence of NGOs in the first place.

Journalists: for foreigners, there were two ways of covering the war—either by entering through Damascus with an official visa (something few managed to do) or entering unofficially and embedding oneself in the Free Syrian Army, Ahrar Al-Sham, or the Syrian branch of Al Qaeda. It was also possible to cover the Kurdish zones, but not until later. At that time, there were only those two options, and many journalists, most of them freelancers not backed by large media outlets, entered to tell the rest of the world what was going on in Syria, to try to sell their articles, and to witness the worst war of the twenty-first century to date. Soon the murders and kidnappings began, especially after the summer of 2013. In September of that year, the journalists Javier Espinosa and Marc Marginedas, and the photographer Ricardo G. Vilanova, were kidnapped by the Islamic State. Nine months later, they were released. In July 2015, it was the turn of Antonio Pampliega, Angel Sastre, and José Manuel López, who spent ten months in the hands of Al Qaeda.

But, as always, it was the local, Syrian reporters who paid a higher price. Tortured, murdered, kidnapped, victims of extortion; but not defeated, not silenced, not suppressed. In areas controlled by the opposition, activists and students of everything but journalism became frontline reporters overnight, telling the stories of that black hole called Syria.

One of them is Peshang Alo.

His leg is in a cast, resting on a chair. His laptop rests on his other leg. Peshang opens folders, shows me photos of Aleppo, clicks between windows, plays videos that he recorded in Syria, opens more folders, searches for his live reports from besieged neighborhoods, deserted streets, collapsed buildings. He has an air of nostalgia about him, like a retired soldier remembering episodes from a war that for him is now over. After almost three months in the hospital, he is now with his family in a rented apartment in the Turkish city of Gaziantep, near the Syrian border. We speak just as he's beginning his rehabilitation: his new life.

"Are you feeling better now?"

"Yes, I'm feeling much better. I was in the hospital for a long time. Before, I felt like I was in jail. Now at least I'm with my family."

"What did you do in Syria?"

"At first, I was on a Kurdish protest coordination committee called *Altaakhi* [Brotherhood], in Aleppo. We organized protests, sit-ins, painted slogans on walls, and gradually began sending the videos we recorded out to TV channels. "

Half an hour after a protest against the regime, security forces conducted a raid, sealed off the streets, and arrested Peshang. He spent sixteen days imprisoned in a basement, blinded by the darkness, not even knowing which branch of the police force was holding him. Then he was handed over to the political police and spent another two months in prison. He was interrogated and tortured. He was lucky that his laptop, with all his videos of battles and protests and images of destruction, had been stolen before his arrest. They couldn't accuse him of anything, only of participating in a protest, so he was released.

"Was that when you began to work as a journalist?"

"Yes, the TV stations began to trust the news and videos I was sending, and started showing them because they were well produced and they weren't propaganda. I did Skype interviews from Aleppo for the Orient News channel, and then they offered me a full-time job as a correspondent in Kurdish and Arabic. I reported on the situation on the ground, on how the front lines were moving, on the bombings and the destruction. . . . And I did reports on education, the displaced population, malnutrition, medical supplies . . ."

"You were interested in the human side of war."

"Yes. There are no hospitals, they've all been destroyed. There are only field hospitals, and they can't help many patients because they're so overcrowded, and there aren't any drugs or staff. I experienced it firsthand when this happened to me," he says, pointing at his leg. "When they took me to the hospital, the doctor told me they didn't have enough staff to treat the wound, and the painkiller they gave me had no effect."

Peshang was filming a documentary in the historic area of Aleppo about the destruction of a mosque, the minarets, and some looted relics. He wanted to show what the mosque had been like before and after the airstrikes. He'd already been there several times, but he still needed a few more shots; that last effort would prove catastrophic. He entered first thing in the morning, recorded some images, and glimpsed the flag of the Syrian regime through a small hole in one of the building's walls. He didn't expect any Syrian soldiers to be posted there. Athough they didn't have a good firing angle, the snipers took aim, and Peshang was shot in the right leg. He was taken to a hospital, but the severity of his injury meant that he had to be evacuated to Turkey. He underwent four surgeries. When his leg finally heals, it's possible that it will be a few inches shorter than the other.

"Why do you do it?"

"Because it's worth it. It's a question of will and determination. The fear barrier has been broken. Some of the journalists now working in the country started the revolution and haven't been afraid for a long time. The regime mostly attacks doctors, journalists, and unarmed activists. Those are the most threatened groups."

"But aren't the Syrian rebels or [the Islamic State] greater enemies?"

"No. If a sniper sees a man with a gun and another with a camera, he'll take aim at the one with the camera. A journalist I knew was running through a combat zone with a camera around his neck, alongside two Syrian rebels, and the sniper shot at him, not at the fighters."

"So the regime identifies you as its enemies because you inform against it."

"But we don't just denounce the regime's actions, but also those of groups like the Islamic State. In fact, the Islamic State is more dangerous for us than the regime, because while we can't enter the areas controlled by the government, the Islamic State is right there among us, in the so-called liberated areas. The regime can bomb you or shoot you, but the Islamic State is in our neighborhoods."

"And they also attack journalists, doctors, and activists?"

"The Islamic State doesn't care who you are, it doesn't discriminate. Its directive is to kill. It's killed a lot of my friends. Others have disappeared, and I don't know whether they're still alive. In their eyes, we are all *kafirs* [infidels]. The only ones who aren't infidels are them. If they catch sight of this," he says, showing a bracelet with the Syrian rebel flag, "you're also an infidel, and they'll come for you."

"How do you work?"

"We began with Skype groups to organize the protests and remind people of the place and time—that was the safest system, the regime couldn't do anything to prevent it. Gradually, we went over to YouTube and Facebook. We uploaded videos so they would have the highest number of views possible. Social networks have been key to the process."

"And didn't people question your neutrality? You were still an activist."

"I have a reputation. People know me. I send news and pictures, and the channel has other ways of corroborating that information. If they saw that what I'm offering them isn't reliable, they wouldn't ask me for more. That's how you work with them. They test you over and over, and in the end, you develop a relationship of trust."

A Doctor Is More Dangerous Than a Fighter

"So really, many Syrian journalists aren't journalists. Or weren't."

"The majority weren't journalists at first; they studied other things. But they work for TV stations, and they have a lot of experience behind them, the experience of this war. So gradually they came to consider themselves journalists."

"What have you heard from your colleagues who are still there?"

"My friend Abu Maryam, for example, was kidnapped by the Islamic State. So was Obayda Albatel, a reporter for Orient News. And Samar, and . . . others were murdered, like Muhammad."

"Muhammad Abyad?"

"Yes. The doctor."

No one outside Syria knows Peshang, Obayda, Samar, or Muhammad. They're journalists and doctors who won't appear in the history books, but who, for those responsible for the war in Syria, for Assad's regime and for the Islamic State, represented a greater danger than their own armed enemies.

Plastic Bottles

South Sudan

> Many of the children collected pieces of shrapnel, played
> with them, traded them. When Baby came back with two
> bits of jagged metal, Olanna shouted at her and pulled
> her ear and took them away. She hated to think that Baby
> was playing with the cold leftovers of things that killed.
>
> CHIMAMANDA NGOZI ADICHIE, *Half of a Yellow Sun*

FROM OUR SMALL PLANE, the city of Malakal looks like a desecrated, uncovered grave site. It's March 2014. We see piles of ash surrounded by dead vegetation. Columns of smoke that show where the huts used to be, furrows of earth covering recent wounds—a reminder that this huge corpse, the second-largest city in South Sudan, has been stripped by war of all it once had: oil, dignity, life. Beside it, the Nile River, the escape route for thousands of civilians, flows on in slow motion, indifferent to the destruction, as if wanting to accompany the canoes departing from its shores.

The tiny plane descends in circles, lurching around—I'm terrified—and touches down on a runway where only armed rebels stand beneath the midday sun, unwisely close to the landing area. I'm accompanied on the flight by Albert Viñas, a mountain man, fisherman, and veteran employee of Doctors Without Borders, who coordinates the humanitarian aid mission in Malakal. Behind the armed men, an exhausted Carlos Francisco, who has been in the area for months and will be relieved by Albert, is waiting for us. We climb silently into the four-by-four and head toward the Protection of Civilians (PoC) site installed in the city by the United Nations: the only safe place in Malakal. In theory.

A dry plain divides the UN compound from the city, which had a population of 150,000—about the size of Pasadena, California—and which until recently was bustling with life. For several days, that no-man's-land was the front line of a battle between government troops of the Dinka ethnic group and rebel militias led by the former vice president, Riek Machar, of the Nuer ethnic group. It is a desolate scene. Boots without owners, plastic bottles, skeletons still wearing military uniforms, more plastic bottles, and corpses devoured by kites and marabous, the carrion-feeding birds that have taken possession of this land.

"They've done a better job of cleaning this place up than anyone," says Carlos as we cross the area.

"They're having a banquet," says Albert.

We're about to arrive at the UN's PoC site, but Carlos asks the Japanese driver to stop the car. In the ditch lies a skull riddled with bullets.

"That's a civilian. He was fleeing to the UN compound, but he didn't make it. They killed him."

"Wow. Come on, let's go, let's go," says Albert, eager to keep going, to turn a new page, to start working.

We enter the UN site: overcrowding and chaos. The peacekeepers—Indian soldiers—live separately from the twenty-one thousand neglected people packed into these allegedly safe camps. They are not safe: as soon as we're inside, Carlos points to a hospital hit by a mortar. We leave our luggage at the camp's base (a word perhaps too sophisticated to describe the large tent where the aid workers live, full of computers, plastic tables, mattresses, electric cords, plastic bottles, mosquito nets, more plastic bottles, and luggage). Then we head into the city.

"BY 2040, we expect to have built an exemplary country: an educated, well-informed country; prosperous, productive, and innovative; caring and tolerant; free and peaceful; democratic and responsible; safe and healthy; united and proud." So proclaims a 2010 document from the regional government of South Sudan, a year before it gained independence and became the youngest country in the world. In 2011, North Sudan and South Sudan agreed to hold a referendum, and *Yes* (for independence) garnered 98.83 percent of the votes. Juba, the new capital of South Sudan, donned its finery to welcome the leaders of half the world and declare independence. It was a democratic moment of euphoria and celebration, in one of the most neglected corners of the world. As with the Arab Spring, which coincided with the independence of South Sudan, the aftermath would turn out to be devastating.

The territory that today constitutes South Sudan already had an embryonic national identity when the British abandoned the region and Anglo-Egyptian rule was dissolved in 1954 to make way for the new state of Sudan, which for decades was the largest state in Africa. The verdant South, home to Nilotic, black, Christian, and animist communities, soon rebelled against the desert, Arab North. The two Sudanese wars (in 1955–1972 and 1983–2005) left thousands of dead and displaced in their wake. Then the Sudanese dictator Omar al Bashir, an Islamist who ended up harboring Osama bin Laden, and the legendary John Garang, the leader of the principal rebel movement in the South who died in 2005 in an alleged helicopter accident, sat down at the negotiating table.

How many times have we read the same story? Garang's death left the Sudan People's Liberation Army (SPLA), a rebel group that was the de facto state in the South, without a leader. Despite being permanently at war with the North, political power struggles at the heart of the group led entire communities to slaughter each other. With the support of the United States, which saw the Arab North as its enemy, two military commanders piloted the independence of South Sudan, which came into effect in 2011: Salva Kiir Mayardit, of the Dinka ethnic majority, who became the country's first president, and Riek Machar, from the country's second-most-important community, the Nuer, who was appointed vice president. Machar was one of the military leaders of the South who had caused most problems in the SPLA, and even received military help from the North—a shameless alliance with the enemy—to fight against other factions in the South.

A new country had been born, but the first years of its life weren't going to be easy.

WE LEAVE THE UN CAMP in an off-road vehicle and head toward Malakal, which is occupied by the Nuer rebels led by Machar. We're joined by two European workers from the International Committee of the Red Cross (ICRC). The mission: to go to the city's only hospital, which has been destroyed and looted, to recover medical supplies and equipment essential for treating survivors.

"How long since the fighting stopped?" Albert asks in the four-by-four.

"Ten days, but the rebel militias are still looting," says Carlos. "I don't know if you saw from the plane, but there's smoke all over the city, and they're still burning down houses. The most recent tension was last week. Machar called to tell us not to leave Malakal because the White Army was looting the city. Machar himself told us, that shows how out of control they are. Though in fact, they're doing his dirty work."

The White Army is a Nuer militia allied with Machar's rebels, but whose massacres and ethnic hatred go far beyond the official party line. It takes its name from the white ash that its soldiers spread on their skin to protect themselves from mosquitoes, in preparation for war.

"So you talk to Machar himself?" I ask in amazement.

"He requested an interview with us. He said we can work in the areas under their control. But we've made it clear to him that what happened at the hospital is unacceptable. And you know what he said? 'This is a war zone. I don't think this is the first time Doctors Without Borders has been in a war zone.'"

We keep going in the four-by-four. We pass white buses with the black letters of the peacekeeping missions: UN.

"Machar's plan is to make Malakal the capital of a new Nuer state. There's this idea that South Sudan can be split into the land of the Dinkas—of President Kiir—and of the Nuers and the other ethnic groups. Coincidentally, the land the Nuers want to claim has all the oil deposits."

Finally, we enter the city. It's been raped, looted, stripped of its identity. Machar's rebels and the White Army operate unimpeded. They are free to steal as they like. We pass one building after another, all of them destroyed. White plastic chairs. Plastic bottles. Dilapidated bikes. Plastic bottles. Scrap metal. Plastic bottles. Bones. Plastic bottles. The clothes of the dead. Plastic bottles. Camouflage fabric. Plastic bottles. Flesh rotting in the sun. Plastic bottles. Dogs.

Plastic bottles.

Plastic Bottles

"Look, those guys have a new bike," says Albert, pointing at two soldiers tooling around on stolen bikes. Albert, with his years of experience, doesn't sigh in the face of tragedy, doesn't put his head in his hands or lament what he sees. Instead, he provides a running commentary on what little life remains in Malakal.

We arrive at the Malakal University Hospital. Until recently, dozens of patients were admitted here. But then the hospital was attacked, and when the medical staff managed to make it back, they found eleven dead patients (some of whom were murdered in their beds), three corpses in the entryway, and some fifty patients who hadn't been able to flee—suffering from tuberculosis, visceral leishmaniasis (kala azar), war wounds—with no one there to care for them. Worst of all, some of them had been trapped and were waiting to be rescued, surrounded by decomposing corpses. According to witnesses, several women were raped. The survivors were evacuated by teams of aid workers to the UN PoC site.

That was just a few days ago. The hospital looks like a freshly painted picture of war, whose first layer of memory is just beginning to dry. Like all of Malakal. We are greeted in a disorganized way by a group of armed men who have made the health center into their own private military base. Carlos knows them. He tells them that we're going to recover the medications that were left in the hospital. No problem, says the man who seems to be in charge. There is no sense of trust, but no immediate threat either: just a vague but persistent discomfort, apathy, blank stares. We also ask if we can take some pictures, as if we were asking to take pictures of a park, and they say sure, do whatever you like.

We start loading the Doctors Without Borders and Red Cross vehicles with boxes of medications for black fever and malaria, clothing, medical gowns, even a generator. In the courtyard, fake South Sudanese pound bills, syringes, bicycle chains, debris: the remains of a deranged, irrational, alcohol-fueled attack (there's also the occasional hip flask), so haphazard that the rebels didn't even go about systematically looting the facilities as they usually do.

It's two in the afternoon and the heat is relentless; we're all sweating rivers, but the hospital is cold—freezing in some rooms—and lost in its own abandonment, the scene of an all-too-recent crime. We greet a couple of soldiers again, smiling—they are everywhere—and, as we keep walking, Carlos says, "Look to your right." I do so automatically, without thinking, and see half a corpse in a state of decomposition: a blackened torso, deep red and pink, boiling under the sun. I avert my gaze and keep walking, as if all I'd seen was a tree, trying obviously not to attract the attention of the soldiers: a kind of tacit acceptance that this is a war, and anything can happen without causing a shock. Not even a grimace of horror, much less a reprimand or a frightened look that might make for any awkwardness.

We keep recovering boxes. Anna Surinyach documents everything she can with her camera, creating a precise record of the maze of horror and violence that is Malakal. We go into another room. To our left, a patient's corpse lies in a corner. The stench is unbearable, and we pull up our white T-shirts to cover our noses, but it's impossible not to feel permeated by death, overwhelmed by the succession of events that began in Malakal on that February 18 in 2014. At the end of the next corridor, on a gurney, lies another corpse. Its right leg hangs down without a foot, which has been cut off. The left leg rests on the mattress, slightly bent; the knee is tilted in an unnatural direction, as if the patient had sought a sophisticated kind of comfort in death.

"Have you seen the tuberculosis ward?" asks the medical team leader. "I want people to know about this."

We inspect the whole hospital, recover all the medical equipment, step on the discarded clothing of those who've fled, and on plates of sorghum seeds. I stop to speak to Carlos in the courtyard, but his words are interrupted by a distant gunshot.

"We have to go."

We finish loading the vehicles with boxes. The operating room seems to be among the least affected. Everywhere else is a tangle of paper, scraps of wood and metal. There are indeed differences between the damage inflicted by humans and by nature. In 2013, Typhoon Yolanda, which laid waste to the Philippines and whose devastating effects on a hospital I witnessed first-hand, was far less selective and capricious in its destruction than this war. When we finish our task, one of the Red Cross workers comes up to me after several hours of working side by side—carrying medications recovered from a hospital devastated by the South Sudanese war creates a strange kind of spiritual connection—and says: "Welcome to Hell."

Like in a movie—perhaps absurd in retrospect, but at the time, difficult to contradict.

SOUTH SUDAN WAS BORN with almost 250,000 square miles, an area similar in size to that of France. The Nile runs through this landlocked country, which is encircled by the Nuba Mountains, the Ethiopian desert, and the dense vegetation of Central Africa. In a country with barely one hundred ninety miles of paved roads, transportation of any kind of goods is a serious challenge. Medical support must be brought by light plane or helicopter, and aid organizations practically do the work of the Ministry of Health.

In 2011, peace between the North and the South was considered one of the keys to improving the situation of the country. South Sudan's independence did not translate into peace along the border. Various territorial disputes, some intimately linked to oil, went unresolved, giving rise to some of the first problems with Sudanese separation. One of the areas most vulnerable to disputes was South Kordofan, Sudan, where thousands of refugees departed for South Sudan, flowing mostly into the states of Unity and Upper Nile (whose capital is Malakal). South Sudan had only just come into being, and already its camps sheltered two hundred thousand refugees.

But this wasn't the conflict that caused so much bloodshed in South Sudan. A secondary war began—this time from within. The Dinka president, Kiir Mayardit, removed the Nuer leader, Riek Machar, from the vice presidency, and months later, at the end of 2013, a war broke out which, while it has been understood in ethnic terms, in fact has more to do with the fragile foundations on which the new state was erected: a polarized society and militarized political structures, a past characterized by guerrilla warfare, the highest infant mortality rate in the world, low socioeconomic indicators, and a total dependence, in terms of its gross domestic product (GDP), on the exploitation of oil reserves, whose northward transportation depends on Sudan.

The youngest country in the world is also one of the poorest.

FIRST NIGHT IN THE TENT. Murphy's law: it's pouring rain. Although the noise inside the tent is at times unbearable, the team seems grateful. "We said we were going to write a book about what happened here, huh?" whispers someone whose voice I can't identify amid the pounding noise of the downpour. When I wake up, it's as if centuries have passed. The sun is shining. In my mind, I hear the voice of a Syrian refugee I met in Lesbos, who described his journey to the Greek Island from Turkey by boat, in the early hours of the morning. "A clear morning," he said. It's a clear morning in Malakal, mild, like an Indian spring: all its beauty and freshness are concentrated in a brief stretch of time, which will soon be obliterated by the sun.

"A clear morning."

Plastic Bottles

We go back to the city again: this time, our mission is to recover whatever is left at the looted Malakal headquarters of Doctors Without Borders, which no one has visited since the recent fighting. First, Carlos and Albert are planning a meeting with the rebels. The streets are still deserted. Every now and then, plastic bottles. A red dress. Wandering shadows. Women carrying pots and firewood. Soldiers. White Army fighters. Corpses. Banks, travel agencies, and markets reduced to rubble. Social science textbooks. Suitcases. Gloves. Deodorant lids. Documents full of information. Machetes. Shorts. A ditch full of Tuskers, the most popular beer in Kenya, with its black-and-yellow logo. On one of the main streets, there's a poster of the president, Salva Kiir Mayardit, with a slogan about the struggle against corruption. Only his face is visible; his body has been stripped away by vandals.

The city is now controlled by the rebels.

We arrive at the base of the military leaders with whom Carlos and Albert will be speaking. I wait in our vehicle with the Japanese driver. A soldier comes up to our window.

"What's up? How are things going with Doctors Without Borders?"

"They're progressing."

"In a few days, everything will be fine. In a few days, you'll be able to move around the city, it won't be dangerous."

We keep waiting in the car. We're in the parking lot of the Palace Nile hotel, a dilapidated complex that's been turned into one of the rebels' bases. Soldiers from the White Army circulate throughout the city, keep on with their looting, and arrogantly brandish their automatic rifles like phalluses. Carlos and Albert finish their meeting and come back to our vehicle, which makes a racket on the way out as it plows through piles of plastic bottles.

We drive through Malakal. The streets make up a perfect grid, like that of a large American city that has no need to build upward and lacks the necessary history to have an old downtown with neighborhoods growing up around it. In just five minutes, we arrive at the Doctors Without Borders building, which was destroyed during the invasion. It's been turned upside down: the same violent chaos as in the hospital, as if it had been the work of the same tormented painter. Notebooks. Tolstoy in French: *Guerre et Paix*. Electrical cords. Pills. Canned food. Tubs of ketchup. A skittish cat. Boxes scattered here and there. A dead dog. Toilet paper. Cell-phone chargers. A novel by Antonio Muñoz Molina. Surgical manuals. We pick up the only things of any use: plastic tables and chairs, generators and boxes. We load it all into two cars and leave.

In the afternoon, back in the UN compound, I meet the survivors of the attack on the Malakal hospital. Around fifty people are divided among several tents, in the suffocating heat. Many have gunshot wounds: most seem to be civilians, but there are also fighters, including a member of the White Army—this is potentially dangerous, since most of the victims belong to the Dinka and Shilluk ethnic groups. The interpreter offers to help me speak to one of the patients, but it turns out not to be necessary, since Ronyo Adwok, who is fifty-nine years old, is a teacher and speaks perfect English.

"The fighting began on February 18," Ronyo recalls, wearing a beige tunic and sitting in the tent with some other civilians. "They shot at my house, I fell over and hurt my leg. Now I can hardly walk. They asked us for money, cell phones, and if you didn't give them anything, they shot you. They beat all of us in the hospital. And then the armed men arrived. They even took a few women. Where are they now? We have no idea."

Ronyo was rescued and brought to the UN compound by aid workers. His whole family fled. He was left alone. He says he used to teach high school history. Unlike most people, he doesn't avoid the subject of politics: he says that Kiir and Machar should sit down and try to negotiate. At the end of the interview, when I hand him the photographic consent form, he quickly agrees, and, while signing, intones, as if reading, the following sentence:

"I/am/responsible/for/what/I/say."

A few feet from Ronyo is Yay Jack Abour, who is thirty-two years old. He tells me that he's a student at the Upper Nile University, which I saw a few hours earlier in the city, forlorn and half in ruins. One of his hands is bandaged; his little finger is missing.

"When the fighting began, I tried to flee and cross the Nile. They shot at me as I was running away. When I got to the river, I realized I wouldn't be able to swim, and that my finger had been shot off. I was stranded there for four days. I took shelter in a church full of displaced people. They wanted to kill us all. Finally, they got me out of there and brought me here."

After speaking to Yay, I watch as medical staff change the bandages on a patient with burns all over his body, who spent two days trapped in a tangled bed in the hospital attacked by the rebels. He has no family with him. It's touching to see the nurses laugh as they wrap him in fresh bandages. He laughs too, even though it's almost impossible for him. It's one of the few pleasant moments of the day.

As the sun goes down, I spend some time talking to Kuol, my interpreter. I ask him about the marks worn by different ethnic groups on their foreheads. The Shilluk, the group he belongs to, wear those scars, little flaps of skin cauterized onto their foreheads, with pride. The cuts are made and then left to heal in the open air. The Dinka and the Nuer wear different numbers of parallel lines across their foreheads. These cuts are part of the initiation ceremonies that mark their coming of age, and, since they are inscribed on the body, they hold deep significance for the wearer.

FOR A FEW YEARS, independence appeared to have deactivated internal tensions, but the historic break from North Sudan failed to end the decades-long tribal rifts between the Dinka and Nuer in the South, the resulting hundreds of thousands of deaths by violence and starvation, and the continued recruitment of child soldiers on both sides. The new country was harboring a ticking time bomb: a vast accumulation of weapons, especially light weapons, and, most significantly, oil deposits.

Oil. As is so often the case, oil was at the heart of the conflict. Oil was discovered in 1978 in Bentiu, another of the cities which, like Malakal, was devastated in the war that began in 2013. The American company Chevron poured over a million dollars into exploring the terrain and identified oil deposits in two separate areas, but in 1984, it suspended its activities due to rebel attacks. Oil soon began to be leveraged as part of the strategy of Bashir's northern regime, which had the pipelines necessary to carry the oil out of the country. The black gold was in the South, but only the North could transport it.

If we take a map of the two Sudans and mark the main oil deposits, one by one, with black crosses, we'll see that they are concentrated along the border, especially in the east. What we see will be much more than a compendium of geological curiosities: if we now mark the most violent battles of the last war with red crosses, we'll notice a striking coincidence. If we superimpose an ethnic map as well, we'll see that the red and black crosses are found along the lines separating the different ethnic groups. Oil, violence, interaction among ethnicities. And, nearby, the border.

AFTER THE FIGHTING, Malakal was abandoned. Its one hundred fifty thousand inhabitants either fled to the UN PoC site, climbed into canoes to seek shelter in other villages, or went upstream along the Nile to look for somewhere safer. One of those areas

was Melut, some one hundred twenty-five miles north of Malakal. I arrive again in a light plane, this time flown masterfully by
a Kenyan major. As we touch down, I see not soldiers, but a group
of South Sudanese people packed into the airport, their multicolored luggage ready for takeoff. There are rumors that the fighting
will spread to this area too. People want to leave.

I climb into the off-road vehicle that will take me to the
Melut camps and watch, engrossed, as the contradictions of Africa
unfold before my eyes. Oil fields next to destitute villages. Power
plants. Crude oil storage terminals guarded by tanks. Dust and
heat. Huts. Women carrying buckets of water on their heads,
untouched by progress. All this under the watchful, guilty gaze of
the Nile, which knows and traverses every part of this country.

There are three camps in Melut, on the banks of the river.
One is crowded with some ten thousand IDPs. The second has
some five thousand inhabitants and is still expanding due to the
arrival of South Sudanese fleeing violence in the state of Jonglei
and other northeastern parts of the country. Many have had to
walk for days; others have been brought there in trucks by the government. Here, the whole population is Dinka, the ethnic group
of the president, whereas the UN site shelters 1,168 Nuer, the
group of the rebel leader Machar. This decision was made to prevent episodes of interethnic violence.

These people have fled from war and are living in a camp, but
since they haven't left their own country, they are not considered
refugees.

There are no adults here who aren't senior citizens; there
aren't even any adolescents. The women provide support for each
other; they gather together, share each other's suffering, weave
their own network of solidarity. Around them, like satellites, dozens of children run around, play, and pester everyone in sight.
Many of them are orphans, but the whirlwind of kids flying

around the camp is so vast that it's impossible to tell which ones are alone and which ones have a mother, or at least have someone to mother them.

Alisa Paul shares a cluster of tents with eight other women. She managed to escape to Melut from Malakal.

"I left my husband at home. I fled. I don't know whether he's dead or in the UN compound. I left on foot with six of my children, we walked for miles and miles with this whole group of women, and finally we boarded a truck, which brought us here."

Upon leaving Alisa's tent, I bump into an eighty-year-old man in galoshes. He radiates charm.

"I'm from Baliet County. I walked here. It took six days."

Elderly men and little boys are the camp's only male inhabitants: the rest are either still at war, in other camps, or dead. The women don't talk about them much.

This is a place of exoduses. People come to this camp in Melut having fled in terror from various points in the North. A backyard of war, an archetypal scenario of twenty-first-century violence: if dozens are dead, hundreds are displaced. If hundreds are dead, thousands are displaced. Who should we be paying attention to? Those who are lost forever, or those who are still alive?

I sit down in the camp to review my notes from the last few days. I read descriptions of destruction and of corpses surrounded by plastic bottles, interrupted only by the jokes of Albert, the fisherman who came to coordinate the aid work of Doctors Without Borders. I smile. I'm beginning to understand everything he's done since he arrived here. And I come across the only serious thing he seems to have said:

"We're working for the living, not for the dead."

PART II

Flights
Who Are They?

Einstein, Picasso, and Alberti were rescued from
their status as refugees, and survived to offer the
world their genius. Had they been born today,
they'd probably be lining up for a bag of food, or
waiting to be sent back to where they came from.

OLIVIER LONGUÉ, *Fleeing to Live*

"I'M NOT A REFUGEE. We aren't refugees."

Akram Jabri, sixty years old, still can't believe it. He used
to have a soap factory in Aleppo, the economic capital of Syria.
He made a lot of money. But his factory was destroyed by fighting
between the Syrian regime and the armed opposition. He left Syria
with his wife, two children, his son-in-law, and three grandchildren.
He paid smugglers to get to the Greek island of Lesbos by boat.

"My factory was the size of this whole port," says Akram, holding his arms out to gesture at the port of Mytilene. His backpack
rests against a graffiti-covered wall. He is waiting to set sail toward
Athens.

FOR SOME ANTHROPOLOGICAL REASON that's difficult to explain,
many Europeans were surprised to see this tide of Syrian refugees
crossing the continent with Nike sneakers, iPhones, and Adidas
jackets. This had a dual effect. On one hand, the realization that
they are *like us*—they work, run businesses, use the same technology as us. A moment of recognition: it could be us. The discovery:

they're people, not because they suffer, but because they exist in the same symbolic universe, inhabit the same economic system, and are connected; we can understand them. Some things, like hunger, are impossible for us to understand since we've dehumanized the sphere to which they belong.

The other effect: why would they need our help? They have money; they pay the smugglers; they're far from helpless. Why don't they sell their phones, their belongings? There are people in greater need. As if it mattered more to the people making that journey to eat every day than to orient themselves and communicate with others farther north, with those who know which borders are being closed and can warn of the dangers; as if a compass weren't what you need most in a desert.

Long lines to charge cell phones, while medical centers were left almost deserted. This was the paradox of the exodus that took Greece and the Balkans by surprise in the summer of 2015. The image was difficult to absorb.

But there is much more to be understood. The Syrian population has become identified with the refugee population, while victims of other conflicts have gone out of fashion. Afghans and Iraqis, fleeing from two of the worst wars of the twenty-first century, sometimes pose as Syrians to improve their chances of being able to cross borders. Even though we are now used to the idea that many refugees have more purchasing power than was previously believed, this is mainly true of those who manage to arrive. The majority are left behind, in countries bordering on the war zones from which they've fled. And that majority comes from some of the countries with the lowest Human Development Indexes: Afghanistan, Somalia, South Sudan, Sudan, and the Democratic Republic of the Congo. But we need a typical refugee profile, and Syrians are the ones who've been chosen to represent it.

Flights

WHAT, THEN, DO THESE (non) refugees have in common? Who are they? Half of them are female. Half, too, are minors. And something essential: they are not nomadic. They are not prepared to live in transit. They learn as they go along, and this book is full of those lessons. They are not nomadic, but rather are sedentary people who have lost their homes and livelihoods. They are not nomadic: the moment they all remember as the beginning of their exile is not when they cross an international border, or even when their homes are physically destroyed, but rather when they cease to exist as a symbolic universe. It's no coincidence that the earliest operations undertaken by many aid organizations were to help refugees: it's an emergency, a moment of complete vulnerability. Human beings forced to explore their limits. They didn't plan for it. They are not nomadic.

And then there's the linguistic problem.

The Geneva Convention says that refugees are people who find themselves outside their own countries. This excludes those who in fact make up the majority of the refugee population: those without international protection, those trapped in Yemen, South Sudan, the Democratic Republic of Congo. These are the refugees who are forgotten because they are not refugees, but internally displaced persons (IDPs).

And the other major linguistic problem, the one that gives rise to so much controversy: are these people refugees or migrants?

The starting point: from a legal point of view, the distinction is fundamental, since one has the benefit of international protection and the other does not.

The battle: on one side, those who add an adjective to strengthen their case, who speak of economic migrants, those who are opposed to a wave of sympathy for refugees that could cause masses of people to take advantage of the opportunity to flee hunger too, those who believe that sub-Saharan Africans are taking advantage of the situation—that's the phrase they use. On the other side, those who are horrified by this discrimination, who can't comprehend why Syrians and Iraqis are given shelter while Nigerians and Gambians are denied it, and who don't focus on the refugees' reasons for fleeing.

One answer is certain: refugees are people. It's an answer that sounds paternalistic and naive. And yet, it's far more profound an answer than it seems because it allows that nearly 1 percent of the world's population into the realm of the human, prioritizing their humanity rather than their circumstances; because it opens the only possible channel of dialogue between host communities and refugees; and because no matter how much we keep talking about refugees, reading books about refugees, and watching news about refugees who are not refugees, it will, unfortunately, be necessary to keep saying that word: *people*. It isn't naive to call them people: this conscious decision contains a desire to reinforce their identity as humans rather than refugees, which is what, for many, defines them, and which is meaningless, since it isn't how they see themselves.

We can't take for granted that they will be considered people because for many, they are less than human.

What's more, in sympathetic quarters, among some nongovernmental organizations (NGOs), and even within political parties, a detrimental view of refugees is gaining support that explains their lives only in terms of their trauma. It encourages pity and condescension, perhaps in response to a kind of moral superiority in the face of others who are unsympathetic. At the center of refugees' lives, it places the bombs, the danger, the inferno; explosions, war, terror. But this version neglects some essential aspects of the refugee experience.

Most of the time, being a refugee is unbearably tedious. It involves days, weeks, months of waiting in line for food in camps.

Flights

Months and even years of struggling with bureaucracy to request asylum, then waiting for an answer, which is often negative. It can take years to reach a destination. Decades to adjust to a new country. This book, this chapter, tells stories of people who've died, who've lost family members, who've ended up in wheelchairs; but it also waits, seeks moments to pause, sits down with them in the shade of a Turkish lemon tree, or on a hilltop in the Democratic Republic of Congo.

These lives must be examined with respect and humility. Among refugees, there are engineers, criminals, mothers, abandoned children, former guerrilla fighters, poets, crooks, poor people, rich people—more poor than rich—potential Nobel Peace Prize winners, potential terrorists. Just as there are among our neighbors.

No, maybe not. Fleeing from a war doesn't make you a better person, but feeling rejected can turn you into a worse one.

In the Shade of a Turkish Lemon Tree

Salwah and Bushra, from Syria

> The wound that births you is as true as an eye that
> when extinguished, would extinguish the world.
>
> Tomás Segovia, *Orphan Song*

SALWAH AND BUSHRA are what journalists call victims of war. Victims of war are smoke, obliterated memories, torn pages—the human anecdotes of conflict. History remembers model weapons, the advance of military troops, epic victories; with luck, it also remembers the true motivations of empires and nation-states: sovereignty, oil, exploitation, the preservation of an economic model. The idea that history forgets the victims of war has become a cliché, and that is the worst thing that can happen to a silenced cause. Only when the tragedy suffered by the victims surpasses the threshold of our tolerance for the pain of others—a threshold becoming higher and higher—do we make time to really engage with their story. Often, we aren't even interested in the ordinary human details: what appeals to us are the limits of experience, a glimpse of violence, and the confirmation that violence is far away.

Between 2012 and 2016, I traveled several times to northern Syria and its neighboring countries, where hundreds of thousands of refugees were arriving, to tell the stories of the war's victims. That was my obsession. I wanted to show the consequences of the worst war of the twenty-first century, and to do so, I needed to find cases that confirmed my hypothesis. Cases. Confirmation. Hypothesis. I took the wrong approach, and I'm embarrassed by how naive I was; I'm ashamed to have thought of victims of war as if they were a product, something to be bought or sold. But it was worth it, because on that hunt for the greatest story, I met Salwah and Bushra—two Syrian women who aren't victims but people, and whose stories moved me deeply; two Syrian women with parallel tales of flight, who I wish could meet each other someday.

Salwah was wounded and evacuated to Turkey. So was Bushra. Salwah is in a wheelchair. So is Bushra. Salwah's father was killed in the war. So was Bushra's father.

What is Salwah's story? She lived in the old city of Aleppo. She was seventeen years old. One day, at dusk, she was on her way home with a neighbor. One of the streets was closed off, so they decided to take another route. As they were about to cross a square, Salwah was shot in the back by a sniper. She remembers how a soldier from the Free Syrian Army took her away from that square, where the air was thick with gunfire. He took her to a local hospital, where she spent the night before being transferred to another medical center.

"There was no one there to take care of the patients, and the hospital was very dirty. Then they said they would have to take me to Turkey," recalls Salwah, who doesn't neglect a single detail of her story.

Her mother managed to get her close to the border, but once there, despite her injuries, she was denied entry into Turkey. Finally, facing pressure from a hospital on the Syrian side, an ambulance was sent from Turkey to transfer Salwah to Kilis, a city in the south of the country that became the main point of entry for Syrians after the war broke out.

"I spent twelve days in the intensive care unit. I had many surgeries in different medical centers. I spent a lot of time in the hospital in Gaziantep, in the south of Turkey. I feel better now, but I can't walk," says Salwah.

And what is Bushra's story? She also lived in the Syrian province of Aleppo, not in the city, but in the surrounding rural area. Bushra was traveling by car along a provincial highway with her mother, father, and grandfather. According to the family's story, soldiers from the Syrian regime attacked the car and forced the passengers to get out. Bushra witnessed, then and there, her father's execution. When she reacted, when she moved, stepping forward to try to prevent it, the soldiers shot her in three different places. The bullets were lodged in her fourth, fifth, sixth, and seventh vertebrae, causing immediate paralysis. Her mother also suffered injuries to her legs and now has difficulty walking. After the attack, Bushra left Syria and was admitted to the hospital in Gaziantep, Turkey—the same one where Salwah received treatment—where she spent two months in intensive care.

I MET SALWAH IN EXILE in Turkey, in an apartment in Kilis where she lived with her mother and three sisters. They were sharing the residence with other refugee families. There was no elevator. Salwah's mother and sisters slept together; Salwah had a bed to herself, a reminder of her disability. Feeling nervous and out of place, the photographer, Anna Surinyach, and I sat with the family around the bed where Salwah lay. After just a few minutes of conversation, Anna interjected.

"We can't do this story in an hour," she said.

That brief statement meant several things. It expressed a shared feeling of guilt: from the moment we sat down, we were overcome by the dismal atmosphere of the apartment, and the first details of Salwah's story—real, vivid, not retransmitted or relayed by third parties—caused the color to drain from our faces. It was too much. But what is *too much*? Weren't we looking for victims of the Syrian war?

We began to question ourselves. What had we come here for? What would the family think of us? Had we no respect for anyone? Beyond expressing a feeling, what Anna meant to say in practical terms, with her usual directness, was that we had two options. We could talk to Salwah and her family for a while, pretend to be recording, not bother them too much longer, and politely say our goodbyes. It wouldn't be the first time. Or we could cancel all our other plans and engagements and suggest spending all day— or several days—with Salwah. It was impossible to do justice to explaining who Salwah was in just an hour of work.

The second option prevailed.

Dressed in a light beige headscarf and a purple checked shirt, Salwah scarcely raised her voice, but when she spoke, everyone listened. She was sweet, sincere, and direct. When we asked her if we could spend the day with her, she agreed immediately, so we continued the conversation in the apartment. She gave a detailed description of the attack she had suffered, but she also insisted on telling us about something which, at that moment, was causing her even more pain.

"I know my husband is somewhere near here with my daughter, in Yarablus, which is also on the Syrian border, but he won't let me see her."

We Are Not Refugees

Salwah was forced into an arranged marriage before the first protests, in the heat of the Arab Spring, which led to the Syrian civil war. She was fifteen years old and lived in Aleppo, where three years later she would be shot by a sniper. In those days, before it was devastated by war, Aleppo was the economic heart of Syria. Not long after she was married, Salwah gave birth to her first daughter, but soon after, her husband assaulted her with a knife and fled with their little girl. She hasn't seen them since.

We looked at the clock. It was midday, time for Salwah's appointment with the doctor. She had to get to a clinic in the heart of Kilis. After folding up the wheelchair, Salwah's older sister picked Salwah up and carried her on her back from the attic, where they lived, down to the ground floor. Out in the street, her mother chain-smoked while they waited for a taxi. Salwah put on a pair of sunglasses that hid her green eyes.

At the clinic, Salwah was the center of attention, and the doctors, nurses, and maintenance staff all showered her with affection. She was comfortable, but she didn't want to spend any more time there than was strictly necessary. After seeing her doctor, she had an appointment with her psychologist, something that seemed to appeal to her more.

We took another taxi to the mental health clinic, not far from there, in the dusty historic quarter of Kilis, a city that had become half Turkish, half Syrian. We went through a metal door and entered an Islamic courtyard, where we waited for the psychologist in the shade of a lemon tree, while Salwah adjusted her headscarf. Whenever I think of her recovery, of how she overcame her trauma, of her new life, I think of the conversation we had with Salwah and her mother beneath the play of light and shadow of a Turkish afternoon.

"One day the psychologist told me a story about a boy who couldn't walk, who had a disability like mine, but which had nothing to do with the war," said Salwah. "That made me realize that there are other people in my situation. There are people with more problems than me. After that, I began to feel better."

We were interrupted by the psychologist, who took Salwah away with her. While they conducted the therapy session in a private room, where Anna managed to slip in for a few moments with her camera, I sat with Salwah's mother, who smoked and smoked and smoked in the shade of the lemon tree. I couldn't detect even a hint of sadness in her eyes that day: only weariness, stagnation, apathy. I entertained her by running around the courtyard with a GoPro camera strapped to my head and then showing her the pictures, in an attempt to put her family's situation aside for a moment—the attack on her daughter in Aleppo, the sniper, the square, the hospital, the impossible border crossing, the life of a destitute family of refugees in Turkey. Her husband—Salwah's father—was killed in a bombing carried out by the Syrian regime, but I didn't dare to ask about him, since neither she nor her daughter had mentioned him all day. It was something that as a journalist I should have found out, but which as a person, I didn't want to know. Had I spent less than an hour with them, I'm sure I would have broached the subject. But at that moment, after so many hours in their company, after entering those lives that seemed engulfed in shadows but which were gradually becoming illuminated, I simply couldn't ask.

Salwah finished her appointment and reappeared in the courtyard. Mother and daughter prepared to leave the clinic and go back to their apartment, where they will no longer hear the bombs of the past.

"Before the war, we had everything. Now we have nothing left," said Salwah's mother, who was obsessed with the idea of returning to Syria.

"Where will we meet next?" I ask, before saying goodbye.
"In Aleppo, *inshallah*." If Allah wills it.

I ALSO MET BUSHRA in an apartment in Kilis. She was twelve
years old. In her case, she was lying on a bed in the middle of
the living room. She was also the center of attention. Her mother
bent over backward to care for her, a community health worker
came to offer psychological support, and that day, a physical therapist was visiting her at home for the first time. People were constantly coming and going, the living room was bustling with
activity: her grandfather, her aunt, friends, neighbors . . .

Bushra's mother fussed over her daughter much more than Salwah's did. The first thing she told us was that when Bushra hears
the footsteps of girls walking to school here in Turkey, it startles her,
and she remembers her life in Syria, when she used to have to get
dressed quickly and run to catch up with her friends. Bushra has
only hazy memories of her school and of the toys her father would
give her during those years in Syria. Bushra broke her silence
only to speak of her father. Her father means the world to her.

"She is very affected by it," said the community health worker,
sitting beside her bed. "She tells me something new in every session about what happened that day, when the soldiers shot her
family. She describes what it was like for her. She has many other
feelings, as well as sadness. Often anger. It's normal for someone
who's suffered the trauma of losing her father and ending up in a
wheelchair. I try to reinforce the positive memories of her father,
which she also has, and banish the negative ones."

"Her father was killed right in front of her, and she talks about
it every day. Every day, every day, every day," said her mother.

As they talked, the physical therapist began his session, trying
to avoid the subject. He pushed Bushra as far as she could go. He
pulled on her hands, stretched her back, tested her limits.

"The most important thing is for the patient to be independent," said the physical therapist. "Harder, harder. Are you tired? Can you do it yourself?"

Wearing red overalls, sitting halfway up, Bushra seemed to gesture in agreement as her head hung down onto her chest. Every shred of her energy was concentrated into that attempt to move, a mass of hope and exertion that made all those who watched her fall silent, that showed just how much she wanted to, one more inch, it's too much, just a little more, try lifting your head. My mind went blank: I wasn't thinking about questions I should ask or not ask, I had no moral dilemmas, I simply observed as Bushra resolutely tried to sit up; she knew she couldn't, but she pushed herself as if she were going to manage it. I lost myself in her determination, in her outstretched arms, in her hunched back that she was determined to bring back to life.

"Now try to relax. Breathe. It hurts, doesn't it? That's good. I'm happy because she can turn around now," said the physical therapist, turning to address us. "Now she's asking me to help her turn over onto her side. Which way? This way? Why do you want to lie on your side like that? Is the TV too far away?"

"I don't watch TV anymore," said Bushra.

A few seconds passed. For a moment, it seemed like the physical therapist had managed to get Bushra to stop thinking about her father, but it was only an illusion.

"My legs hurt when I'm trying to sleep."

"And how do you try to get to sleep?" asked the physical therapist.

"I think about my father, I'd like to join him."

"You shouldn't be thinking about death. You should be proud of your father. He didn't want to die, somebody killed him."

By the end of the session, Bushra was exhausted, but she seemed pleased. She admitted that of all the people who come to help her, the physical therapist is her favorite. He smiled proudly. Bushra's mother was the only one who didn't let herself rest, who couldn't stop turning things over in her mind, who wanted to delve into and try to explain the precise extent of her pain.

"I'm not sad for myself, that my leg was injured. I'm sad for her," said her mother. "Before, Bushra used to run along dirt roads. Now look at her. And she gets very afraid, too. Let me tell you something. One day we heard distant gunshots, and I fell on the floor in fright. And when she felt afraid again, she thought she was being shot in the neck. She said, 'They hit my neck, they hit my neck!' She thought they were shooting at her."

Oblivious to the adults' conversation in the living room, Bushra was deftly swiping her thumb across the screen of her smartphone.

"She used to just watch television, but now she's happy because she can at least move her fingers, that's why she's always on her phone," said her mother.

Who can blame her? But she isn't just playing with it. As we're getting ready to leave, I notice that the background on the screen of her phone is a photo of Bushra with her longed-for father, yet another victim of the Syrian civil war.

Bushra smiled.

Because of an Iranian Accountant

Nesime, from Afghanistan

> Who am I, who are you,
> how are we to know that our identities are stable,
> that we shall not flow into *otherness*,
> as do wind and light and water?
>
> GEORGE STEINER, *Extraterritorial:*
> *Papers on Literature and the Language*
> *Revolution*

H E WALKS SLOWLY across an unending desert on a sweltering summer day in 1984, alongside thousands of Afghans who, like him, are fleeing from war. The young man Kazim Kazimi, the poet Kazim Kazimi—he's already a poet but he doesn't yet realize it—crosses the sand where foreign armies are defeated again and again, that parched cemetery of empires, into Iran, the new home of millions of refugees. "I will march along this high-way, into the scorching wind," he will write years later. "On foot I came, and on foot I will leave."

I am obsessed with stories of people that also tell the story of a country, a war, a revolution, a political process, a social movement.

We Are Not Refugees

The Syrian exodus, the largest of the twenty-first century so far, can be told through a young woman's diary. Most Syrians have known peace: now, new generations are beginning to appear that have known only war. But the Afghan exodus isn't new: it began in the 1980s with the Soviet invasion of Afghanistan, and since then, the tide has only swelled. It has its poets, like Kazim Kazimi; it has its liturgy, its soul-searching, its history. "Death is always bitter, but death in exile, death in loneliness, death in a land where no one understands anything you say, is even more cruel," writes Layla Sarahat Roshani (1960–2005).

No other people, in the last half-century, has suffered the secret pain of exile as much as the people of Afghanistan. No refugee — no *non*-refugee — has been so ignored: history has immortalized the mystique of this land where empires have foundered, but it hasn't traced the paths of the millions of Afghans who have fled.

The story of this Central Asian exodus can be told through the escape of one Afghan widow: Nesime. She was born in 1979, the same year that the Soviet Union invaded Afghanistan and the country was plunged into the cycle of violence from which it has yet to emerge.

"I was very little. I remember my parents, I remember the bombs. We went to Iran."

Nesime's children scamper around the apartment. She and her family now live in Zeytinburnu, Istanbul. The boys jump up and down on mattresses, draw with colored pencils, constantly make mischief. Indifferent to their merriment, Nesime keeps talking, fumbling through a rush of words, gazing straight ahead. When she speaks of her roots, of her childhood, of the first time she had to flee, she seems to speak not only of herself, but of history, a shared destiny, a public tragedy encapsulated in her story, in her private suffering.

Because of an Iranian Accountant

"We were Shi'ites, but being Afghans in Iran was a problem. We didn't have the same rights as everyone else."

On December 25, 1979, 7,700 Soviet soldiers were flown into Afghan bases, while the 108th Motorized Division headed to Kabul, where the Soviet soldiers immobilized the seventh and fourteenth divisions of the Afghan army and disarmed the troops of the Ministry of the Interior. On the 27, KGB troops attacked the presidential palace, killing the president, Hafizullah Amin.

The Soviet invasion had begun.

Ten years, a million civilian deaths, and five million refugees later, the war ended. And other wars began.

The main destinations for refugees were Iran and Pakistan. The Pashtun, of the Sunni denomination, were welcomed into the homes of Pakistanis of the same Pashtun ethnicity. It was there, on the Afghan-Pakistani border, that the mujahideen or Islamic freedom fighters' resistance against the Soviet invaders was organized. By that time, a certain Osama bin Laden, in those days almost completely unknown, was operating in the area unimpeded. That was the distant seed, planted and nurtured by U.S. and Saudi Arabian intelligence agencies, of the radical Islam that flourished in the aftermath of the Cold War.

The Shi'ites, a minority in Afghanistan, who usually speak Dari—a dialect of Farsi—took refuge in Iran. Like Nesime. Despite many shared cultural codes, integration wasn't easy. Then, as today, refugees were leaving countries at war and arriving in developing countries that treated them like any migrant population. They had no special, much less international, protection, but local people assumed that their arrival couldn't be prevented. They needed to be assimilated.

Nesime married an Afghan, and her family began to prosper in Iran. The Soviet war and the civil war among the mujahideen that followed it were over, but in 1996, Mullah Omar, the one-eyed priest who donned the cloak of Muhammad at the Shrine of the Cloak in Kandahar, came to power as leader of the Taliban. The refugees were reluctant to return. In Pakistan, they felt at home. In Iran, despite the exploitation and ethnic discrimination they faced, at least they were safe.

"We couldn't own property," recalls Nesime, "and my husband had an illegal textile factory. It was working out well. Then the Iranian police found out and closed it down. They requisitioned his papers and deported him to Afghanistan, along with the rest of the workers."

That was in 2000, when the Taliban regime was in its death throes, and before the attacks of 9/11, which would trigger the American invasion. Those were the years of darkness, of sky-blue burkas, sharia law, and public executions in the Kabul stadium.

"When my husband was deported to Afghanistan, the Taliban asked him where he'd come from. When they found out he'd come from Iran, they put him in jail, since the Iranians are their enemies because they are Shi'ites."

Nesime's husband wouldn't last long there. He planned an escape with a group of fellow prisoners, taking advantage of a night when there was only one guard on duty. They tied him up and managed to flee, but the Taliban pursued them across the desert, the same desert of exile, the same ocean of dust and stone, the same scorching wind blowing in their faces that the poet Kazim Kazimi had suffered as he fled.

"They tried to hunt them down. They had no shoes. They ran across the desert and through the mountains. Finally, they reached Iran. My husband was sick, he couldn't walk, he couldn't stop shouting. The doctor told us he was going to die, but gradually he began to recover."

Because of an Iranian Accountant

The family resumed their life in Iran, where they lived between Tehran, Mashhad, and Jom. Her husband reopened the factory. On the other side of the border, in Afghanistan, another invasion was beginning, the post-9/11 American invasion, the search for Bin Laden in the mountains of Tora Bora. The Soviets had named their intervention Operation Storm. The Americans called theirs Operation Enduring Freedom. Different names, but in Nesime's eyes, the same war. She had no intention of returning: her home was now in exile, where another story, another destiny began to be woven.

"We had a nice life and a small factory. We needed an Iranian accountant to act as a front, so the same thing wouldn't happen to us again. But we didn't know he was a Christian."

It might seem like just an insignificant detail, a remark by an intolerant Afghan woman who didn't want Christians around her. But the Iranian accountant befriended Mehdi, the eldest of Nesime's seven children, and made it his mission to convert him to Catholicism.

"My son was a good Muslim. First, we noticed that he wasn't getting up to eat before sunrise during Ramadan, like the rest of us. Then we noticed that he would disappear into his room to pray on Sundays. He had converted."

Their son's decision, in a frightened family of Afghan refugees in Iran, caused a torrent of family strife. They asked him to give up his new religion, to "go back to being a Muslim." Just as they were beginning to feel at home, they suffered another kind of ostracism: that of their community, and of the society that had welcomed them.

"My brothers and sisters began telling me we were no longer part of the family," says Nesime, as tears begin to fall from behind her small, rectangular glasses. "They said my son was a disease.

'Get away from here!' they shouted. When one of my nephews died, they wouldn't let me go to the funeral. We couldn't go to weddings, we couldn't go to our relatives' houses. They tormented my son, and threatened him."

All this causes her much more pain than the war. Her family's rejection: a private, personal anguish she carries with her as a mother and as a refugee. A *mistake* that she made her own, a sentence to flee yet again, an unforeseen persecution, a story that combines the great ills of our times—politics, religion, borders—in the worst possible way, where the obscure and unfathomable reasons why humans make life impossible for one another rise to the surface.

"The Iranian government also wanted my son to convert back to Islam," says Nesime as she glances at the clock and we hear a key turn in the door of the apartment. "We even signed a letter promising we would try to persuade him."

It's one in the afternoon, and Mehdi, the son who converted, arrives home from work. He has just turned seventeen. He works in a textile factory in Istanbul along with his younger brother, who is thirteen. Skinny and poised, with a kind expression, he sits down on the couch, unperturbed by the presence of notebooks, pens, and cameras. He answers my questions willingly but asks me not to take up too much of his time since he needs to have lunch and get back to the factory.

"They tormented me, they beat me, they did things to me I can't mention here, in front of my family," says the young man, who now suffers from epileptic seizures. "I feel awful whenever I remember it."

The memory of that pain doesn't seem to be attached to Mehdi's physical suffering, but rather to the knowledge that he was harming his family. But despite this, his spiritual decision would remain firm and irrevocable.

Because of an Iranian Accountant

"Why did you do it?"

"I had a friend who taught me about Christianity, and in the end, I converted. My mother has always supported me because I'm her son, she's always been there for me," says Mehdi. "All this is my fault. I feel terrible because if it weren't for my conversion, we wouldn't have fled, and nothing would have happened to my father."

His father: a silence descends. His father isn't here. Mehdi gets up to go and eat, and his younger siblings follow him into the kitchen. Nesime resumes the story, now that her son has left the room, and explains why her husband isn't there.

"We decided to leave Iran. Our situation was very dangerous. We couldn't withdraw money from the bank because the factory was in the Iranian accountant's name, but we had a small amount of money and some gold. We went to Tehran, and from there we tried to cross into Turkey illegally, through Urmia and Van. We had to walk along the border for twelve hours. We saw dead bodies, it was terrible. There were three groups of us, we were in the middle one. The Iranian police caught us. The first group stopped, and we stayed quiet. We were in the middle, so we didn't know what to do. There were gunshots. Five people were wounded, two of them children. We started running. We kept running and running, and I thought my husband was there with the rest of our group. We ran for miles, until dawn. But my husband was gone."

Nesime assumes that her husband was shot to death by the Iranian police. While she believes that this is what happened, the loss is especially painful because it is unconfirmed. I don't dare to ask her if she's considered the possibility that her husband might have escaped, or that he may have survived, but he didn't want to return to his family. I don't know if it's more cowardly to ask this question or not to ask it.

We Are Not Refugees

The family now lives in this modest apartment in Istanbul, and they've requested asylum through the UN Refugee Agency, but they complain that the bureaucratic process is dragging on, and have little hope that it will bear fruit.

"We want a place where we can live in peace. When we arrived here, my son kept screaming. He was anxious, he thought our family were going to send Afghans here, to attack him. He's afraid of the Afghans in this neighborhood. In fact, we didn't want to request asylum for fear that they would find us. Other countries aren't interested in us. We're human beings, but it doesn't matter to them. If anything happened to us, they wouldn't care. My husband's relatives said they would follow us wherever we went, to do away with my son. I'd like to go to Australia. As far away as possible."

We finish the interview, and I start playing with the children. They're making an almighty ruckus and I take a couple of punches. I keep a drawing by one of them: Argentine soccer star Lionel Messi with the number 10 on his back, some dark blue stripes, an oval-shaped ball, a sun shining brightly, a soccer field that looks much more European than Afghan. I leave the apartment to go and get something to eat with the Afghan interpreter. He savors his *pide*—a kind of Turkish pizza—with relish, oblivious to all that surrounds us. We begin to forget Nesime's story. One more story.

A few days later, I went to the Greek island of Lesbos and spoke to the Afghans who, in that distant summer of 2013, were already boarding boats to Europe. I thought that might be the only possible way out for Nesime and her family.

Two years later, I went back to Lesbos and followed the refugee trail toward northern Europe. Greece, Macedonia, Serbia, Croatia . . . the blockades, the waiting, the humiliation. The majority of the refugees were Syrians and Afghans. I imagined Mehdi the Christian, now the head of his family, leading a group of Afghans across the border between Greece and Macedonia. On the buses, I saw Afghan women with rectangular glasses and blue headscarves, any of whom I thought might be Nesime. I looked everywhere for her. Few stories like hers encapsulated every kind of persecution that a human being can endure: bombings, fanaticism, the police. I imagined the family arriving in Sweden and presenting their request for asylum, which would be rejected since they couldn't provide documentation of the persecution they'd suffered, because they couldn't provide documentation of the destruction of their hometown that had occurred in the 1980s, because they couldn't provide documentation of a permanent war that belonged in the public domain, because they couldn't provide documentation of their status as refugees.

All this wasn't just because of an Iranian accountant.

The Forgotten Lake Kivu

Birihoya, Julienne, and David,
from the Democratic Republic of Congo

> They're not heroes, they don't want recognition, or
> fame, they don't even want to talk to me for longer
> than it takes to smoke a cigarette. They don't want
> to be known for running their tongues, only to have
> their tongues cut out.
>
> ALBERTO ARCE, *Blood Barrios: Dispatches*
> *from the World's Deadliest Streets*

E XODUSES. Human masses. Thousands carrying sacks, bags, suitcases. Endless rivers of people: the elderly, hunched over; swift-footed women; children who have no idea what's going on; men in distress. Desperate flights. Humanitarian corridors, columns of civilians escaping extermination.

These elements exist, but they don't tell the full story of this world in movement. In African countries where violence has become deeply embedded, especially in places like the Democratic Republic of Congo, displacement becomes more of a background murmur; something just as painful, but ordinary, routine, at times imperceptible.

The Forgotten Lake Kivu

In a village called Kalungu, on the Congolese side of Lake Kivu, dozens of people are packed into a dilapidated building that is either destroyed or half-finished — it's difficult to tell which. That whiff of cement, that feeling that any minute now, it might collapse. There are improvised fires, people organizing into groups; anxiety. Birihoya Bokani, sixty years old — a spotless white shirt, beige pants two sizes too big — sits in the building's entrance with his seven children. The photographer, Juan Carlos Tomasi, and I approach him: he confirms that he's here because he hasn't been able to find anywhere to stay, because he doesn't have a plastic tarp from the UN Refugee Agency, and because he doesn't know where else to go.

A ruined house crammed full of people is a warning sign: if there are dozens of people, it's because thousands have fled here. Yet another battle, the latest conflict, the same attacks on villages as always.

"We left Ufamando [dozens of miles north] because the Interahamwe militia burned our houses down. Many people burned to death. They killed the people who were out in the fields, too. There were cases of sexual violence. They killed my neighbors, they killed nearly four hundred people. Many died in the hospital. Others managed to take refuge in the rain forest."

Among the dead were his wife and two of his children.

"They shot at my wife as she was fleeing from our house."

No one saw him arrive, but Birihoya fled the inferno, yet another of those small infernos that make up this world of nonrefugees.

"WE ARE NO LONGER YOUR MONKEYS," the first leader of the independent Congo, Patrice Lumumba, is said to have proclaimed in 1960. Governed for decades as a private property of King Leopold II of Belgium, this stunning African territory, which holds in its depths an enormous wealth of natural resources, was saddled both before and after independence with some of the most stereotypical labels applied to Africa. All the elements were there: a cruel and exploitative (post) colonial period, foreign mercenaries, mines, greed, pillage, corrupt national authorities, military coups, Cold War intrigue, intervention by the U.S. Central Intelligence Agency (CIA), Che Guevara's travels, and the romantic, anticolonial myth surrounding the figure of Lumumba, who was later murdered by the Belgians. It was one of the continent's most traumatic processes of independence.

From this chaos emerged the dictator Mobutu Sese Seko, who ruled with an iron fist and imposed his cult of personality for several decades. A special friend to the CIA, Mobutu led one of the largest campaigns of mineral exploitation, corruption, and nepotism of the twentieth century in Africa. Following the end of the Cold War, and facing a loss of prestige in Africa and the rest of the world due to corruption, Mobutu threw in his lot with the small neighboring country of Rwanda and backed the Hutu regime of Habyarimana. The Rwandan genocide of 1994, led by the Hutu organizations in power and especially the Interahamwe militia, the Hutu guerrilla group, killed some eight hundred thousand people in just a hundred days, but the echo of those massacres can still be heard in the neighboring Congo. At that time, a million and a half Rwandan refugees arrived in eastern Zaire—as the country was then known—to the territory of the Kivu.

The consequences of the two wars of the Congo (1996–1997 and 1998–2003) were felt all across the region. Paul Kagame, the new strongman in Rwanda, conspired to place Laurent-Desiré Kabila in power in the Congo. In the second conflict, known as the Great African War, 4.5 million people were killed. The war ended officially in 2003, but in the Congo, there is no such thing as life after war. It is one of the most emblematic chronic conflicts on the planet. International fatigue has caused one of the African countries with the most legitimate claim to media attention to be forgotten. There is no new story to tell about the Congo, and yet every story that can be told about the Congo is new.

WE WALK ALONG THE SLOPE where the internally displaced persons (IDPs) are living, through a green ecosystem of tents, huts, and shelters that has sprung up around the building where I met Birihoya, that dilapidated building that insists, with its contrasting color (the color of cement and construction), on looking like the central attraction. Juan Carlos Tomasi, a veteran photographer with Doctors Without Borders, who has been traveling in Africa for decades, gets annoyed by the children and tries to get everyone out of his way, shouting at them to let him take his pictures. There's nothing affected or self-important about the fuss he's making—it's just a natural way of relating to people who don't take him seriously, who gather around and keep bothering him.

"You guys are a pain in the neck!"

An improvised soccer game gets underway, which serves to divert people's attention so that he can take a picture or two, but most of all he's just having fun, enjoying the feeling of being in Africa, which is what he likes best.

Nestled into a clearing on the slope is a medical center packed full of women. At one end, Sezage Delice, a nurse, runs an independent clinic out of a kind of hut: a table, a computer, a bed with a mosquito net, a couple of chairs. We knock on the door. The patient, Batasema Tulinabu, speaks in a low voice, almost a whisper, but she invites us in, wanting to tell her story.

"I was planting crops in a field when a stranger attacked me. He told me he'd been looking for me. I asked him, couldn't he tell I was eight months pregnant? He said he didn't care, then he raped and beat me. I didn't tell my husband anything. Then I started having problems with my uterus, gave birth prematurely, and lost the baby. My husband and I both fled."

Batasema now comes to Sezage's clinic for treatment.

"We have nothing. I always think about how poor we are. I sit here and think about my life, and all I see is poverty. My husband can't work because he's disabled. There was even a time when I thought of leaving him, but then I realized I couldn't. We're very close."

We ask about her husband. She tells us he's waiting outside. Hottel Kisandro, forty-eight years old, sticks his head through the door of the clinic. Friendly but frail, he comes in and shakes our hands. He's wearing a torn checked shirt. He sits down beside his wife, who until now had worn a serious look, but can't help smiling when she sees her husband.

"After the treatment, she began to improve," he says, and they leave the appointment together.

Segaze sits back in her chair and shuffles through some papers. As a nurse, she provides treatment to the victims of sexual violence who have arrived here. She has helped fifteen patients in the last month, she says. She is familiar with the problems and the fears faced by these women, the vast majority of whom have been raped and forced to flee under threat of violence.

"Many women are afraid to seek treatment because if people find out, they end up stigmatized by their community and families. They aren't accepted. Men reject them and they can't find partners, because people immediately associate rape with sexually transmitted diseases."

We spend the whole morning with Sezage. Tomasi takes photos of all the women who pass through the clinic.

The Forgotten Lake Kivu

"Can I take your picture?" he asks a Congolese woman after conversing with her for a while in the hut.

"Of course. How will you remember me if you don't?"

ACCORDING TO A REPORT by the *American Journal of Public Health*, about 1,152 women are raped every day in the Congo, although statistics offered by the United Nations are lower. Forty-eight women every hour. This is the country that uses "rape as a tool of warfare." The Congo is the "world capital of rape." These phrases appear in virtually any article about the country. In this conflict, militias rape women to destroy the moral and social fabric of the enemy. Some studies dispute these figures, attempting to demonstrate that rape is common throughout the country, not just among the Kivu: the epidemic extends far beyond the setting of this conflict.

By focusing only on the logic of war, do we run the risk of dehumanizing the suffering of rape survivors? Of representing it as just one more ingredient—normal, natural—of conflict? Of legitimizing it, even? Of speaking only of "victims," and not of survivors? Among the Kivu, yes, I found stories of villages being attacked, militias' strategies to destroy the enemy—humiliations, children of rival armed groups being stigmatized—but mostly I saw something much more obvious, to which little attention is ever paid, but which has a profound impact on the lives of thousands of women: rape is a weapon of forced displacement. Not even a bombing is so effective at ousting entire villages. I've spoken to Syrian refugees who wanted to go back to the inferno of Aleppo, I've spoken to Central American migrants who did not take a dim view of returning to neighborhoods controlled by gangs, but I haven't spoken to a single Congolese woman who'd been a victim of sexual violence during an armed attack who wanted to go home. Not to mention everything that comes after this attack on their bodies and their homes: sexually transmitted diseases, families torn apart, losses of livelihood.

The Congo is a crisis no longer considered urgent because it's been going on too long.

IT'S OUR LAST DAY at Lake Kivu. We stay in an enclosure—for what it's worth—that serves as a base of operations for the Doctors Without Borders team. Because the EuroCup soccer final between Spain and Italy will soon be played and the staff are feeling relaxed, they've promised us a special meal, instigated by the constant complaints of Tomasi, who ironically calls the place "Ritz Hotel."

"There's a delicious cheese nearby, in Goma. Why don't you buy some? We need to take good care of people, man."

After days of a diet of nothing but potatoes and fufu, a form-less paste made of cassava root, a mouthwatering new menu is unveiled: potatoes crowned with sardines from Lake Kivu . . . and fufu. Tomasi bursts out laughing.

Our next destination is Kalonge, farther inland, into the rain forest, miles and miles of dirt and roadblocks. On the way, we see trucks packed with soldiers, pickups carrying civilians and plastic barrels, endless life, the vitality of the Congo, grasslands and wooden houses. We visit a hospital where the American nongovernmental organization (NGO) IMC is working. There, we meet more women who want to tell their stories, who ask Tomasi to take their picture, who share everything, who remind one another of the details of their lives—"That was two years ago," "You've been here three months"—who don't want to miss this opportunity to be heard.

Julienne Akilimali is one of those who insists most on speaking. She wants to be the first. When she sits down with us, she shakes her head as if wanting to forget, as if wanting to speak to forget.

Julienne's village, Idunga, far from here, was attacked by the Interahamwe militia.

"The first time they came, armed men came to my house and raped me. The rest of my family escaped. They kidnapped my daughter, who is fourteen, and took her into the forest for six months. They got her pregnant. When she came home, we welcomed her happily, but then the same men came back, raped me again, and killed my husband."

That was six months ago. Her daughter had the baby, who was born with the stigma of being the child of a Hutu enemy. They live together here in Kalonge and have no intention of returning to Idunga.

"I don't want to go back, I'm not planning to go back. The same thing would just happen again. I'm beginning to feel better now, but I'm still in emotional shock, and I relive what happened to me over and over. I've been displaced, I have no money, I have no husband, I have no home, but I'm feeling better now."

The other women gather around Julienne as she tells the story they already know, and which they all share, in one way or another. The web of solidarity they have woven is what keeps them alive, the only thing that provides them with any safety or certainty.

None of them are refugees.

ACCORDING TO THE UN Refugee Agency, Africa is the region of the world that receives the highest number of refugees — 4.4 million in 2016. It's a striking statistic, but there is another, more permanent one, which provides a better explanation of population movements in this corner of the world: since 2002, the number of IDPs in sub-Saharan Africa has remained stable, at around twelve million. Furthermore, the Democratic Republic of Congo is included among the ten countries with the highest number of displaced people since 2003.

We Are Not Refugees

What do we know about these people? If they've been away from their homes for so long, wouldn't it be logical to think that we'd have more information about their humanitarian needs? On the contrary. The more time passes, the harder it is to know what's happening to them. Population movements become more complex, routes are redrawn, and new, smaller conflicts emerge. As a result, it becomes impossible to keep track. And we always quote official data from the United Nations, or from other organizations with access to government statistics. But how many people have really been forced violently from their homes? Here, it's impossible to know.

In the last fifteen years, the number of IDPs in the Congo has not dipped below one million, peaking at up to three million in 2003. And within the Congo, the area where that enormous human washing machine spins fastest is North and South Kivu. One of the last major insurgencies, that of the Tutsi M23 militia, supported by Rwanda, caused a new exodus to be added to the displacements brought about by old conflicts. A palimpsest that always appears to be the same, but which is subject to constant tectonic shifts.

OUR ROUTE THROUGH the Kivu region, one of the most beautiful areas of sub-Saharan Africa and one of its great battlefields—armed groups locked in power struggles, coltan and gold mines—ends high in the mountains. We leave Lake Kivu, the humidity, and the grasslands behind. Here, there is a breeze. From a jagged promontory in the town of Bisisi, we see the expanse of forests and villages unfolding before us, whose recent history speaks of suffering and guerrilla warfare.

A young man in a gray checked shirt and jeans wanders among the tents sheltering the IDPs who have come here to escape the conflict. His name is David Enabukonjo. Tomasi, the photographer, asks him to tell us his story in an abandoned church on top of this hill. There, we will be able to talk in peace. David balances his crutches on the ground with some difficulty and heads toward the church: a stone structure with beams of light passing through it.

"When the Interahamwe men arrived in Cibinda, my town, they began burning houses down, killing people, and raping women in front of their children. I tried to escape, but I got shot, and the bullet went through my thigh. My family looked for me after I was injured, but I hid in the rain forest for a few days and they couldn't find me."

In the end, they did find him. The International Committee of the Red Cross (ICRC) evacuated him to the provincial capital, Bukavu, so he could have surgery. Now that he's recovering, he has traveled to the area where his family is hiding, to this remote, peaceful promontory where civilians have fled in search of safety: another improvised refuge that gives shelter to those leaving destruction behind, another of the peripheral scenes of Africa's wars, another haven of peace in which—for a few days, for a few weeks, for as long as the evolution of the battle's front line allows— the nonrefugee population will try to forget the sound of gunfire.

PART III

The Camps
Where Do They Live?

At the end of this day there remains what remained yesterday and what will remain tomorrow: the insatiable, unquantifiable longing to be both the same and other.

FERNANDO PESSOA, The Book of Disquiet

THE REFUGEE CAMPS ARE A SIGN OF WAR. Camps are scars — some disappear, others suppurate, becoming infected — reminding us that there is war, that there has been war. They are a sign that thousands of people have had to be shut in, with their stories of violence and their marks of suffering, because they were no longer safe anywhere else. They are a sign that what's happening in the country next door isn't just sporadic bombing and fighting, but a war that leaves only the possibility of fleeing. They are a sign that all we could do for these people fleeing the inferno is toss them into a wasteland where nobody wants to live.

There is no law in the camps: only lies. Although technically, the host country is responsible for protecting the camp, it's often the refugees themselves who organize to look after their own safety. There are other, closer authorities: that of the UN Refugee Agency, which coordinates humanitarian aid in many of these camps, and that of the local and international nongovernmental organizations (NGOs) that work there. There is no law, only competing rules, like those dictated ad hoc by committees that the refugees create to assert their rights.

We Are Not Refugees

If twenty thousand North Americans sought refuge in a camp in Marseilles, what would happen? What law would prevail? How many conflicts would be generated by the overlap between the self-management of the camp's inhabitants, the French authorities, and the presence of aid organizations?

Refugee camps are a prefabricated response to people fleeing. They're like an IKEA home for all the world's refugees.

Are they?

We may imagine that this is so, but according to the UN Refugee Agency, half the world's displaced population is living in "private accommodations." In other words, in the homes of relatives, of whole communities that open their doors to them, and often of strangers. One of the most extreme cases is that of the Afghans who, since the 1980s, have sought refuge in Pakistan. As Pashtuns, they share a culture with their neighbors, and, although camps like the one in Yalozai were established, they most often stayed in the homes of Pakistanis. They also built their own. And at the end of 2016, many found themselves forced by the Pakistani authorities to return to Afghanistan en masse, to a country still at war, which was no longer their home.

And those who do live in the camps? They live under the plastic tarps provided by the UN Refugee Agency, some of them even in prefabricated houses, but also in precarious tents made of sticks.

Camps are a Band-Aid solution. In times of war and humanitarian crisis, they are indispensable because they allow concentrated aid to be given to those who need it most, the necessary logistics to be deployed, protection to be provided. These days, refugee camps often include schools, soccer pitches, places of worship. Many international humanitarian aid organizations were founded to help large groups of refugees staying in camps.

But they're expensive. In the long term, they have no economic or political justification. They cause ghettoization, and they reproduce the logic of war. To state the obvious: not all those who flee are innocent civilians. The good and the bad are each present, if indeed it can be said that there are good and bad people in war. Young girls, guerrilla fighters, mothers—and sometimes those guilty of genocide, as in the case of the Hutu in the Congo. The camps can be manipulated: armed groups take advantage of the opportunity to infiltrate them, seeking safety, using civilians as human shields. And once there, they use the members of their ethnicity, of their sect, of their community, to fuel hatred.

The camps often cause environmental problems. Land use. Aquifers. Competition for natural resources with the local, host community. And the conflicts that this generates: host countries are poor, and the grievances that arise among communities can have catastrophic consequences.

We have become accustomed to the United Nations (UN) fund-raising to help refugees. Funds being channeled into these camps without any long-term vision. Summits attended by contributing countries. In this marketplace of contributions to one crisis or another, the crises begin to compete. Help given to Syria is taken away from the Central African Republic.

And then what?

The camps represent a struggle to survive. Here, the law of the survival of the fittest applies. Anyone visiting a refugee camp for the first time notices a vague sense of hostility, an underlying tension. And one more thing: camps are increasingly prisons, and refugees are suspects. There is no such thing as freedom of movement.

War doesn't end outside the country at war.

This chapter contains stories about Zaatari, the largest Syrian refugee camp, located in Jordan. About UN compounds, the singular model for refugee camps in South Sudan. And about migrant shelters in Mexico, which are not refugee camps but which reproduce some of the same dynamics among a population—in this case, Central Americans—who are often neglected in the discussion of the international protection of refugees.

Despite their contradictions, many civilians do find shelter in refugee camps. The bombs no longer fall on them there—although attacks on camps, especially on camps for internally displaced persons (IDPs), are not infrequent. They are more likely to receive help in the camps than anywhere else. But these are not places where they can regain control of their destinies. It's impossible to develop personal and community autonomy there. For human beings, progress is in the future, in what lies ahead. But there is no horizon in the camps, only waiting. Dignity is elsewhere.

Dignity is recovered when you get your life back.

The City of Refugees

Zaatari (Jordan)

> In countless corners of the camp, the whiff of urine
> betrayed the proximity of the latrines; each time a
> maintenance truck emptied the septic tank, the stink
> spread through all of Zaatari.
>
> JAVIER ESPINOSA AND MÓNICA G. PRIETO,
> *Syria, Country of Broken Souls*

CARAVANS, CARS, BICYCLES.

A twenty-year-old refugee woman wrapped in a black niqab and a beige jacket crouches and aims a digital camera at the largest Syrian refugee camp: Zaatari, Jordan, with a population of eighty thousand. Photography is her therapy.

Balls, fences, plastic barrels.

"I always liked photography, but I'd never tried it before. I'm a very emotional person and it works for me, it allows me to express myself, and gives me some relief."

Cooking pots, baskets, water tanks.

Fatima arrived at Zaatari in November 2013, after her husband was murdered in Ghouta, on the outskirts of Damascus. She entered a period of depression from which it was difficult to emerge. Then she met Brendan Bannon, an American photographer who at the time was conducting a workshop for refugees with the United Nations, and it changed her life.

Ruckus, mischief, children kicking up dust.

"When I take photos, I'm expressing myself. My emotions reveal themselves. If you know how to read a photo, you know how I'm feeling at that moment, when I took the photo."

Fatima has an intimate relationship with her surroundings and a radical artistic stance that nothing needs to be added, that everything is already there, waiting to be captured.

"I don't like this big camera. I prefer small ones, because I can take photos like this, without warning. Otherwise, people get agitated and start crowding around me."

Roads, schools, smiles.

Fatima now teaches photography. She has cameras, pens, and notebooks at her disposal, and she asks her students, who are thirteen or fourteen years old, to go out and take photos, to capture the decisive moment.

She's behind the camera. She isn't used to being the center of attention. Since we're interviewing her, Anna Surinyach crouches down and takes her picture. For a moment, each stays in the same position—they compete, conspire, are one and the same; each looks at the other in her Western mirror, her Eastern mirror.

They smile.

Relection, light, image.

Zaatari.

THIS IS ONE OF THE LARGEST refugee camps in the world—and one of the newest. The Syrian war, which broke out in 2011, caused millions of refugees to seek shelter in neighboring countries. In Turkey, although there are camps, the majority live outside them: in cities, towns, squares, apartments. In Lebanon, there are no refugee camps: they live in settlements, with Lebanese hosts. In Jordan, since the beginning of the crisis, Zaatari has been the quintessential refugee camp, the emblematic location, the visible wound, proof in the form of endless rows of tents—and later, of prefabricated houses—of the destructive power of the Syrian war.

It isn't a refugee camp so much as a city-refuge. A Little Syria. Here, nothing is temporary: everywhere you look, there are fruit stands, clothing stores, mannequins, bicycle repair stands, children riding donkeys pulling carts.

But Zaatari exudes melancholy. Despite the bustle of the markets and the children racing on their way to school—today they have exams, and they're being very unruly—there's a strange atmosphere of neglect and resignation. The reason? The city of refugees is not some paradise to which whole families have fled, leaving the bombs behind forever. Some families have been separated. Some people are lonely. Some aren't thinking of seeking refuge in Western countries. Some consider returning to Syria. Some do return there, to join their families.

I visit the house of a refugee. Her name is Mays, and she is twenty-one years old.

"I arrived here two months ago. I was at home, in the province of Daraa. They opened fire on our house with artillery. My legs were injured, and I was evacuated to Jordan. My husband and my four children were left behind in Syria. I hope they can come and join me here; if not, I'll have to go back."

I ask her if she could apply to be resettled in a Western country.

She answers that Canada has already offered her asylum.

"I don't want to go to another country, I don't want to feel foreign. And my family is still in Syria."

Her story repeats itself again and again. Not only among refugees who have been left alone, but among families who have managed to flee but don't believe that this is the solution to their problems.

I knock on the door of another prefabricated house in Zaatari—long streets and avenues of caravans and tents—where a friendly family shows me the clothing and jewelry that they're making and selling to try to get by.

"We were near the border between Syria and Jordan. An unbelievable number of bombs were falling, and mortar fire. . . . I remember once we counted 113 mortar explosions in one day," says Abu Ali, fifty-three years old. One of his sons was murdered by the Islamic State in Damascus, and another was imprisoned by the regime and dragged behind a truck until he was killed.

In Zaatari, Abu lives with his wife and his other sons who are seventeen, nineteen, and twenty-six, but despite the pain they've left behind, his family does not want to forget Syria.

"Canada called us. I think we ought to go, but she says we shouldn't," he says, pointing to his wife. "She wants to buy a house next to her son's grave."

Canada is the only country actively seeking refugees in the Zaatari camp and offering them asylum. Although some prefer not to leave, there are long lines of Syrians in the camp who want to apply. What passes almost unnoticed is the constant trickle of buses leaving the camp.

Buses headed for Syria.

WHEELCHAIRS. I'd never seen as many wheelchairs in my life as I saw in the Zaatari camp. Amputees, paralytics, the war-wounded. There's only one hospital in this city-refuge to which patients can be admitted. It's located at the edge of a highway, next to a school, has forty beds, and is managed by Doctors Without Borders. It used to be a pediatric hospital, but was turned into a rehabilitation center for patients wounded in the Syrian war, where they can recover after surgery, after their initial trauma.

Inside the facility, young patients joke among themselves. Some are trying to recover from amputations. Others are working on trying to walk again. Layaly Gharaybeh, who supervises the care work, says the patients' diet consists of meat and eggs because they need as much protein as they can get.

But she believes that their main challenge is psychological.

"Many of the people we see here will be dependent for the rest of their lives. Some of them accept it. Others don't."

Amani Al Mashaqba, one of the center's psychologists, joins the conversation. She oversees the patients' mental health care. She points to a kid in a wheelchair. His is the case that most concerns her.

"He arrived four months ago. He was depressed, very depressed. He was afraid of speaking to anyone, to the patients, to the people caring for him. He wouldn't speak to me for a whole month. I asked his cousin to help me get him to express his emotions. I spoke to his family on the phone, too, so they could give me some guidance."

Hassan—not his real name—is wearing a gray hooded sweater. He is fifteen years old. He keeps rolling his wheelchair back and forth in a kind of nervous tic.

"Four months ago, I was at a funeral," says Hassan. "I was reciting the Koran when the army attacked. Everyone scattered. 'Leave the dead behind!' people shouted as they fled. Then a plane dropped two barrel bombs. I don't remember anything else after that."

Hassan suffered injuries to his leg and his whole left side. He lost his sight in one eye, but his doctors are optimistic: they think he'll be able to walk again. The problem—once more—is that he's alone. Hassan was evacuated to Jordan while his parents remained in Syria. They're trying to leave, but so far they haven't been allowed. Refugees encounter obstacles not only in Europe, but also far nearer, at their very point of origin. The most painful thing for Hassan isn't his leg, but being so far from his home and his family.

"Before, we used to play soccer in the courtyard behind our house. Some of us were Barcelona fans and others were Madrid fans." He recalls, continuing to slide his hand over the wheel of his chair, as if wanting to kick a ball. "My family sends me pictures on my cell phone, but that's not enough. What is a person without their family?"

In theory, Hassan has the typical profile of a Syrian who would be given priority on an asylum application. In practice, though, Europe won't offer him refuge—and neither will the United States. But his mind isn't on Europe. He says he wants to recover as soon as possible. If his parents aren't able to cross the border and make it to Zaatari, the city of refugees, it will be he who, by his own means, on foot or in a wheelchair, will return to the inferno of Syria to join them.

"My parents haven't tried to go to the border because they know that if they do, they'll have to wait months to cross. If they don't come in two or three weeks, I'll go myself."

If Hassan ever walks again, he will walk toward Syria.

HOW WAS ZAATARI, that city-refuge of abandonment, built? Why is it causing families to be separated? Like so many other cities—in Europe, in the Americas—this city is best explained not by its center, but by its periphery. A few dozen miles south of Zaatari, near the Syrian border, a town beats to the rhythm of war. This is Ramtha: gazing into the distance, you can see the Syrian hills from which columns of civilians flee. Here, only three miles

from Syria, the bombs no longer fall. This is the entry point for
the wounded. Only they can enter; all other civilians are denied.
Ambulances arrive, carrying patients with wounded eyes, spines,
legs, and the authorities decide who can and cannot come in.

This is where the separation of families begins.

In Ramtha, there is a hospital where these patients are treated.
It has dozens of beds. Every day, between five and seven patients
arrive. Around 20 percent of these are under the age of eighteen.
Here, the most direct and brutal consequences of the violence
can be seen: children missing legs or eyes, or with abdominal
wounds, fractures . . .

Not only that. Here, of course, there are many rebel fighters.
"Yalla! Yalla!"

At the entrance to the hospital, getting some fresh air, a patient
in a wheelchair keeps shouting "Come on, come on." In this
moment, the words have no particular meaning. It's a way of vent-
ing, a cry of enthusiasm. Qusai Ismael, twenty-eight years old,
fought in the ranks of the rebels against the Syrian regime.

"I was riding in a pickup truck during a battle, and the helicopters began firing. They killed six people."

He lost a leg, but he says he'll go back to Syria as soon as he
can, to fight again, or to do whatever it takes to put an end to
Bashar al-Assad's regime.

Ten days before we met, his first son was born.

Qusai is one of the few who agree to talk. Most of the patients
are afraid, especially the civilians. In the first ward in the hospital,
a toothless man of about fifty approaches me and asks me to tell
his story, but not to reveal his name, not to give too many details—
to tell only what's essential. He was in the city of Nawa when a
helicopter—flying "about 150 feet from the ground," according to
him—dropped two barrel bombs, one of the weapons used indis-
criminately by Assad's regime.

"I saw them coming," he says. "I grabbed my daughter and we ran, but after a while I couldn't see anything—I had blood in my eyes, I was wounded. I have wounds on my hand, my left foot, and my abdomen. They took me to the border, and I felt like every part of my body was on fire. My family is okay, but I want to go back to Syria to be with them."

It's unusual for relatives to be able to cross this border between Syria and Jordan unless they've been wounded. They can't get permission, they're denied entry, the process is delayed. So many decide to go back.

I leave the entrance and go up to the second floor of the Ramtha hospital, where there's another room, with some of the most serious cases. The names in the next few sentences have been changed. There's Muhammad, a two-year-old boy who lost his sight in a tank attack. There's Amina, a four-year-old girl who lost a leg. There's Amal, a five-year-old girl trying to recover her sight in one eye.

All these children were victims of the same attack. They're siblings. This is how Saquer, their father, tells the story:

"We were in our house, I had just brought some sweets home for the family. I heard a noise and went outside to see what was happening, and right then, the house was attacked by a tank. I had four children. The youngest, eight months old, was killed. The rest were wounded."

The young, stout Saqer doesn't raise his voice. He tells the story in whispers. His wife, Marya, interrupts him.

"We got married in 2011, right at the beginning of the war. I was pregnant when the earliest protests began. Children remember what happens. One of my daughters is always saying, I lost my leg because of the war. And the other one remembers bleeding out of her eye. She lost consciousness during the attack, but she remembers everything."

The City of Refugees

Amal, the five-year-old girl who remembers everything, captures our attention by playing with a purple balloon and putting it in her mouth.

"All these years we've suffered bombings, shootings by snipers . . . but now they've attacked our house. And in the news, they said they'd killed four terrorists. They were talking about my children. They were saying my children were terrorists."

The mother clenches her fists. This hospital in Ramtha is the beginning of the journey. She knows this. Soon they will go to a refugee camp; then, who knows? Outside the hospital, we hear a procession of cars full of Jordanian students celebrating their graduation from university. The hills of Syria are only a few miles away.

Soon they will leave this place, the border. Next stop: Zaatari, the city of refugees.

Open-Air Prisons
Malakal (South Sudan)

> "If we leave, the south will fall into the hands of
> the government in Khartoum, and the rebels will
> be crushed within a month." We all knew that was,
> effectively, what would happen, because there is
> no peacekeeping mission to protect these people.
>
> BRU ROVIRA, *Africas*

IN THE BEGINNING, David was unknown as a photographer, but gradually his popularity increased. At first, he wasn't working; just playing around, taking pictures of his friends. Then he began taking pictures of friends of friends, and then of strangers. Word soon spread that there was someone in the camp with a magic wand: someone who could alter a picture of you, change the background, transform the landscape. He received more commissions. "Why don't you start a business?" people asked him. The quick fix: he began summoning his customers to a pharmacy in the market. But the demand kept growing. David was overwhelmed, and finally he convinced a friend to lend him a space to set up his shop: DD Studio. He sees about fifteen customers a day. Business is booming.

"Now everyone knows me, because I take their pictures. They're always calling my name, but I have no idea who they are."

This bald man with a goatee, wearing a Manchester United T-shirt he rarely changes, runs the business of the moment at the market in the UN Protection of Civilians (PoC) site, a camp for the displaced in Malakal, South Sudan. David used all his savings to buy a digital single-lens reflex (SLR) camera, an up-to-date computer, and a printer. Outside the door to his grimy studio, people line up to have their picture taken. David then sets about editing the images with Adobe Photoshop.

"Look at this photo. The little boy is dressed in blue. What shall we do with him? Sometimes the customer arrives with a clear idea of what they want, and they ask for a border of hearts, like here. I add the hearts, but I also duplicate the image of the boy, and change his outfit."

David flips through photos of his neighbors in the camp. These images could be used to illustrate the word *tacky* in any dictionary. A celebration of the kitsch: bucolic landscapes, fake flowers, childish decorations. Women dressed up in Western outfits; men made to look taller, posing proudly.

"Their clothing needs to match the background, but the background can't be prettier than the main subject of the photo. What's most important is the person."

The naïveté of these images throws me off, touches me, and makes me laugh, until gradually I begin to realize their depth, their true significance.

"I put this little boy next to a big stuffed bear, because he's always playing with it."

Often his customers tell him exactly what they want the photo to look like, but sometimes they don't mind if he lets his imagination take flight. As David keeps showing me his catalog of Photoshopped horrors, he tries to explain why he's been so successful.

"When they leave here, they'll be able to look back on what their life was like. The photo is the story of the time they spent here."

"But these Photoshopped images," I protest, "don't look anything like where we are" — the UN camp in Malakal, one of South Sudan's open-air prisons, set up to prevent massacres.

"Look at this photo," he says, showing me a picture of a young girl in a white T-shirt and a black skirt, posing in front of a skyscraper. "This is Dubai! New York, Paris, Dubai . . . people want to go to those places, but they can't. So what do they do? They ask me! 'I want to be in Paris.' Well, in this photo, you're in Paris. They want to be in other places, other countries. They want to be among flowers, because here there are no flowers."

THE TASK OF THE JOURNALIST is to go, see, tell, and not return. Our memories become a collection of snapshots of horror from all over the world. Although they might rust and become distorted or replaced by others, these frozen images linger in our minds. But it's almost always more difficult to capture a continuous story, an uninterrupted narrative that would allow us to explore the causes and consequences of conflict; the situation both prewar and postwar.

In places like Malakal, where there is no such thing as postwar, this is even more the case.

We had left Malakal — plastic bottles, 150,000 inhabitants fleeing along the banks of the Nile, more plastic bottles — plunged into an orgy of violence between Dinka government troops and Nuer rebels, just after the outbreak of the civil war. At that time, in March 2014, 21,000 people took refuge in the UN PoC site. It was then that South Sudan received all the media attention that can possibly be received by a country like South Sudan. One year and nine months later, when I returned to Malakal and the situation seemed much calmer, almost 50,000 people were crammed into a third of a square mile: 32 square feet per person—far less than the 150 square feet that international standards recommend.

The UN compound isn't only one-third of a square mile; that's just the space reserved for its displaced inhabitants. The PoC is a large, fenced-in site, occupied mostly by the United Nations and various nongovernmental organizations (NGOs). A city of humanitarian aid, with generators, all-terrain vehicles, vacant areas reserved for logistics and storage, prefabricated houses with air conditioning—even a Hard Rock Cafe Malakal, where you can buy warm beer. The peacekeepers—Indians and Bangladeshis—circulate in their armored vehicles, play soccer on a pitch that could accommodate dozens of families, strut around showing off, and give the occasional slap to a couple of sparring adolescents, but when the moment of truth arrives, they are neither present nor expected to show up.

On February 17, 2016, twenty-five people died in an attack on the PoC. First, the soldiers failed to prevent the entry of weapons into the camp, and then later, when the conflict broke out, they failed to intervene. They even blocked the exit of the inhabitants attempting to flee the fighting. Similar events occurred in several parts of South Sudan and were often passed off as ethnic confrontations among civilians. The pattern repeated itself: if allegiances shifted outside the camp, if there was fighting outside, this was reproduced on the inside. Armed groups infiltrated these open-air prisons, from which only women emerged occasionally to gather firewood.

The Malakal PoC has always been unique. Not just because it's one of the epicenters of the war, but rather because it's the only PoC where different communities coexist, divided into five sections, or neighborhoods: the majority are Shilluk, but there are thousands of Dinka, Nuer, and even some Darfurians. In this miniature representation of Malakal, the contradictions are egregious. In the rich, spacious area of the PoC, there is an enormous humanitarian machine that should be providing aid to the internally displaced persons (IDPs). In the poor areas, dozens of women carrying their yellow jerrycans to water-collection points are surrounded by trash, crowded markets where people struggle to push their way through, and gutters through which sewage trickles, pursued by insects.

What are the PoCs? Why were these camps built in South Sudan? From the beginning, this was a war on civilians, on entire communities. The consolidation of these centers supervised by peacekeepers responds in large part to the specific nature of the conflict. An armed group attacks a city, and the people—a community—flee to the only place where they believe they can be safe: with the United Nations. Some 240,000 IDPs live, or at least survive, in these PoCs in South Sudan. Each center usually provides shelter to one of the country's main ethnicities—Dinka, Nuer, and Shilluk.

At first, the United Nations was satisfied with its decision—almost an obligation—to establish the PoCs. When the civil war broke out in mid-December 2013—with all the diplomats and aid workers packing their bags and preparing to go home for Christmas—the doors of the UN compound in Juba opened even before the IDPs arrived. And it isn't a bad solution; during those days, perhaps thousands of lives were saved, and they continue to be saved today. The problem is that PoCs began to be established in other places—Malakal, Bentiu—according to the same logic, but these camps were originally devised for an emergency, not as a long-term solution. When the United Nations opened the doors of its compounds, it didn't imagine that the IDPs would stay within its military perimeter for years, or even months. The rush into embracing this strategy has had catastrophic effects: military leaders thousands of miles away making humanitarian decisions because one of their battalions is deployed in the PoC, an outrageous lack of coordination between UN agencies and NGOs, and a bureaucracy that has prevented the population from receiving aid and protection at the most crucial moments.

Anna Surinyach, who always goes wherever necessary to capture the precise images of injustice, is talking to the inhabitants of some flooded tents in the PoC. As she positions herself to take a picture, she steps into what looks like a stream of sewage and sinks up to her knees. Some children point at her and burst out laughing.

Nearby, a separate area where the tents aren't so packed together captures my attention. It's occupied by containers and large tents used by the United Nations for storage. There are two abandoned patches of wasteland: the ground is covered in trash, broken glass, and plastic, which a whirlwind of children, without any school to attend, are getting stuck in their bare feet.

"*Kawaya! Kawaya!*"

This is the Shilluk word for "white man." This is one of those places in Africa where children, though they see white people every day, pinch you to see if you're real, to confirm your substance, touching you like you're an alien. In one of the vacant areas, the children swing vigorously on some swings surrounded by junk mixed with broken glass: a huge dumping ground for manmade waste, like the backyard of an industrial plant. On the adjoining piece of land, the nonrefugees of South Sudan live in storage containers of faded colors—blue, green, red, yellow: these are the most recent arrivals, and no one knows where to put them.

At the door to a caravan, I stop to talk to Lucia Daniel, who wears a long blue tunic, a black necklace, and very short hair. A three-year-old boy sleeps in her arms. I ask if he's her son. She says no, he's her grandson; his mother disappeared and Lucia has been left to take care of him. In this tiny caravan—almost a prefabricated unit, with everything ready for habitation—live six people.

"I lived in Malakal before the war began. During the conflict, one of my sons was killed by a stray bullet. That's why I wear this black necklace. My daughter, this boy's mother, disappeared."

"She didn't disappear! You know what happened. Tell them," a neighbor listening in on the conversation says. I'm stunned. I don't have the necessary cultural codes to understand the situation. Is this a reproach? She doesn't seem to want to humiliate her. Does she want her to face the truth—to say it out loud?

"They say my daughter went north, toward Melut, by public transport," says Lucia, her head hanging low. "She went by herself, without telling me, and without taking her son. She left him behind with me. The vehicle was attacked by armed men, and all the civilians riding in it were killed."

Lucia is distraught; she doesn't want to accept that her daughter is dead. She says she doesn't know where the little boy's father is, either, that he disappeared during the fighting.

She regains her composure. Then she gets angry. "The living conditions are terrible. There are no latrines, and people shit wherever they want. In Malakal, things were much better than here."

"FIDIA IS SEVEN MONTHS OLD and weighs less than nine pounds," says Xavier Casero, a doctor. "If she'd been born in the West, she'd weigh almost twice as much."

The Nile—the White Nile, when it flows through this region— tells the story of hunger and war in Malakal. Here, the river isn't just a river, the source of life: it's a battlefront, a line separating armies and ethnicities. When the fighting broke out, civilians fled in canoes, with bullets whistling at their backs. They are still fleeing in canoes to this day. These are the lucky ones: many were killed as they fled toward the river, the only escape route left.

The White Nile flows through oil deposits, encampments, vegetation, semiarid lands. The White Nile is a strategic zone, a battleground, a trading area, but above all, a transit camp for IDPs, an area of population movements, a quagmire that no one wants to set foot in, but a last resort for staying alive one more day. On the eastern bank of the White Nile, the Malakal side, the Dinka are now in charge. On the Western side is the so-called Shilluk Kingdom, the axis on which this war turns: in the beginning, its military leaders supported the Dinka, and then they supported the Nuer. Light military boats float on the river, shooting at the enemy. In 2015, the government, led by a Dinka, bombed both sides. It used an ancient and deadly strategy of warfare: closing the river off to traffic so that the Shilluk, on the other side of Malakal, would starve to death. The result: the Shilluk, many of whom had fled the fighting in the first place, undertook an exodus in reverse; now they were fleeing from hunger.

But what is war here, and what is hunger?

In Malakal, they are intertwined: war is made of hunger, and hunger is made of war.

"We've saved her life four times. She's spent more of her life in the hospital than outside of it," Dr. Casero continues. We're in a Doctors Without Borders hospital with almost fifty beds, about three hundred feet away from David's photography studio. An invisible umbilical cord connects it to the rest of the PoC. The same patients—mostly children—are admitted over and over. The reason: catastrophic conditions in the camp. On top of displacement, people are suffering from illness and malnutrition. There's no use in recovering when you keep returning to the same uninhabitable place.

During the time I spent in the PoC, at least one person died each day in the hospital, where you could hear the echoes of their families' desperate cries. This was a common situation in a humanitarian emergency, but one that was inappropriate to the moment, since the fighting had begun more than two years before. Inaction was dragging dozens of people into the abyss.

The hospital is a huge, ventilated tent, half of which is dedicated to treating children. I read the notes pinned to the beds: the patient almost always has more than one illness. "Epilepsy and malaria," reads the chart on the bed of a young South Sudanese patient. "Malaria and anemia," reads another. Babies with malnutrition and tuberculosis, all cared for by this doctor, who can't stop gazing at Fidia, with an inscrutable look in his eyes.

Cradled in her mother's arms, wearing a threadbare pink sweater, Fidia sucks constantly at her mother's breast. She doesn't move; she barely cries. No one knows what came first—the malnutrition, or everything else. She has tuberculosis; she's had pneumonia; she's suffered hunger. This is the fifth time she's been admitted to the hospital. The overcrowded conditions her family endures in the PoC leave her frequently on the verge of death.

"Now we're saving her life all over again."

Dr. Casero knows what will happen, but he speaks only of the immediate future—a few minutes, a few more hours. You can tell from his appearance that he's a perfectionist: he walks around the hospital with his shirt tucked in; pants and belt neatly fastened; short gray hair; clean-shaven; spotless glasses. His appearance and discipline help the patients recover, I tell myself. Dr. Casero now examines Josephina, who is five months old. Every ounce matters: she now weighs six pounds, three ounces: five days ago, she weighed six pounds, four ounces. She's wasting away. The doctor suspects that she has tuberculosis. She also has marasmus: a disproportionate skull, her temples pulsing vigorously beneath her encephalon, a swollen belly, her skin loose and dry. The doctor decides to adjust her nutrition program: she also has Down syndrome and heart disease, so she needs a higher caloric intake.

"The prognosis is bad, because sooner or later the heart disease . . ." the doctor stops himself. "But we have to try everything we can to save her."

In the other bed is Mary James, four months old, who has already been admitted to the hospital three times. It's sweltering, but her mother keeps wrapping her up.

"She's the crown jewel, the most difficult case," says Dr. Casero. The little girl is wearing a pretty orange dress with hearts and a black stripe. She's having trouble breathing: her head moves every time she inhales. Her hair is mussed, and she has a tube in her nostril.

"She has tuberculosis, and some kind of genetic illness. You can have malnutrition from not eating, or because you're sick. In this case, I think it's the latter. The problem is figuring out what she has. This girl is suffering from a chronic illness, but I don't know which."

With the current treatment, Mary James has gained almost nine ounces. She's a success story.

"She was in a desperate condition," says Sara Mayik, her mother. "I hope she'll get better soon. There are too many people in this camp. If people go back to Malakal and the city is safe, I'll go back right away, but at the moment, we can't."

I look at the doctor. I'm overwhelmed by his serenity. I look at him again. There's something about him that unsettles me, a strange sensitivity. I don't dare to ask any more about the little girl. He seems to think that she's going to die, but that they must still fight to save her. A few hours later, before going to sleep in the section of the PoC reserved for NGOs, I notice the book that he's reading on the dining table: *Hunger*, by Martín Caparrós. We talk about literature and journalism, and he goes over to his bed, which is covered by a mosquito net, and comes back with something he's written. It's the interior monologue of a six-foot-tall boy who is dying:

I need another dose of morphine—please, nurse. Talk to the doctor and give it to me. Or don't talk to anyone, and just give it to me. Or, better still, don't give it to me, and just talk to me. Nobody ever talks to me, they just ask me how I am, knowing I have no answer, because I don't have the energy to respond. They make like they're talking but they're not talking, they just do their job, which isn't talking. Talking isn't a job, except for politicians who make decisions and start wars and close hospitals and set up tents and tear down dreams. Nurse, doctor, you, everyone . . . speak to me, I don't want any more drugs that aren't words. I want to feel you near me, I want your touch. The only time I feel it is when you take my blood pressure. Hiding behind your medical equipment, you distance yourselves from my skin because it's getting colder and colder, I can tell. My hand falls onto my thigh, I can't lift it anymore, but I can feel that my thigh is cold, getting colder and colder.

I read and reread the words, the desire for human touch, the cold thigh. If I could choose a single place in the world to set up an office for processing urgent asylum applications, a place from which planes would fly bound for the West, loaded with people in need, I would choose the Malakal PoC site because it seems to me that each of Dr. Casero's words was forged from a hundred stories of hunger and war.

The Spirit of the Migrant Shelters
Ixtepec (Mexico)

> I will build the biggest wall you have ever seen.
> U.S. president DONALD TRUMP

"**H**E THINKS HE'S A HERO. He's only thirteen."

It's raining. There aren't many people at Father Flor María Rigoni's shelter. The entrance is guarded by two blue phone booths. Inside one, someone has scrawled "El Salvador." But this isn't El Salvador anymore; this is Tapachula, on the other, less important Mexican border, the southern one, without any walls. This is one of the first stops—near Guatemala and the Suchiate River—for Central Americans attempting to cross Mexico to reach the United States.

We're welcomed by Father Flor María, an Italian priest sporting a long, mystical white beard. He has many years of experience in humanitarian aid for people fleeing violence—he's worked in Africa with the UN Refugee Agency and has opened three migrant shelters in Mexico. From his office, his words transport us to the border between the Congo and Angola, where, he says, he witnessed unclassifiable illnesses and irrefutable proof of the existence of shamans and the efficacy of voodoo. His team, more focused on questions of daily life in Tapachula, says that these days, more and more women and children are making the journey. Before, only one in thirty of the people staying temporarily at the shelter were women, but they now make up 40 percent of the total.

Based on the people resting, waiting, or passing the time in the shelter's courtyard, as far as I can tell, the proportion of men and women here seems approximately equal. I walk around the courtyard and strike up a conversation with a frail, sixty-two-year-old Salvadoran, who keeps his cap on the entire time. His name is Miguel Ángel Reyes.

"In El Salvador, we had a stand selling French bread and other baked goods. A month after we opened, some gang members came and started charging me a weekly payment of twenty-five dollars. That was a hundred dollars a month, but after almost a couple of years, some guys from the Mara Salvatrucha came and told me we were going to have to give them five thousand dollars. We had to hand it over on April 28 or they were going to kill us. You can't mess with those guys."

Miguel Ángel isn't making the journey; he's not on his way to the United States. He's not going anywhere. He has requested asylum through the Mexican Commission of Refugee Aid (Comar) and is waiting for his application to be processed. He is convinced they can't deny him; the reasons he left his country are very clear.

"I'm not here because of poverty, but persecution. Those of us who work, civilians, working people, are being hounded. The only people who are safe are the gang members, and anyone who doesn't join them ends up dead."

Miguel Ángel disappears into one of the rooms in the shelter and comes back with a notebook. In it, he has written some nos-

talgic poems composed during his exile. He reads me one, titled
The Wayfarer or the Migrant:

I find myself where I shouldn't be,
And in a place where I shouldn't wake.
I don't know what will happen
Or what path I might take.
Life is about decisions.
When my land I've had to flee,
I'll go the way I must go
To become a refugee.
Thank you, my Mexican brother,
For giving me shelter and bread in your country.
You have a big, human heart
And have made an immigrant happy.
From my land, I come fleeing
From a filthy, cruel society,
That contributes nothing
To a life of peace and tranquility.
It pains me to speak ill of my people
But this is the sad reality
And it even seems shameful to me
To be telling this truth now.

In a corner of the courtyard, Anna Surinyach talks to another
Salvadoran family torn apart by violence. The mother—she asks
us to call her María, not wanting to give her real name—is traveling, or was traveling, with three children: five, seven, and thirteen
years old. They crossed the border into Mexico from Guatemala
five days ago. They're only at the beginning of the journey, but
María is having doubts, since The Beast, the cargo train on whose
back Central Americans ride to reach the United States, is too

dangerous. María ran a clothing store in El Salvador, but gang members were demanding a hundred dollars from her every week.

"I had to borrow the money. After two months, they were asking for a hundred dollars every three days, and I had to support my whole family," says María, huddled next to one of her children in a corner of the courtyard, leaning against a column.

So the family decided to flee. Her mother—the children's grandmother—went to "a safe place" in El Salvador, which in fact turned out not to be, since in El Salvador, it's difficult to find anywhere safe. The gang members—the same gang members who had demanded money from María—tracked her mother down and threatened her. María heard news of this when she was already in Mexico, about to arrive in Tapachula with her children. Her thirteen-year-old son was very upset.

"He was already traumatized, because he'd seen a woman get killed in the street in El Salvador," says María. "The police knew he'd been at the scene of the crime and interrogated him, but he was too afraid to say anything. Now maybe those memories have come back to him. He didn't want to see his grandmother die, so he went racing back towards the border, towards El Salvador. Just yesterday."

That's hundreds of miles: to get to El Salvador from here, that thirteen-year-old boy will have to leave Mexico and cross all of Guatemala.

"My mother shouldn't have said anything. Now I have no idea where he is," says María, trying to hold back the tears rolling down her cheeks. "He thinks he's a hero! He's only thirteen."

In the shelter run by the priest with the white beard, a rumor was circulating, the same unfounded rumor heard in every shelter, along every road and train track in June 2014: that undocumented children who entered the United States would be legally allowed to stay. In the first six months of that year, more than fifty thousand children had entered the United States unaccompanied. Statistics showed that this exodus wasn't anything new, and that in fact it had begun long before, but in those weeks, migration in the region—one of the most significant regions in the world when it comes to population movement—had reached a turning point, and perhaps a point of no return. Images of children being detained at the border were shown around the world, and people spoke of crisis—that word that says it all—and of children going missing at the border; of a generation driven into exile by the violence in Central America, even though the violence had been going on for years; of a massive northward flood (the media found the adjective *massive* to be indispensable). The United States and Mexico responded with public campaigns and changes in the way that immigration laws were implemented: detentions in the United States were reduced by half, but then they increased again, and the problem remains unsolved. Statistics fluctuate, and the number of arrivals and detentions of Salvadorans and Hondurans rises and falls like the stock market, but the problem continues to fester. After the so-called "crisis" of unaccompanied minors arriving in the US, the issue once again fell into neglect by the media, but with the arrival of Trump to power, the scenario has changed—not only has the new president promised to build a wall, but he has even ordered National Guard troops to be deployed at the border.

The humanitarian drama, though, began earlier, much earlier than that 2,000-mile-long northern border of concrete, desert, and border patrol agents, which does nothing to stem the flow of migrants in constant search of new routes, despite the danger they face on the journey. There is already a wall almost seven hundred miles long, an intermittent artificial barrier composed of steel, fences, and surveillance systems that President Donald

Trump has promised to complete and turn into "a big, beautiful wall."

But the drama began—begins—at the southern border.

And the children could not have arrived in the United States alone: in many cases, they traveled the route with guides, migrant smugglers known as *coyotes* and *polleros*.

According to Amnesty International, the country that deports the highest number of children isn't the United States, but Mexico. In 2015, six months after the shift in migration policy in Mexico, authorities detained more than twenty thousand children from Guatemala, El Salvador, and Honduras. Although the UN Refugee Agency estimated that half of them were eligible for asylum that year, the Mexican authorities (i.e., Comar) offered refugee status to only forty-four children.

Now people were beginning to speak of the violence there, in that triangle of silence: of the gangs' control over the territory, of women and girls being raped, of the recruitment of minors by gangs, and of what was therefore an inevitable result: people fleeing violence. And those people could not—should not—go back: those who leave, asylum-seekers, become even more vulnerable upon their return because the gangs consider them to have disrespected their authority; because if they're victims of violence, then they've witnessed events that the gangs do not want to become known; and because they are assumed to have money. For all these reasons, they become targets.

Honduras: a higher murder rate than Iraq. El Salvador: the highest murder rate in the world. The civilians escaping this horror, in this part of the world, fulfill to the letter many of the requirements established in the UN Convention Relating to the Status of Refugees for requesting asylum.

Despite this, they are referred to as migrants.

The Spirit of the Migrant Shelters

That word only means people who migrate, people on the move, but it also means more than that, since it silences the gangs and extortion and murder: migrants in pursuit of the American Dream—nothing to see here, just migrants fleeing poverty; they may be suffering from hunger, but there's nothing unusual about that. These migrants fit perfectly into a space in our minds that is different from the space reserved for Syrians, Iraqis, or Afghans. When we say *migrant*, the profile we have in mind is of a young man seeking a better life.

They are not refugees.

BYRON SOLARES is only a few minutes from losing consciousness. His life is about to change forever. He's riding The Beast, the freight train that he hopes will take him to the border with the United States. People are pursuing him to attack and rob him. Byron leaps from car to car, escapes danger by running over the train's steel back. Just as he's in mid-flight, the train shudders: Byron loses his balance and falls. He breaks his tibia and fibula. He's taken back to Guatemala. Twenty days in a coma.

"All I remember is that some firemen from my country picked me up and took me to the hospital. I woke up on December 27 and just gave my mom's name and phone number so they could call her, because everything I had was stolen. And I was in a coma, with a bunch of tubes attached to me. I'm out of there now, but it's tough, because when I saw myself like that I didn't want to go on living. I've had surgery on my stomach, my arms, my jugulars, I've had tubes in my chest. They told me I pulled them out. I lost my leg because they left it too late to operate, I tried to get a new one for a year and a half, the last material they tried cost me nearly thirty thousand quetzales [over four thousand dollars], and I never got my leg, or the material. I don't know what the hell they did with it. The doctor told me that if they didn't amputate, I could die. I decided I'd better sign the letter of consent, so they could amputate."

Four and a half years later, now in a wheelchair, Byron went back on the road. He crossed the Guatemalan border and arrived in Tapachula, in Chiapas, Mexico. And he stayed in the Jesús el Buen Pastor [Jesus the Good Shepherd] Shelter, which is also known as *doña* Olga's shelter, which is also known as the "shelter for the crippled."

"This time, I'm planning to stay here in Mexico. Now I hope to walk again, but with a prosthetic. I have no choice. I lost my leg. I lost part of my intestines too, but I'm alive, thank God," says Byron, sitting in his wheelchair with red tires. He's wearing green khaki shorts and a blue T-shirt. He's stout, but his chest is taut and sinewy, like that of an athlete. We talk in the middle of a rain-soaked courtyard, accompanied by two birds in a cage that has been left there, awaiting its owner.

After his accident, the accident suffered by so many migrants—again, *migrants*—Byron thought it would be impossible for him to ever find a partner. He made the fatal journey, the first one, just after his wife had left him and taken everything he had. Or at least that's what he says.

But Byron says he's staying at this shelter for now, that for the moment, his mind isn't on the United States. He pulls faces, makes insinuations, excuses himself for not being more explicit because we're in the courtyard, and someone might hear us; we're in the shelter of Jesús el Buen Pastor. He's met someone here, but he can't tell anyone because this is a house of God.

IN TAPACHULA, there are two shelters, or *albergues*: the one run by Father Flor María, from which the thirteen-year-old hero set off for El Salvador, and the one run by *doña* Olga, where a man who lost a leg riding on the back of The Beast found love again. The shelters are also called—they prefer this name, it's the one they use on their signs—Casa del Migrante [Home for Migrants]: a place where those on the trail can access food, showers, and sometimes medical attention. The sporadic network of camps and settlements woven at the periphery of a war in the Middle East or Africa, following a major route or a river, here becomes a string of shelters—*albergues*—scattered along the railroad, pulsing to the rhythm of The Beast.

Missionaries, Good Samaritans, nongovernmental organizations (NGOs), religious organizations, charities.

In some shelters, migrants are practically under house arrest: their comings and goings are monitored, even forbidden. The general rule is that they can stay only a limited number of days. They are segregated by gender, in rooms packed with bunks, as in a holiday camp, but without the amenities. Calendars, crucifixes, and images of saints and virgins hang on the walls. The dense aroma of religion seeps into every corner.

The main communal areas are the showers, the dining room, and the courtyard. Laundry is a tense affair: after days of travel, migrants can now wash their clothes, and sometimes the lines are interminable. The shelter attempts to involve migrants in the cooking, cleaning, and maintenance of the communal areas. When they aren't working, the residents organize checkers tournaments. The women do each other's hair. Friendships blossom. But conflicts are also unleashed, usually among kids who've fled Central American neighborhoods where violence reigns with impunity.

The shelters are dormitories of flight, boardinghouses where experiences are shared, dining rooms where people begin as strangers, but where everyone ends up knowing everyone else; a moment of respite from the journey, a chance to gather strength—

though some don't want to stop for even a moment, staying on the road whenever they can, heading north; strange sanctuaries offering safety from theft, extortion, kidnapping; islands, almost always of peace, on one of the most dangerous journeys in the world.

I DON'T KNOW WHY, but I don't trust him. Nelson is wearing a pair of Ray-Bans. He's twenty-one years old. My prejudices are immediately awakened, and I suspect him of being a gang member. He takes off his sunglasses, and the area around his eyes glistens with two purple shiners. He says when he crossed the Suchiate, a group of young men, tipped off by the money changers on the other side of the river, immediately attacked him and robbed him of two thousand Mexican pesos. He was beaten up as soon as he set foot in Mexico.

"One of them grabbed me. I turned to look at him and then the other kid told me not to, and he punched me here and again here, then he took out a knife, but only a small one, because they weren't even all that brave. By then, my friends were on their way. They punched me and left me with these bruises. The swelling's gone down now, thank God. Now I feel a little better. I'm ready to catch the train."

"Are you going to report it?"

"What's the use of reporting it? I want to get to San Luis Potosí. I don't want to report anything."

Nelson freely admits that he's migrating for economic reasons. He doesn't want to go to the United States. He wants to stay in Mexico, in San Luis Potosí, where his employers are holding a job for him in a barbershop.

"I already took the train a year ago or so, I was in San Luis Potosí almost a year, but then I went back to see my mother for her birthday, and now here I am again. The last time, everything went well; they say it's more dangerous this time around."

The Spirit of the Migrant Shelters

This shelter, in the town of Arriaga, north of Tapachula, where The Beast begins its journey, has an air of conflict about it. As soon as you enter, there are cubicles where the migrants have had to leave all their belongings. In the outdoor courtyard, spacious enough to avoid fights, the men—almost all of them are men— give me an icy reception, look at me with suspicion, and obviously want me to leave. Miniature ghettos, small groups, bare chests, young men recovering from their wounds.

Gradually, I begin to overcome their resistance and speak to some of the migrants, like Nelson, who was very eager to talk, but in general not even soccer—an overused resource, but one that's effective all over the world—serves to break the ice. People speak in whispers, so I try to blend in, adapt to my surroundings, make myself part of the scenery. I sit down beside a soft-spoken Honduran man who reveals his story slowly, as if drawing back a curtain. Leaning against a wall, we both stare ahead, as if permanently on alert. Walter Antonio, thirty-four years old, has neither a wife nor children. Sometimes he speaks in the first person. Sometimes he uses the royal *we.* "I had a job working for a company, for Nestlé, that didn't cover my living expenses. I had to quit, and with what they gave me when I quit, I decided it was time to emigrate. I went to Ciudad Hidalgo and took the train from there to Medias Aguas.

"We went down from Medias Aguas and stayed in Veracruz," he continues, "working for a while, and that's how we traveled, little by little, until we got to Tamaulipas. We were there five days, and then we crossed the river and made it to Brownsville, Texas, in the United States; we paid a taxi driver twenty dollars to take us to Harlingen, stayed there and worked for a while, earned some money, lived there for six months, and then went to Los Angeles.

"When we got to Los Angeles, we had no work for a while,

about four days, and then I got a job in a restaurant with some Koreans. I was with them for a while and then I moved to Culver City and worked in a restaurant called The Cheesecake Factory. I worked there for a while but I couldn't handle the pressure—I was tired all the time, and I had two jobs. I went somewhere else, started working for a while, and one day I left at one in the morning, after working late. I was riding my bike on the sidewalk. I didn't even have a light, and that's not allowed in those cities. I was carrying a fake ID, and the police stopped me and asked to see it. You know this is an offense? I said yes, and he arrested me and took me to the police station."

Walter Antonio keeps telling the story in his listless voice. He was released, but then arrested again and taken to Orange County, where he was detained: according to him, this was racially motivated. In the end, he had to choose between going to court and risking a fine of twenty-five hundred dollars or signing an order of deportation. He signed. All of this happened a year before our conversation.

(During his presidential campaign, Trump proposed to deport 11 million undocumented immigrants. After his election, he reduced his promise to "two or three" million people with criminal records. Between 2009 and 2015, Barack Obama had deported 2.5 million—a record not often discussed.)

Walter Antonio set out on the journey again.

"The gangs are very active in Honduras right now. What happened to me was threats, organized crime. They think if you've been deported, you must have money. And they started threatening me and demanding payments. Once you have no money left to pay them, you might even get killed. Sometimes you can't live in peace even in your own home."

This time, as soon as he arrived in Mexico, Walter Antonio requested asylum. He waited eight months. During this period, asylum-seekers must sign in regularly at the same office and go through an interview process. They are not allowed to leave.

Then the answer arrived.

"They told me they'd investigated my case and they hadn't found anything, so I told the young woman: if they'd investigated me properly, they wouldn't have denied me my refuge."

My refuge. My asylum. I had never heard those words from the mouth of a Syrian or an Afghan, much less from a South Sudanese or a Central African. With his record, it was highly unlikely that Walter Antonio would have been granted asylum. He himself admitted that, at first, he left for economic reasons, but this time was different. He was aware of his rights, and specifically of his right to seek refuge. It wasn't granted—he had a feeling it wouldn't be—but he knows it's his right. It's unusual for Central Americans to stop and spend months in a Mexican city waiting for an asylum that they know will never be granted. It's a sign of patience, and of faith.

And when the negative response arrives, what next?

Exodus.

Walter Antonio is leaving. Heading north.

"Eight months, and nothing. It's risky here too, on the trail. . . . Right now, they're saying the crime has gotten worse. I don't know what will happen to us. I'd like to go back to the same border with the United States, to Tamaulipas, where I went before. I've already crossed twice there, so I feel more confident about it."

This is how the system works. The system criticizes those who try to slip through, but the system itself doesn't invite them to take a number, to proceed by official means. Instead, it drives them to try to slip through. The system works because it lies so shamelessly that everything it says appears to be true.

Everything seems to be as it should.

———

VIOLENCE IS THE DRIVING FORCE behind exoduses. It is the root, the reason, the trigger. In many parts of the world, the violence continues after departure, on the journey, but few countries of transit are crueler than Mexico. In 2015, 58 percent of Central American migrants treated by Doctors Without Borders suffered one or more violent incidents on the trail. And nine out of ten showed signs of anxiety or depression as a result of the journey. Theft, extortion, assault, including sexual violence that all too often affects minors—both girls and boys. Organized criminal groups that extort money from migrants along the trail—charging them for the right to climb onto The Beast, to board a bus, to continue on their journey.

And kidnappings, many kidnappings. What is the logic behind them? Why kidnap those who have the least? Because an entrepreneur, a politician, or an actor would be sure to attract the attention of the press and the police, but nobody cares about the fate of Central Americans kidnapped in Mexico. If migrants are kidnapped en masse, and their families can be contacted to pay a modest ransom, within a few days their kidnappers can make the same amount of money. These wholesale kidnappings, with victims held in safe houses, take place on a complex chessboard where drug traffickers, cartels, migrant-smugglers, petty criminals, and security forces all play a part, and the latter not only turn a blind eye, but are sometimes also perpetrators of the violence themselves.

"Most are afraid of not seeing their families again, so they're stressed right from the beginning," says Miguel Gil, a psychologist. "There are groups of migrants who talk about nothing but violence. 'Here's what happened to me.' 'What happened to me was worse.' Whether it's true or not, the effect starts to take its toll. They hear stories from other people, then repeat them. It's gossip. They go days without sleeping. They're predisposed to the violence."

The Spirit of the Migrant Shelters

The psychologist says that migrants think it's normal for the gangs to charge them to get through, and they don't see it as violence. That's why he speaks of migrants who are "predisposed" to violence. They're used to it, they expect it, and they accept it. They almost want it to happen, just to get it over with as soon as possible.

"Many are unaware of the state of their mental health," Gil says. "They have physical symptoms, like headaches or other aches and pains, insomnia, or loss of appetite. The doctor sends them to the psychologist. Then they come in and we start talking, they tell us they've been attacked, and everything that's happened to them on the trail starts to come together. And they make the connection. How long have you been getting headaches? Since leaving my country."

Some people are assaulted as soon as they set foot in Mexico—like Nelson, the suspect kid in Ray-Bans—when they still have twenty-five hundred miles to go to get to the United States. And then there's the feeling of guilt.

You knew what would happen to you. Why did you do it? You're afraid to tell your parents, who stayed at home. You're afraid to tell your sister, or your friends, who stayed behind in Tegucigalpa. But most of all, you're afraid of disappearing, and neither your parents, nor your sister, nor your friends ever finding out what happened to you.

IN THE DINING ROOM, roast pork is being served. Dozens of Hondurans are watching TV. It's the group stage of the soccer World Cup: Honduras is playing France. The silence is deathly until at the last minute, toward the end of the first half, when Wilson Palacios, one of the players most applauded by the audience, is given a penalty and sent off. Karim Benzema scores a goal.

"They always do that to the little teams," says one young man.

"That's the only way they can beat Honduras," says another.

Discouragement reigns. Those in the front row are chopping onions for dinner—work here is done in community. Green tubs, tortillas, baseball caps, tortillas, necklaces, more tortillas. The French team's second goal drives many of the viewers from the dining room, away from the large cluster of people in front of the TV, and from a result that seems destined to favor the opposing team. Leaning against a wall, several young men are absorbed in lively conversation.

"I left my country on Sunday," says Jorge Hernández, a twenty-one-year-old Honduran. "I didn't know what day it was today, but I knew Honduras was playing."

Today is Sunday again. It's been a week since Jorge left Honduras.

"They brush up against them and it's a penalty," says Raphael Andino, a fifty-year-old computer technician, still absorbed in the game. "This is the second time I've made the journey. I got picked up and deported from the United States a year ago."

In his words, there is a combination of pride—"The best Honduras team was in 1982; they played with heart"—and angst—"I'm bitter, there's no work in Honduras and I have three children." Benzema scores the 3–0 goal, and the snout of a train appears outside Father Alejandro Solalinde's shelter. The Beast is getting ready to leave.

These Hondurans will soon forget the match with France—another, much more important one has just begun.

Father Solalinde's shelter is one of the most well known in Mexico. Its official name is Hermanos en el Camino [Brothers on the Trail], but everyone knows it by the name of its charismatic founder. The shelter is in Ixtepec, in the state of Oaxaca, still thousands of miles from the United States. Four hundred migrants slept there the night that it was established in 2007, and some twenty thousand people pass through its facilities every year. The train that appeared after the France-Honduras game was one of the last to arrive loaded with migrants. Since then, most arrive on foot and in precarious conditions because the Mexican government has forced them off the train. This is the shelter with the most pleasant atmosphere: the dining room, the open-air spaces, the friendly volunteers.

The shelters are also called refuges: there, nonrefugees take refuge and can feel safe. Father Solalinde's shelter shows how the situation is changing, the route shifting. I'm told before the soccer game that until recently, the shelter was packed, the courtyard and entrance crammed with people sleeping on the floor. Now only a few dozen people are here, and most are not just passing through, but rather, for a range of reasons, have decided to stay longer. The refuge fills and empties to the rhythm of The Beast, which, each time it pulls into Ixtepec, unloads hundreds of people who must wait for the next train to arrive, to go on with their journey.

When does the next train leave?

Is it raining in Arriaga, where these steel animals begin their journey?

Gossip, rumors, sometimes fights.

I'm captivated by a tiny figure leaning against a multicolored mural depicting Father Solalinde and his family. His name is Gustavo Adolfo. He makes flowers. He doesn't grow them but fashions them, crafts them by hand. He weaves the flowers out of colored thread and sells them to earn a little money. Friendly and serene, he immediately agrees to tell me his story. At twenty-five— he looks older—he's a globetrotter, a go-getter, and this isn't the first time he's made the journey.

Gustavo Adolfo is from Guatemala. The first time he entered the United States, he went through Tamaulipas. He got caught a total of eleven times at the border. The last time was the worst.

We Are Not Refugees

"I spent two months in jail in Tucson, Arizona. After two months, I got out and they sent me to Mexicali. I tried again but I decided to go back once I was halfway there, because if they'd caught me again, it would have been six months."

His story reminds me of Walter Antonio, the young Honduran who was deported after being caught riding his bike on a sidewalk in California. Both are single and childless, both managed to get into the United States: both achieved—achieved?—the American Dream. For now, Gustavo Adolfo will stay in Ixtepec, but then he wants to go farther than usual, to Canada. He might change his mind in a few days or a few weeks, but he's sure to keep selling his hand-woven flowers.

The Salvador Moreno family from San Pedro Sula, Honduras, is staying for a few days in the same shelter. Juan Ramón is traveling with his deaf-mute brother and three of his children, who are fourteen, fifteen, and twenty-five. The fifteen-year-old is a left-footed kid in love with soccer who hasn't missed a single beat of the France-Honduras match and who spends every spare minute kicking a ball around; in this shelter, there's even a soccer pitch. Two of the children have the same mother; the other has a different one. The goal is for them to make it to the border so the sons can go on to Houston, to join their mothers.

Juan Ramón speaks with effortless and moving eloquence. Leaning up against a corner, beneath a crucifix, and surrounded by pots and pans, he reflects on the importance of family, protecting his loved ones, and the twists and turns of life.

"Honduras is in a state of collapse, there's a lot of violence. Right now, my city, San Pedro Sula, is considered one of the most dangerous in the world. My son and I were dealing in merchandise, clothing. They won't even make an exception for a woman selling five pounds of corn tortillas there. They make her pay the war tax. And it doesn't matter whether it's a criminal or a cop who gets you, it makes no difference. They'll always rob you. They have a license to steal."

The family was driven to flee by extortion. But, as is the case of many migrants, the worst was yet to come. They were attacked on the first leg of their journey.

"They stripped us completely naked, took away our clothes, made us empty out our backpacks and take everything out of our bags, ordered us around while they searched through everything. And then they told us, get dressed and get out of here, nothing happened, don't go telling anyone; but even so, they kept us there forty minutes, naked, crouched down with our faces to the floor, threatening us with a bullet to the head. My brother didn't understand what was happening, he's deaf-mute and he's in a different world, so he wanted to know what was going on; they forced him to understand by kicking him."

Juan Ramón is a river of words.

"I think that was traumatic for my kids, it's a terrible experience I wouldn't wish on anyone, for us to be there as a family, me as their father and they as my kids, and all of us there naked. I wouldn't wish it on anyone."

Unlike most victims, Juan Ramón reported the attack. He is now at Father Solalinde's shelter, waiting for a humanitarian visa designed for migrants who've suffered violence while making the journey. But just today, after the interview, he finds out that Cristian, his eldest son, is not going to wait for the response to that application. His mother, in Texas, has sent a *pollero* to take him up—here, people always talk about going up, about the North; there's a strange sense of verticality, which is much more absolute than in other places.

"We're dismayed," says Juan Ramón. His sons don't know how to react. He looks as if he's possessed by a spirit.

PART IV

Routes
How Do They Travel?

The new globalization of movement has reinforced
the long tradition of popular economic hostility to
mass immigration . . .

ERIC HOBSBAWM, *Globalization,*
Democracy, and Terrorism

I TYPE THE WORD "ROUTES" into Google and find airline and
bus schedules. I type the words "migrant routes" and find
human traffickers, refugees trying to forge another path to Europe,
Central Americans crossing Mexico to reach the United States.

These are the routes closest to us, but they are not the most
traveled. Routes leading from south to north, from poor countries
to rich ones, are the minority: more than 90 percent of Africans
displaced by violence are still in Africa. Populations most often
move from south to south, both within and between developing
countries, and this book travels to the Democratic Republic of
Congo, South Sudan, and the Central African Republic to tell
that story.

But let's talk now about the routes that lead north—the most
dangerous ones.

In 2017, the International Organization for Migration reported
6,142 deaths along migration routes across the world—an insignificant figure in terms of the big picture, which doesn't tell the
whole truth: the truth can be known only by the Mediterranean

sea bed and the Bay of Bengal; the dunes of the Sahara Desert, and the labyrinths of disappearance in Mexico.

That year, the Mediterranean swallowed up over 3,000 lives—a record figure that's even more painful when we consider that in 2017, fewer people arrived in Europe (172,301) than in 2015 (over a million). These figures speak of the cruelty of European countries, but also of the greed and inhumanity of the mafias that keep packing more and more people into inflatable boats. Supermarket goods: the more products that can fit in a box, the greater the efficiency. Cost-benefit calculations. The commodification of human beings.

Where do they come from? In 2017, the principal nations of origin were as follows: Syria, Nigeria, Guinea, Côte d'Ivoire, Morocco, Bangladesh, Gambia, Algeria, Eritrea, and Iraq. Many of these countries have a history of violence and political persecution.

It's said that not all those who arrive are refugees. This is true in the worst sense, since they're unlikely to be granted asylum. Are there also people who have tried to reach Europe for purely economic reasons? Yes, of course. But these categorizations— who qualifies as a refugee and who does not, who has the right to migrate and who does not—are not only perverse but useless when it comes to understanding this world in movement.

Let's not bother to discuss the morality of separating people into groups. There are ideological—and legitimate—opinions on both sides. Let's start from the beginning: do these categories tell the whole story? For example, those leaving Libya aren't in fact Libyans, but mostly sub-Saharans. We'll meet some of them in the pages that follow. A boat full of Nigerians and Gambians is the perfect image for a British tabloid to stir up xenophobia: from what war are they fleeing? Let's not even waste time by pointing out that Boko Haram has caused an unprecedented crisis of displacement in Nigeria and its neighboring countries. Or that many Gambians are suffering persecution in their own country.

Rather, let's listen to what they tell us: many of them had migrated to Libya, and then decided to flee because the chaos of the post-Gaddafi era resulted in a racist campaign of extortion, theft, and worker exploitation that became simply unbearable. These people became (non) refugees after they'd left their own countries. Should they go back? The desert is another Mediterranean Sea, where dead bodies don't get counted. It's better to go to Europe.

This is but one example: the reasons driving people to migrate are complex. Some of the Syrians who speak in this book hadn't yet suffered the consequences of war when they decided to flee. The promise of a better economic future was also a factor.

A SIMPLIFIED SKETCH of the routes leading from south to north goes as follows.

From Africa, there are two major points of departure: West Africa and the Horn of Africa. From there, the route leads to the north of the continent—Libya, and to a lesser extent, Egypt. From there, to the Mediterranean Sea, and from there, with luck, to Italy. Spain, a pioneer in the violation of human rights and the installation of razor-wire fencing, closed its borders long ago. Only a few more than six thousand people arrived in Spanish territory by sea in 2016, although the figure tripled in 2017.

From the Middle East—and beyond, because Afghans must traverse Pakistan and Iran before arriving in Turkey—refugees cross the Aegean Sea, and then follow the route through Greece and the Balkans that the European Union made a deal with Turkey to close off. As a result of this deal, the flow was diverted toward the central route, the most lethal, which leads through Libya.

From Central America to the United States, the route leads across Mexico—amid robbery, kidnappings, rape—to come up against the huge wall that President Donald Trump is now planning to complete.

All these routes have something in common: they're controlled by human traffickers. In the absence of any action by nation-states, hundreds of thousands of lives are left in the hands of unscrupulous groups whose foremost priority is profit. But here, there are also gray areas: it's common for the owners of migrant boats to be arrested and accused of trafficking when in fact, they are often merely quick-witted refugees—as perhaps is the case of a DJ whom we will meet soon. There are also *polleros* and smugglers who say: they're going to try to do it anyway—I'm just helping them along, and trying to make sure they do it in the safest way possible.

Business grows with the walls. The walls grow with business.

Since the fall of the Berlin Wall in 1989, more than forty countries have built barriers of one kind or another. The fall of the wall was the metaphor for the end of the Cold War, the end of the competition between two distinct worldviews. The world was opening up completely; a new order had been established. But since then, countries all over the planet have only raised more electrified fences and continued to shut themselves off from the rest of the world. The explanation provided is national security—safety from terrorism, from illegal immigration, from refugees. The world is made up of fences and barriers, far beyond just a few notorious cases, like the wall between the United States and Mexico, or the Israeli West Bank barrier.

It's increasingly meaningless to differentiate between walls and fences: modern borders are sophisticated contrivances that, with their design and their technological virtuosity, show off the superiority of the state that builds them. The medieval concept of a solid wall is prevalent mostly in xenophobic political language, of the kind used by Donald Trump. Borders almost never consist of an actual wall, but rather a metallic chain of barriers, razor wire, sensors, security cameras, areas of desert, wire fences, signal inhibitors.

Power declaring its technological arrogance.

Power declaring its primitive political ideals. Which are so very modern.

Waiting for The Beast

Central America—The United States

> The place is stained red by the blood of migrants, some say.
> The place makes you whimper like a dog, others say.
>
> OSCAR MARTÍNEZ, The Beast: Riding the Rails
and Dodging Narcos on the Migrant Trail

A PAINTED YELLOW RAMP with dark lettering boldly tells us where we are: "Welcome to Paso del Coyote." This is Ciudad Hidalgo, one of the main points of entry into Mexico from Guatemala, on the Pacific coast. Here, beneath the bridge where customs and immigration are found, flow the waters of the Suchiate, a river crossed by makeshift rafts loaded with goods, sacks of rice, clothing. And people.

Each day, trade moves languidly down the river, watched over by the large metal structure that links the two countries. On one side, Mexico: opportunity, a vast territory to cross, the promise of a better future, the train, the *migra*, or immigration officials. On the other side, Guatemala: Central American poverty, unending violence, the place where the escape begins.

Waiting for The Beast

Raft operators gather on the riverbank, waiting to transport people and goods, although traffic is light today due to the weather. Rafts carry passengers from one side to the other to go shopping, but also groups of migrants intending to try their luck in the North. They are easy to spot since they wear backpacks and disappear immediately into Ciudad Hidalgo, either on foot or by bike taxi, whose drivers wait patiently for their customers. All this goes on under the watchful eye of the federal police, who often accept bribes from smugglers and don't bat an eyelid when they see us taking pictures.

Small boats keep arriving in Mexico to the rhythm of the music played on the Guatemalan side of the river. One of the raft operators tells me that there used to be more people "passing through," which is to say more migrants, but in 2005, Hurricane Stan swept through, taking train tracks and bridges with it and interrupting rail service from Ciudad Hidalgo and Tapachula to Arriaga, farther north. Things used to be slightly easier for the migrants: back then, they crossed the river and immediately boarded the train. But now, once in Mexican territory, they must walk or take public or private transport, first to Tapachula and then on to Arriaga. On their way, they will try to avoid the *migra*, and so they will take the less-traveled routes.

The migrants step off the rafts, climb a slope, and disappear immediately in groups of five, ten, fifteen people. I walk behind several groups who have no time to lose, who don't want to pause for even a moment. I walk past the city's defunct train station and approach two young Hondurans, Mario René and Fredid. The tracks, watched over by a railroad employee, are covered by a layer of moss. Surrounded by locomotives and derailed freight cars, Mario René and Fredid tell me they've already tried to cross Mexico once, but they were deported by the *migra*.

"We crossed the river and stayed right here overnight. We left for Tapachula early in the morning on public transport, but when we go there, they made us get off and asked to see our papers. The *migra* got a hold of us, locked us up for two days, then sent us back to Honduras."

The very day they were sent back to their country, they set out again on the same journey. From Honduras to Guatemala. They crossed the river, again. Today, the train tracks of Ciudad Hidalgo. Tomorrow, they'll head north.

"In Honduras, the violence is very tough. You can't work in peace there. Because if you work hard and make sacrifices and start making a little money . . ."

Mario René doesn't finish his sentence. He lights a cigarette. His travel companion rummages around for some food in their backpacks. The two friends languish in the ghostly train station, waiting for the weather to improve so they can set out again.

MEXICO'S 714-MILE-LONG southern border separates the states of Chiapas, Tabasco, Campeche, and Quintana Roo from Guatemala and Belize. The border with Guatemala is 594 miles of rain forest, rivers, and mountains.

The Pacific route, which cleaves to the coastline, is one of the most traveled. This is the route that Mario René and Fredid will take. What comes next after Ciudad Hidalgo and Tapachula, as soon as they've entered Mexico, is one of the toughest stretches of the journey: the Arrocera, from *arroz*, the Spanish word for rice. The Arrocera is a key place name in the migrant vocabulary, and it inspires the same look, the same respect, the same fear that I later saw in the eyes of refugees crowded into small boats crossing the Mediterranean. The Arrocera, which takes its name from an abandoned rice cellar, is an area of over one hundred fifty miles of overgrowth, which cannot be crossed by train. Migrants make stretches of the journey on foot and by VW camper or *combi* — the legendary hippie van, transformed into a form of public transport — getting off to avoid police inspections, dodging checkpoints, fleeing from the *migra*.

This is where Juan Ramón, the Honduran possessed by the spirit of the migrant shelter, was attacked; where Nelson, the man with the black eyes, was beaten up; where Mario René and Fredid were taken into custody. A territory of crimes and robberies, of rape and extortion. The Arrocera: a territory of impunity. The migrants will not report their assailants since they too are fleeing from the authorities. The conditions are ripe for abuse and exploitation. Of the weakest.

After Guatemala, after the Suchiate River and the Arrocera, comes Arriaga, still in the state of Chiapas. The Beast sets out from here. In these days of June 2014, the bad weather, caused by Hurricane Boris, is hindering its departure. A freight train has been derailed somewhere up ahead, and they're waiting for a crane to come and lift it back on. I go to the train station first thing in the morning and talk to a group of migrants led by a man with a bushy beard, who seems to have the answers to all my questions.

"I was interviewed. I was on TV. [Gael] García Bernal interviewed me, and someone from Televisa, too."

It's easy to tell that he's a *pollero*. The others look at him to ask permission to speak, seeking his approval. None of them wants to be interviewed, or even just talk casually. The boss forbids it. I walk along the tracks and come across three black men who say they're from Belize. They don't want to talk either. I wander around some more. I strike up a conversation with a Nicaraguan and some Salvadorans. Until I tell them I'm a journalist — then they send me packing. One of them, by way of an apology, shrugs his shoulders as if to say, "I'd love to, but you know how it is." The weather is bad: a cloud of nerves, suspicion, and rumors settles over the Arriaga train station. An absence is also weighing the atmosphere down: in the surrounding hotels, hundreds of people are waiting for The Beast to leave again. Staying in those rooms are the migrants traveling with guides, with *polleros*. Migrants pay these guides a fee of thousands of dollars for a series of attempts to make it to the United States—usually three. The fee includes room and board, like a kind of tourist package. The size of the fee determines a range of privileges, such as the right to travel on a "protected" train car, thanks to an advance payment made to the gangs or other criminal organizations. Women and children tend to travel with *polleros*, on organized trips, to avoid mishaps. But that doesn't guarantee anything. Sometimes the *polleros* and the executioners are one and the same; often, women are prostituted, or forced to sleep with their guides in exchange for their services.

The Beast sets out from here.

A MYSTIQUE HANGS AROUND the train tracks; they are part of a whole ecosystem, a way of understanding the world. The emotions, thoughts, and dreams of migrants are forged by the clatter of the train, its relentless forward march, the way it grinds to a halt like an exhausted mammoth. Waiting for this steel animal to depart Arriaga for Ixtepec, a hundred miles to the north, everyone in this city sustained by the train tracks, as if by a river, remembers the last time the freight train stopped here, and everyone contributes to the circulation of old rumors, fresh news, and all kinds of hearsay about the misfortunes of the passengers riding The Beast.

Lupita and Miguel, who work in a Doctors Without Borders clinic near the train tracks in Ixtepec, say that for the last few days everyone has been talking about the same thing.

"On May 28 we were giving a talk, and there was an accident,"

Lupita says. "We found a twenty-three-year-old Honduran woman on the train tracks. When the train arrives, it slows down, and a lot of people are so desperate that they jump off."

"The train was long; it had sixty cars," Miguel continues. "It stops and then moves suddenly to position itself. When it starts up again, the air rushes through all the cars."

"We were about seven hundred feet away," says Lupita. "We helped them until the ambulance showed up. The boy is in the hospital, he lost a leg. And she's going to have her arm reconstructed."

Yenny Guardado, a twenty-six-year-old Salvadoran woman who has just arrived in Ixtepec, riding on the back of The Beast, is horrified.

"They told us about the boy too. It makes you think: a little boy who's only just turned two, already without a foot. Just imagine. It changes your life completely. It's unbelievable. I told my husband, I'm not getting back on that train."

Yenny doesn't want to keep going. Her husband is going to try to make it to Mexico City, but not her. She wants to turn back.

"Our money began to run out on the way. We've made it this far. My goal was to get to the United States, but I realized on the way that the journey is tough, very dangerous. I've asked myself whether leaving my girls was really worth it, just to follow this dream we all call the American Dream. At this point I've realized my daughters need me. I can't keep risking my life, I can't risk anything happening to me, or getting killed and leaving my girls alone in El Salvador. So I've decided to go home."

The Beta Group, which offers protection to migrants, will pick her up today and take her to the immigration authorities so she can be deported to El Salvador. Yenny has only seen the beginning of the route—Ciudad Hidalgo, Tapachula, La Arrocera, Arriaga, Ixtepec—but she is horrified.

"We crossed Guatemala just fine, by bus and taxi, and it seemed like an easy journey until then, but coming into Mexico was very different. I had to walk for over two days, I couldn't take it anymore, the sun, the exhaustion. My husband and I made it to Arriaga in a *combi*, and then we got on the train," says Yenny. When she talks about The Beast, her round cheeks flush with a strong pink tone that contrasts with her brown skin. She remembers:

"As we were leaving Arriaga, the train was long, there were a lot of us, and suddenly it stopped, and my husband says to me, 'That's not good, something's going to happen.' At the time we were riding on a long car down below because we didn't want to ride on top, and he got up onto the step to see what was happening. You could hear some motorcycles. They boarded the train, then the women started crying and shouting. We put our backpacks on and he says to me, 'If I tell you to jump off the train, we jump: run and hide, and don't move.' I was nervous, shaking, wondering what was going to happen to us. A lot of people had machetes; some of the migrants tried to scare the thieves away by making a lot of noise. Then it was over, and the train kept going. When we arrived, we realized not all of us had got down from the train, that some thieves who'd gotten onto the train had taken two of the women away with them. Unbelievable. And I told him, I'm not getting back on that train."

An orange pickup is waiting by the roadside. Yenny slings her backpack over her shoulder, her passport in one hand, and says goodbye to her husband, with tears in her eyes. The men in bright orange shirts—the people from the Beta Group—open the door to the truck. Yenny and her husband no longer make eye contact; they just hold onto the tips of each other's fingers, and then let go.

When will they see each other again?

Waiting for The Beast

"You leave full of hope, with a dream, and the journey sucks the life out of you. It isn't worth it. It isn't worth leaving your children alone just to follow a dream."

FARTHER INLAND, the vegetation persists. I drive through towns with beautiful, poetic names: Ixtepec, Atalaya, Tierra Blanca. But despite its immaculate name, Tierra Blanca—white earth—is a city under the control of the Zeta cartel. Here, the Pacific route meets the one coming from Tenosique, farther east.

I wander along the train tracks and see several groups of migrants lying back in the gravel, waiting for The Beast. There are gang members among the backpackers—tattoos, hostile stares. I approach a group of Salvadorans who have moved away from the tracks and are resting beneath the shade of a tree. They're anxiously waiting for the train that will take them to Lechería, near Mexico City. From there, the trail branches into four major routes that lead to various locations on the border with the United States.

They are all in the shade, except José Armando Pineda, sixty-two, who watches everything with fascination. He is taking The Beast for the first time. He says that a sixteen-year-old boy fell from the train he took to get here, and lost a leg.

"I don't know how he'll get around when they send him back to his country. This is a very risky journey."

José Armando watches the tracks. The train is several hours late. With no question to prompt him, he says: "Well, I like the train. It's nice . . . everyone gets excited when the train comes."

It's true: when the steel animal appears, its sound rings out clearly, with no voices or shouting in the background, as if people were showing their respect for The Beast with a vow of silence.

No, this train isn't going to Lechería. They'll have to keep on waiting.

"I just went for a shower," says José Armando. "I was feeling down. Now I feel more limber. I'm ready to jump, like a parachutist from a plane."

LECHERÍA, less than forty miles from Mexico City. A girl cries on the train tracks.

"I wanted to see if God would give me the blessing of crossing to the other side, because I want to go to the other side, to the United States. My family didn't want me to come because they say the train's very dangerous, that they catch people, they beat people up, people fall. To be honest, I've been really scared."

Raquel Julieth keeps her baseball cap on. The visor hides her tears. A boy with curly hair—unruly, dark brown ringlets—smiles next to her, as if he's oblivious to the story she's telling, or as if he's just heard it before, or as if he's carrying part of the weight of it for her—I'll never know which.

"I want to give my son a better future. He stayed behind in Honduras, with my mom. I spoke to Mom just a week ago, and told her I was OK. She cries when we talk, she gets scared. She knows these routes are dangerous, with everything you see in the news."

But something happened to her as soon as she arrived in Mexico.

"I was working in Tapachula and I was attacked. I got beaten up. I was in bad shape for about two weeks. They brought me with them as best they could," she says, glancing at the curly-haired boy, "and they couldn't even carry me because I was so hot, I had a fever for almost two weeks. I couldn't eat anything."

"Yeah, there was a group of five of us and she was alone, and sick," says the kid, "so we said look, there's a girl who got beat up, and she's from Honduras like us, we've got to help her out, so we all agreed that we would. That's how I met her, about two weeks ago we met and got together, and we've decided that we're in love."

"They beat me up because I didn't want to give them what I had, they beat me all over," says Raquel Julieth, who continues her story without acknowledging what he's just said. "I made the journey sick like that. I couldn't walk, I had a fever, I couldn't swallow or lie down."

"She got sick and just wanted to stay under a bridge and sleep."

"I couldn't stand the fever anymore."

"She couldn't take it anymore. People were staring at her because she was so sick she didn't even fix herself up, she couldn't even take a shower."

"My head was swollen from where they hit me with rocks, they beat me really badly. They cut me up, too. Now I'm eating again. I've been in bad shape; I don't know, everything I've seen has upset me."

Raquel Julieth doesn't say whether she was raped. She says she wants to get on The Beast and keep heading north.

SOME FOUR HUNDRED THOUSAND people enter Mexico each year, most with the goal of reaching the United States and achieving the American Dream.

In July 2014, the Mexican government launched a plan to limit migration and set in motion a system to prevent people from climbing aboard The Beast, under the pretext that the freight train made them more vulnerable. The name says it all: they call it the Plan Frontera Sur [Southern Border Plan]. Mexico deployed thousands of police and soldiers and set up checkpoints to prevent migrants from continuing on their journey.

The result was a significant increase in detentions and deportations: 198,141 in 2015, as opposed to 127,149 in 2014. It can't be said that they didn't try any other solutions: asylum requests have also increased exponentially, from 8,052 in 2010 to 56,097 in 2015. The problem is that the cases where asylum is granted still only number in the hundreds. Asylum isn't a realistic option for those fleeing violence. Exile is statistically improbable.

The route, with the train tracks as its vertebrae, was deconstructed. While it may have been cruel and dangerous, The Beast had schedules, times, stations, and routines that allowed humanitarian and charitable organizations to deploy their services at key points and provide assistance to migrants along the trail. Now, no longer do hundreds of people arrive from the train to Father Solalinde's shelter; no longer do teams of aid workers await the arrival of the migrants passing through Lechería: those on the trail have been forced to flee into the hills or the forest, to seek alternative routes which are full of regions like the Arrocera—ideal territories for criminals to rob and rape with impunity. This is a sign of our times: forcing the migrants off The Beast erases the problem by claiming that the train that was devouring migrants no longer exists, and that the amputations, attacks, and tragedies aboard the freight cars are now only myth, history, a thing of the past.

Before, the microcosm of the train and its tracks provided a backdrop to this network of crime, extortion, and human trafficking that allowed people to imagine it as a coherent narrative. Now, the journey is even more dangerous, and it lacks the mystique of the train that previously attracted the attention of the media. New, invisible routes are traveled on foot or in shared transportation. Now, for example, trucks make the journey loaded with Central Americans, many of them minors, at risk of being suffocated on their journey to the U.S. border.

They pay thousands of dollars to ride in those trucks.

Donald Trump's racist campaign speeches sounded the alarm, but once again, they focused mainly on the border, on the wall that already exists and that he wants to expand. States fighting immigration of any kind have long been aware that these isolated measures tend to be merely cosmetic, that it's necessary to address the root of the "problem," and that the most effective strategy is to externalize the border by transporting it to another country. That's the irony of the Plan Frontera Sur: a plan more American than Mexican; a border, constructed before Trump, that is more American than Mexican.

While Mario René, Fredid, Yenny, Raquel Julieth, and the boy who lost his leg riding The Beast were attempting to travel north to the United States, Vice President Joe Biden was traveling south to their countries, to prevent them from continuing to go north. Biden traveled to Central America to resolve a crisis — that of migrants fleeing their repressive and often deadly homelands — which is in fact an American crisis. The U.S. government promised to send aid to Honduras, Guatemala, and El Salvador. The following year, it promised more — up to seven hundred fifty million dollars.

Backpacks. Human traffickers. Security forces. Shifting routes. Agreements with third countries. The purchase of borders.

A refugee crisis?

Europe discovered those words in the summer of 2015.

The Route of Shame

Turkey—Greece—The Balkans

> And if we've held on by the loins, clasped
> other necks as tightly as we could,
> mingled our breath with the breath
> of that person
> if we've closed our eyes, it was not other than this:
> simply that deep longing to hang on
> in our flight.
>
> GIORGOS SEFERIS, *Flight*

IT'S RAINING, AND THE BORDER IS CLOSED. Three thousand people trapped in the mud: half of them lie, resigned, beneath shiny thermal blankets; the other half wander, desperate and shivering from cold, in search of a solution to a problem that's out of their hands. There are no tents in this camp on the border between Serbia and Croatia because this isn't a place to stay, because Serbia wants those fleeing to leave its territory as soon as possible; nor is there any movement, because the flow of people toward Northern Europe is being reorganized, and because right now, Croatia doesn't want to let anyone in.

The Route of Shame

There's trash everywhere you look, as if the downpour were causing it to sprout from the earth. At the side of the road leading to the border, a woman is having an anxiety attack: she's just been reunited with a relative whom she had lost track of during the journey. She shouts, then faints, and people come to her aid. She is soon revived.

The woman is from Afghanistan. I can't understand what she's saying since I speak neither Dari nor Pashtun; perhaps I don't want to understand what she's saying. We spontaneously start speaking Urdu, the language of neighboring Pakistan, which she speaks brokenly, and I fumble my way through. She tells me that she has four children—I see them by her side, wrapped up in enormous blue rain ponchos, clinging to her with their eyes screwed tightly shut to keep out the rain. She tells me that they've been waiting two days to cross into Croatia and that they can't stand it any longer. She asks me to help her cross the border, tells me I have the power to do it, grabs me by the hand and cries, "You can do it, come on, let's go, don't leave me here!"

Around us, the elderly in wheelchairs, babies, teenagers, more desperate families. In the background, beyond the border, as if presiding over the scene, flies the flag of the European Union.

IN THE SUMMER AND FALL OF 2015, European public opinion discovered the continent of refugees without refuge. It had been formed long before, but until Europe saw its outline, until it saw the faces of the millions fleeing from war each year, it didn't react. It had to see inflatable boats—dozens, hundreds, thousands— arriving on the Greek island of Lesbos, loaded with Syrians, Afghans, and Iraqis. Farther north, at the border between Greece and Macedonia, it had to see the police spraying them with tear gas. It had to see the crowds of civilians crammed into trains in Macedonia, an image not without painful historical echoes. It had to see people from all kinds of backgrounds traversing rivers and obscure paths across the Balkans, countries that had suffered so much in the 1990s. It had to see detention camps, closed borders, the shouting, the tears.

Most of Europe had to see all this, to experience a moment— a few weeks, a few months—of ferment. Of indignation, of a scent of change in the air, of the feeling that nothing would ever be the same again. TV news, front pages, tweets, the #refugeeswelcome hashtag, banners of support in German soccer stadiums, welcoming parties at the Vienna train station.

And European public opinion had to see an image that served as a catalyst, as a symbol of this supposed awakening of conscience: Alan Kurdi, the three-year-old Syrian boy found dead on a Turkish beach after his boat, heading for the Greek island of Kos, had capsized. In those days, Syria was entering the fourth year of its war, and far more horrifying images had emerged—and continue to emerge daily—from that country. The Syrian war still wasn't a source of indignation in Europe. But that picture, taken by the Turkish photojournalist Nilüfer Demir, was a slap in the face for the continent. That picture didn't just speak Arabic—it spoke English, German, Spanish, and French.

Several months later, it no longer spoke any language at all.

WHAT IS THE STORY behind the most famous migration route of the last few years? Does the Syrian war fully explain it? If the war had already been going on for four years, what prompted that great exodus in the summer of 2015?

In 2015, Turkey became the country that hosted the highest number of refugees, or "temporary guests," as Ankara calls them: a total of 2.7 million, the vast majority of them Syrian. The Turkish-Syrian border is Syria's longest: 511 miles. A border crossed by thousands of jihadists who traveled to the country to fight Assad's regime, and, in the opposite direction, by Syrian civilians fleeing the war in the north of Syria.

One of these civilians is Muhammad, the olive-skinned construction worker who convinced me that a journalist is more dangerous than a fighter, whom I first met on the Syrian side of the Bab al-Salam border pass, and who invited me to speak with him in the tent where he lives with his wife and five children. I speak to him in April 2013, but his suffering began not with the war, but long before, in 1993.

"I was talking to some friends. We were having an argument about politics. I told them that Hafez al-Assad, Bashar's father, sold the Golan Heights to Israel. Somebody leaked my comments to the authorities, and I spent eleven years in jail. Eleven years! Eleven years without seeing my family, because the regime wouldn't let me. Eleven years for a couple of words," says Muhammad between mouthfuls of food. Today's menu is scrambled eggs, salted green peppers, and lentil soup. Accompanied by his family and some neighbors who've joined them for lunch in their tent in this internally displaced person (IDP) camp in the old customs area, Muhammad recalls the last few weeks: they fled the bombing in Aleppo, a few dozen miles from here.

"They destroyed our house in Aleppo. They killed the people who stayed. There were so many bodies, they couldn't even be buried. I want to go to Turkey because it isn't safe even here. There are bombings, the planes fly over us. The children are terrified."

Muhammad sips his coffee. He can't stop smoking. One cigarette after another. His goal, he says, is to get to Turkey as soon as possible and work in what he knows best: construction. Until then, neither he nor his family will feel safe.

"What's happening now in Syria will be engraved in our children's minds for a long time."

We Are Not Refugees

AT THAT TIME, it was still possible for foreign journalists to cross to the Syrian side and speak to the civilian population. Black flags were beginning to fly in the north of the country, but not until weeks later did it become evident that entering a Syria controlled by armed opposition groups, among them the Islamic State, wasn't so much a lottery as almost a guarantee of being kidnapped. Since then, media coverage in places like Aleppo and the rural area surrounding it has depended on local journalists, often activists turned reporters (like Peshang Alo, whom we met earlier) and the foreign media has lost touch—if indeed it ever was in touch—with what was going on there, at the point of departure. That was the first reason why they had no idea what was about to happen.

That same year, 2013, I meet Hassan Nasser, forty-two years old. He lives in a basement in Istanbul with his wife, two sons, and an exceptionally gifted three-year-old daughter whom I watch as she frees up space on a smartphone to download an app and even skillfully handles a borrowed single-lens reflex (SLR) camera. Her proud father, dressed in a green T-shirt bearing the suggestive slogan "De puta madre" [Fucking awesome]—just like that, in Spanish, an expression with which he seems unfamiliar—tells us that he participated in the earliest protests against the regime in spring 2011.

"From the beginning, I was very active. I was one of the protest leaders. We were peacefully asking for freedom."

The Syrian security forces went looking for Hassan at his house: he leaped from the third floor and injured his back. A year later, he sought refuge in Turkey. Now he spends his days in Istanbul worrying about the injury, which prevents him from working. He is desperately seeking a cure: some doctors say he needs surgery, others say he doesn't; he wouldn't be able to afford it anyway.

Hassan's family wasn't exactly poor in Syria. Hassan spent ten years in Saudi Arabia, working for a travel agent. He did business in construction and manufacturing. In his hometown of Kesweh, on the outskirts of Damascus, he had a successful clothing store. Now the family survives however it can without an income, he tells me while watching his children, Yaman and Yanal—brothers, but complete opposites—who sit beside him, one on each side, on the couch. Yaman is twelve, very quiet, and a Real Madrid fan. He wants to be a mathematician, and when the war is over, he wants to go back to his country. Yanal is eleven, enjoys attention, and is a Barcelona fan. He shares a bed with Yaman in their basement in Istanbul. He wants to be a journalist and to try his luck in Europe. Divergent forces in the same family: Syria versus Europe, the attachment to home versus the desire for a better life.

"If we go, we'll do it legally," says Hassan. "Many Syrians enter Europe illegally with smugglers, but it's very dangerous. My family can't do that. To go to Europe, you need to have your papers in order."

My cell phone rings. On the screen, I see the code for Turkey: +90. Before I can answer, it stops ringing. It's a missed call, which used to be common before everyone started using apps, but now just exasperates people. It could be anything, but for me, it's a good omen: when I conduct in-depth interviews with refugees, I give them my number no matter where they're from, and when they complain that it's a Spanish number, I tell them to call me and hang up so I can call them back. For years, a missed call from a foreign number has been a reason to get excited.

I return the call and am surprised to hear a voice in Arabic.

"*Suhufiin 'iisbani!*"

Spanish journalist! I recognize the voice, hoarse from smoking: it's Muhammad, the construction worker trapped in the IDP camp at the Syrian border. He tells me that he's in Kahraman-mara, in the south of Turkey. That I can visit him.

A month later, I arrive in this gray, lethargic Turkish city with an unpronounceable name. We've agreed to meet at some build-ings under construction. Muhammad comes down from one of them, except that Muhammad is no longer Muhammad: his name is now Yahya. In Syria, he was afraid of retaliation and asked me to use another name, but now I'm allowed to use his real one.

"My wife and five children are at the Kilis 2 refugee camp. We arrived a month ago. I've found work here in construction. When the Muslim holiday of Eid comes, I'll go and spend a few days with my family at the camp."

I go with him to the apartment he shares with some other Syrians who, like him, are working illegally—refugees were pro-hibited from working in Turkey until 2016. Now his daily routine has changed: he gets up early, goes to the construction site, and leaves at around five in the afternoon. Muhammad/Yahya show-ers and sits on the mat in the living room. He now sips tea instead of coffee, but he still speaks incisively of his experiences.

"The fear gets into your body, like an illness."

Muhammad/Yahya lights another cigarette, with a vacant look in his eyes. He's no longer in Syria, but the anxiety still pursues him relentlessly.

"You can't get away from that feeling of fear. When you hear the sound of a plane, your mind goes back to the past. It isn't easy to get over it."

Throughout the conversation, he seems downcast, afflicted by the passage of time. This is when homesickness and longing take hold, when war and destruction, now hazy memories, are left be-hind and give way to a new scenario of uncertainty, where a dif-ferent language is spoken, and codes are no longer shared. This is when "home" passes from being a reality, into something distant, idealized, impossible. Now, "home" is no longer within reach, or easy to speak of without a sigh of longing; "home" has become something literary, abstract: something that will not return.

"I miss my country. My village was destroyed several times. The Syrian army destroys everything and kills everyone. My dream, twenty-four hours a day, is to go back to my country, to my village . . . when you're away from home, you can't relax. Right now, since I can't go back to Syria, I'd go to any other country where I could be safe."

As Muhammad/Yahya plays nervously with his cigarette, tears well up in his eyes.

IT'S A TRIP OF REUNIONS. After seeing Muhammad/Yahya, I visit Hassan, the Syrian who lived in a basement in Istanbul, with the sons who were Madrid and Barcelona fans. They're still living there, but their family has grown. His daughter, Zein al Sham, a little girl with a mischievous face, now fills their home with joy, and Hassan is besotted with her.

"When she was born, they said we had to go to the Syrian consulate to have a passport issued for her. The consulate told us we had to wait six months and pay 300 euros. We don't have that kind of money," says Hassan in the living room, always keeping one eye on the TV. The Syrian passport—the paperwork—is a requirement for the little girl to be granted a residence permit. His daughter, born in exile, is now stateless, undocumented. Many would say "illegal."

The basement seems smaller and gloomier: Zein al Sham isn't the only new arrival in the last six months. A cousin of Hassan's has moved in after having fled from Egypt, where security forces broke into his house. Before, five people had been living in this Istanbul basement; now there are thirteen, living in less than 250 square feet.

"We have no financial resources. Yesterday I had to ask a Syrian in the neighborhood for some money. It's a loan—I'll have to pay him back."

Hassan says he has no plans for the future. He is overwhelmed: the family's problems keep piling up, and the physical agony of his back continues. It's becoming clearer and clearer to him that his dream of going back to Syria will now be more difficult to realize: day by day, the bombs bury the family's hopes of returning home. His mother, the only member of his family who stayed, and with whom he often speaks via Skype, is still there. She has met her new granddaughter, Zein Al-Sham, only on the computer screen. Hassan fears for her life.

"I spend every day glued to the TV, to find out what's happening in Syria."

Where to go? Hassan knows he's unlikely to be offered asylum in any European country. He knows the process could take months, years. He still says his family cannot risk their lives on a rubber boat, but he no longer talks about going "legally," and he no longer criticizes the smugglers. The balance between his sons' wishes has been broken. The dream of his son Yaman, the little boy who wanted to go back to Syria, is drifting further and further away, while Yanal's wish—Europe—is becoming a more and more clearly defined possibility. The one who before seemed crazy now seems to be the most rational. What's impossible now is Syria, not Europe.

DEEK GETS UP AT FIVE in the morning. His sister has made him a hearty breakfast. As he devours it, he wonders if he should say goodbye to his mother. They haven't spoken in months, and besides that, she's sick. In the end, he decides to leave without a word, getting in the car with his father and brother. Feelings of regret will stay with him for the whole journey.

The Route of Shame

It's a long drive: the car stops at a gas station to refuel. Deek—
he asks me to use his last name, not his given name—is a twenty-
one-year-old Kurd from the city of Raqqa, which will soon be
transformed into the de facto capital of the Islamic State in Syria.
After an indeterminate stretch of time, he arrives in the village of
Tell Abyad—meaning "white hill" in Arabic—one of the Syrian
border crossings that has seen the most conflict. Deek crosses the
official border with his passport.

"Oh! You're from Raqqa? Good, go ahead."

Deek enters Turkey alone; his father and brother stay behind.
The family has agreed that Deek should try to achieve his dream.
When he was very young, he already wanted to go to Russia, Can-
ada, the United Kingdom. He began studying English and went
to live in Damascus for a while, though Raqqa was still his home.
This is the moment: Deek will not stay in Turkey.

Now he is outside Syria. A taxi takes him to a Turkish city
whose name he can't remember. After a two-hour journey, he has
no intention of resting and goes immediately to the bus station
and buys a ticket to Istanbul. The trip is long and dull. Twenty-
two hours later, he's in the great metropolis. There, he contacts
some smugglers, and soon he is traveling again, this time toward
the west coast of Turkey, toward Izmir, a city on the Aegean Sea
through which Iraqis, Afghans, and Syrians pass frequently to the
rhythm set by the bombs. From Izmir and other nearby locations,
the smugglers launch precarious vessels loaded with refugees,
sailing toward the Greek Aegean Islands. Deek boards an inflatable dinghy with twenty-five other people, among them two children, all trying to reach Greece. He's afraid: it's dark, and the boat
is very small. It's five in the morning again, the same time he left
his house without saying goodbye to his mother. Dawn is break-
ing. "A clear morning," he remembers. The Greek police spot the
vessel and approach it. The refugees panic, thinking that the

police will send them back to Turkey; the boat's helmsman speeds up. In the end, the police stop the boat, but they help the passengers get to the Greek island of Lesbos. They allow them to stay overnight in the port of Mitilini, the island's capital. The police then take them to the station, where they remain under arrest for a day. Then they give them some papers written in Greek and let them go, according to the protocol for temporary stays.

"Then we were free."

DEEK'S JOURNEY could be any one of the thousands reported in the news beginning in the summer of 2015, but in fact, it happened in April 2013. The route—the beginning of the route—already existed, and was already killing people. Shortly before Deek set out, seven Syrians drowned in the Aegean Sea. The Greek coast guard was terrorizing refugees by threatening to turn them away. Cases of so-called pushbacks were becoming more frequent: that's why Deek and his fellow travelers attempted to flee when the Greek boat came into view. Although the media didn't shine a light on this exodus, it was a historic moment: since 2004, most of those arriving in Greece had been Afghans, but in 2013, for the first time, most were Syrians. That year, the number of arrivals in Greece rose from 3,600 to 11,400: more than three times as many in just one year. During those years, (non) refugees began traveling by sea: until then, the overland route, farther north through Evros, had been the most traveled. In the summer of 2012, the Greek authorities built a fence in the region and deployed two thousand border agents to stem the tide of migration. The result: the population flow moved south, to the Aegean Sea.

At that time, the Village of All Together, a local charity supporting refugees, was entering the last phase of its operations. Since the authorities were placing refugees in enclosures of approximately

30 square feet, this group established the Pikpa summer camp to accommodate them. It was an emergency solution that guaranteed a minimum of humanitarian standards: medical attention, food, drinking water. When I visit the camp in May 2013, it's already closed: only two Afghans and two Somalis are left. Dead leaves, empty caravans, cold blankets. A single shoe. The archaeological remains of those who've moved on. At that point, despite the peace of the island, a new exodus was in the making, which would arrive in Europe with full force two years later, and would require humanitarian efforts far more powerful than the Village of All Together, with volunteers not just from Greece, but from all over Europe.

In May 2013, in the port of Mitilini, there are only fifty-five migrants and refugees. They're living in poor conditions, in containers monitored by the coast guard. When I approach some of these people who've fled, to talk to them, the coast guard doesn't try to prevent me. I say hi to the aid workers from Doctors of the World and enter the port enclosure. Most of the people here are Afghans. I approach a couple of Syrians in a corner, shielding themselves from the sun. One of them—with a well-groomed beard, Ray-Bans that seem welded to his dark face, hair perfectly slicked back despite the sea voyage—tells me that he was a soldier of Assad's regime, and that he deserted. That he tried to join up with the armed opposition groups but was rejected. That he understood that he had to flee if he didn't want to die. That he crossed into Turkey and paid a smuggler to get to the Greek islands.

"Being in Assad's army is impossible if you're a Sunni [the branch of Islam to which most of the armed opposition belongs]. If you're a Sunni, you have to kick the prisoner three times as hard. You always have to prove yourself more than the others. They always suspect you."

We Are Not Refugees

He doesn't tell me his name. He speaks in a whisper, for fear his travel companions might overhear him. He languishes in the port, waiting for his turn to receive the papers that will allow him to remain temporarily in Greece and take the ferry to Athens. This soldier in Ray-Bans is from Latakia, on the west coast of Syria, but he was called up to join the ranks in Hama, a hot spot in the early months of the revolution.

"Everyone wants to desert, but you have to be really brave to do it. The day I deserted, I ran away. I had no idea where I was going, I just ran, and a soldier who was a friend of mine was shooting at me. He had to do it. It was his duty."

Along the route, he could barely speak to his family because they'd begun to receive threats. Nor did he speak to any Syrians on the journey because he trusted no one. That's another problem faced by Syrians fleeing the war: the sectarian nature of the conflict fuels suspicion. No one trusts anyone, the war can't be left behind—it travels with you, along with its infernal logic, its ability to sow division and create ghettos, allegiances, factions.

"Why did you desert?"

"It wasn't for me. I'm not a murderer."

From this port, Syrians and Afghans set sail for Athens. First, they spend a few days—or weeks—in custody at the Moria police station, where they have their fingerprints taken and are issued with a certificate allowing them to remain legally on Greek soil; in fact, it's a deportation document: a month to leave the country, or three months, if they're Syrian. They go immediately to the port, buy a ticket to Athens, and depart. Deek, the young Kurd who didn't say goodbye to his mother, is one of twenty-five refugees boarding one of those ferries alongside the tourists. They arrive in the Greek capital first thing in the morning.

"No, I don't have words to describe how I'm feeling. I feel free, and happy to have left Syria," says Deek as he glimpses the

Acropolis, his face bathed in sunlight. As he disembarks from the ferry, his fellow travelers keep walking, but two officials take him by the arm and pull him aside. He's cornered by a man in a suit and a blonde woman with the face of a bureaucrat. The conversation moves quickly since Deek speaks English. They put him in a car. They're from the European Border and Coast Guard Agency, also known as Frontex. Welcome to Athens, Deek.

Two years later, in Skala Sikamineas, in the northeast of the island of Lesbos, inflatable boats with up to seventy refugees on board are arriving constantly. Numerous cars patrol the dusty coastal highways. They're all following the rescue workers from Proactiva Open Arms, a nongovernmental organization (NGO) working to raise awareness about the situation in the Aegean Sea, rescuing and providing aid to refugees who, upon their arrival in the European Union, in Greece, find themselves not knowing what to do.

It was in Lesbos that a lifeguard and sea rescue company from Badalona, Catalonia, was transformed into an NGO that would later attract much attention and go on to save many more lives on the most dangerous route: the central Mediterranean route, from Libya to Italy.

A boat approaches the shore, the cars park at the edge of the beach, and a swarm of lifeguards, volunteers, and photographers prepare to welcome the refugees. The Proactiva team signals for the refugees to land in a safe place and avoid crashing against the rocks. Some throw themselves into the water before reaching the shore, but all arrive safe and sound. Mothers and children embrace, people arrive with injuries, others change their clothes. Well-organized groups of Greeks collect the fuel and engines from the inflatable boats.

We Are Not Refugees

Muhammad, an eighteen-year-old Syrian, is among the recent arrivals. He has a small digital camera slung over his shoulder. He's traveling alone: he says that he's an economics student and wants to attend a European university. He has traveled the same route as everyone else: he left Syria, boarded a truck with dozens of other people bound for the west coast of Turkey, and from there, boarded a boat to Lesbos.

"I can't live in Syria. People are dying every day. Now the Russians are bombing us, too. I have a one-month-old son. I hope I can be reunited with him one day. I want to live in Europe."

This isn't the best time to talk to Muhammad. He's in a hurry. The volunteers give him some coffee. "Thanks," he says, "this coffee is really strong, let's keep going." Weeks earlier, the refugees had to traverse the whole island to get to the police station, get their papers, and proceed to the port to leave for Athens. Cab drivers were on the lookout for them and charged them as much as they possibly could. A whole economy has grown up around those escaping the bombs: vendors, hotels, stores. A "tourist" trail, fraught with scams and expenses for the refugees.

Now Muhammad and his traveling companions can take the buses leaving from Skala Sikamineas. First, the buses take them to the Kara Tepe camp, farther south on the island. After a few days there, the travelers can go to the Moria police station, around which an improvised camp has been established, where the living conditions are appalling.

If the camps are overwhelmed, then naturally, the port is too. In 2013, I had to follow Deek and his twenty-four fellow travelers closely to board the ferry and accompany them on their journey: now thousands of refugees languish in the port, and there is even a ferry destined exclusively for them, which costs sixty euros, as opposed to the forty-eight-and-a-half paid by tourists. The small but great indignities of being a refugee in the twenty-first century.

The Route of Shame

In 2015, a record number of people arrived in Greece: 856,723, compared with 43,500 in 2014, and 11,400 in 2013. The Syrians who were still hanging on in their country became convinced that there was no end in sight: they packed their bags and invested all their savings in trying to get to Europe. Turkey was just a transit country. They belonged to every social class, but those with more purchasing power were clearer that their destination was northern Europe.

"MY FACTORY WAS THE SIZE OF THIS WHOLE PORT."

This is Akram Jabri, a Syrian sitting on some ramshackle steps in Lesbos with his family. The Syrian who gave this book its title. The Syrian who says that he is not a refugee, that we are not refugees, that refugees are everyone else: *refugee* is a word for the poor, for the dispossessed.

"Now we want to go to Oslo, but what I'd really like to do is go back to Syria and reopen my business. We were making fifteen hundred dollars a day. My factory was the size of this whole port."

But his factory no longer exists. His children say he was "almost blinded" when he saw the state it had been left in by the fighting.

The family waits patiently to leave Lesbos.

A few hours later, two ferries depart for Athens. These ferries are a world map of populations fleeing from war: the majority are Syrians and Afghans. In an outdoor cafeteria on the boat, where everyone is smoking anxiously, I see a couple who can't stop fooling around and kissing each other. Perhaps it's the first moment of peace they've enjoyed in a long time. Her: a purple jacket, a scarf with a pattern of blue, gray, and pink stripes and circles. Him: a leather jacket, bent glasses, the hope for a new life in his expression. It's the same part of the ferry where I spoke with Deek, the Kurd who was intercepted by Frontex. It's inevitable; he reminds me of Deek, so I go over and talk to him.

We Are Not Refugees

Adham has escaped from the Yarmouk Palestinian refugee camp, on the outskirts of Damascus. His grandfather fled Palestine after partition in 1948, and took refuge in Syria. Adham belongs to the third generation of Palestinians to have lived there, who are now fleeing en masse.

"I'm a math teacher. Assad's army killed my brother and my father. The Islamic State is in Yarmouk, too. Life is impossible there. So I decided to flee with my girlfriend."

He had to pay the Syrian branch of Al Qaida one thousand dollars to pass through the checkpoints dotted around the country, from Yarmouk to Aleppo, on the northern border with Turkey. Hidden in trucks, like cargo. Across the desert, through the olive groves. Once in Turkey, he paid another thousand euros to be taken to the west coast and loaded onto an inflatable boat headed for Lesbos: a kind of tourist package, because that's how human trafficking worked, and still works today.

"I've never seen Palestine, but it's in my heart, in my eyes. Oh, Palestine! I love Palestine. I want to go to Germany, and then one day I'll be able to travel to Palestine."

He can't say "return," since he's never set foot in the land of his ancestors.

WE ARRIVE AT THE PORT OF ATHENS: the same light that bathed Deek's face that morning now settles on Adham's features. This time, there's no Frontex. I follow Adham, who's moving at full speed. During those weeks, the route through Turkey, Greece, and the Balkans became a true obstacle course: inflatable boats, long waits, ferries, buses, taxis, roads. I'm joined by the photographers Edu Ponces and Anna Surinyach. From our appearance, we could be just another group making the journey—Afghans, Syrians—so we follow Adham onto a bus that's just for refugees, which takes them to Idomeni, in the far north of Greece, on the border with Macedonia. We wait there patiently in the transit camp. Things are moving quickly. We mingle with the refugees and pass through the Greek police checkpoint. It's dark, and we cross an unlit pathway, and then reach another camp, the one on the Macedonian side. We sit under a large tent, in the mud, waiting for the border to be opened. Some people are shouting, but in general the refugees are impeccably civil, unlike the Macedonian police, who laugh and shout unnecessarily, since everyone is calm. Our only plan is to accompany them on their journey, with little regard for the consequences. Adham crosses the border and we follow him, but the tripod sticking out of Ponces's backpack catches the attention of an official, who tells us to stop.

"Passport."

We show our passports.

"Spanish? What are you, refugees? Come with me."

Like dozens of other reporters—"You aren't very original," the superintendent would later tell me—we were detained and required to pay a fine of two hundred fifty euros. We had to sign an order of expulsion and agree to leave Macedonia within twenty-four hours.

We get going as soon as possible and try to catch up with Adham. We head to the station and climb aboard a dilapidated train, hoping it will leave for the border with Serbia, along with the rest of the refugees. It's three in the morning: there's nobody here, so we snooze on the seats. A furious conductor expels us from the train, and we end up having to take a more traditional route: a bus to the capital, Skopje, and another bus to the border. When I manage to contact Adham by text message, he's already at the border between Serbia and Croatia. We still haven't left Macedonia.

Once in Serbia, we rejoin the river of people—Bangladeshis, Pakistanis, again Syrians and Afghans—pursuing their dream. We walk along a dusty path, surrounded by farmland. Some British journalists are using a drone to capture this cinematic moment: columns of humans with backpacks—children, elderly women, young people, mothers, grandfathers. Serbian taxi drivers pull up alongside families with babies, trying to convince them that for ten euros, they can take them to the registration point in Presevo in no time: many people bite, since they don't know how short a distance there is left to walk. In just a few minutes on foot, there are buses that will take them to the same place for free.

From Presevo, we board another bus full of refugees. It has Wi-Fi, which is the most important thing—more important than food or water, which most can buy for themselves. This is another key to the aid organizations' failure to help these people: what they were dealing with wasn't a nutritional crisis in Africa or a war in the Middle East, but a crisis of human rights and dignity. These people's needs were different: their most urgent requirements were communication and orientation. If bombs began to fall tomorrow on Barcelona and I was forced to flee, the last thing I'd leave behind would be my cell phone.

Between the tremendous snores of the passengers, I notice that the bus is moving very slowly. It makes many stops. For something to eat. For a cup of tea. For people to stretch their legs. There's an increase in police checkpoints, which are constantly stopping the bus. Hungary has just closed its borders. The tide of people is rearranging itself: a new route is being forged. It's no longer Serbia–Hungary–Austria–Germany: it's now Serbia–Croatia–Slovenia–Austria–Germany. Thousands of people are crowded on the border between Serbia and Croatia, since the latter allows only a limited number of people to enter each day.

We drive in circles around the Serbian town of Sid, near the Croatian border. Confusion reigns. Until, suddenly, the bus stops in the middle of nowhere.

The Route of Shame

"Yalla! Yalla!"

In a mocking tone, the Serbian police shout at the refugees in Arabic, telling them to "hurry up!" and take a dirt road that, now that night has fallen, leads somewhere unknown. Everyone obeys without saying a word. We walk with them until we realize that if we keep going, we'll have the same problem we had on the border between Greece and Macedonia. We turn around and manage to arrive in Sid. Then we discover that in fact that wasn't the *official* border: faced with so many arrivals, the desperate Serbs—behind the backs of the Croatians—were trying to push these refugees into crossing the border via that path in an attempt to get rid of them as soon as possible.

Waste management.

The next day, we approach the *official* border. I use italics because this isn't really the border either: during those months, a circuit of informal borders was created for the refugees to cross. The authorities made them cross at illegal passes set up only for refugees, and then registered them so they could continue their journey. They forced them to underline their status as illegal migrants. That was the solution that the countries involved were offering to the flight of hundreds of thousands of people.

It's raining, and the border is closed. Three thousand people trapped in the mud: half of them lie, resigned, beneath shiny thermal blankets; the other half walk, desperate and shivering from the cold, in search of a solution that's out of their hands. In this camp on the border between Serbia and Croatia there are no tents, since this isn't a place to stay, because Serbia wants those fleeing to leave its territory as soon as possible; nor is there any movement, since the flow of people toward Northern Europe is being reorganized, and since, at the moment, Croatia doesn't want to let anyone in.

I couldn't help the Afghan woman cross the border. She had

to sleep there with her children, in the mud, and wait for Croatia to open its border. When it did so—the humanity of the Croatian police contrasted starkly with the Serbs' rudeness—the hysteria dissipated within half an hour. They crossed the border at full speed—the young people pushing the children and the elderly—and went on their way. The Afghan woman also crossed. From the apocalypse to nothing. Puddles, rain ponchos, shoes, bags, a filth that emanated exhaustion and desperation. Just before the Croatian fence, which stood open, a little boy had abandoned a toy. A teddy bear was the only one left behind in the mud. The rain had stopped. After the parentheses of Macedonia and Serbia, the refugees had again entered the European Union. Or at least the flag flying above them suggested as much.

Only four months later, the European Union came to a historic agreement with Turkey to stop the exodus. It bought a border from the Turkish president, Recep Tayyip Erdogan, for six billion euros. It threatened those who dared to cross with being returned to Turkey.

Arrivals in Greece decreased precipitously, from more than eight hundred fifty thousand in 2015 to less than two hundred thousand in 2016, and then thirty thousand in 2017. Now only one route was left—the most dangerous, the one that has caused the highest number of deaths in the twenty-first century: the central Mediterranean route. The one that begins in Libya and has only two destinations: Italy or the bottom of the sea.

Libyan Waves

Mediterranean Sea

> You are nothing more than a boat at the end of its journey
> Nothing more than a mute script.
>
> CLARISSE NICOÏDSKI, The Color of Time

T HESE WAVES ARE FLAMES.
  While sailors dressed in red coveralls pull (non) refugees from the Mediterranean Sea and nurses in latex gloves and short sleeves rally to treat their injuries; while a white inflatable dinghy that until a few minutes earlier was transporting the hundred people crowded onto it now sails empty, adrift, carrying only soaked T-shirts, bandanas, good-luck charms; while African children cry on board at the sight of a sea that nearly killed them; while all this madness takes place on the high seas and the sweat streams into my eyes, I decide to pause. I stop running up and down the lower deck of the rescue boat snapping photos; I stand still for a moment and watch the sea's waves—the sea of my childhood, the sea of my life—crest and turn into flames: everything is an immense blue fire of war, flight, and European contempt, consuming thousands of Somalis, Syrians, Nigerians, Ethiopians, Gambians . . .

We Are Not Refugees

That ghostly fire didn't swallow up Westerners; I myself needn't be concerned about those wave-flames. Nowhere else had I seen with such clarity the abyss that separates the privileged from the dispossessed. The scene on the open sea, like a hyperrealist painting, a few dozen nautical miles from Libya, clarified that thought even more. On that blue threshold between Europe and Africa, life began to gain meaning and to be worthy of the efforts of the authorities. A few nautical miles determine where *civilization* begins; where people, once here, become considered people; where African reality ends, and Western reality begins.

On that blue tapestry surrounded by oil rigs whose lights shone faintly by night, merchant vessels bound for Tripoli, British frigates with bare-chested soldiers lifting weights on deck, there was an essential story that needed to be told. With time, reviewing my notes, writing and rewriting, I realized that the essential thing wasn't the rescue boat and the spectacular logistics it entailed; it wasn't the adventure of the European idealists trying to save the (non) refugees; it wasn't even the route traveled by those fleeing, those who risked being devoured by marine flames.

The essential story was an encounter among five people. Five people I met during my time on board the *Dignity I*, a Doctors Without Borders rescue boat. A captain from Santander, a temperamental aid coordinator from Italy, a shrewd sailor from Mallorca, a Nigerian baby who'd never been to Nigeria, and a Gambian DJ who was evacuated by helicopter. Five people who were ordinary when separate; five people with nothing in common, but who converged at a moment of immense historical significance—the so-called refugee crisis; five people whose paths would never have crossed were it not for the fact that we live in a world of war and flight, a world of desperation and injustice, of hope and the search for freedom.

A world of exodus.

Libyan Waves

PACO GARCÍA ABASCAL was convinced that this was *his* mission. The veteran captain had received a call from an aid organization asking him to command a boat—no one knew which boat yet—off the coast of Libya, to rescue the thousands of people setting sail across the Mediterranean in dinghies and fishing boats. The fact that a nongovernmental organization (NGO) that had always worked on dry land—in the Democratic Republic of Congo, or South Sudan—was somewhat quixotically abandoning its natural habitat to enter the fathomless depths of the sea illustrated the moral bankruptcy of some European governments and political institutions that didn't care if the Mediterranean turned into a cemetery, so long as they prevented more sub-Saharans and Arabs from arriving on European soil.

A native of Santander, Captain Paco accepted the proposal and recruited a trusted crew accustomed to the Cantabrian Sea, and some sailors from the Balearic Islands. Now they needed to search for a boat. They found it in the frigid North Sea. It was called the *Furore-G*, and it had been built in 1971 as a fueling boat for Scandinavian oil rigs. Life took a new turn for this contraption. It got a new home, a new purpose, and even a new name. It was renamed the *Dignity I* and transferred to the Mediterranean Sea, to accomplish the noble mission of saving lives.

The *Dignity I* wasn't designed as a rescue boat, but it managed to become one. A clinic was established in the cabin to treat those who were injured, deprived of oxygen, sick, or pregnant. At the stern, there was a spacious lower deck covered in boards and tarps to provide shelter for hundreds of people. Up above, on the top deck, a space was also set up for those who'd been brought on board. Bottled water and food kits were stacked in the storeroom—cheese, chicken, crackers—to be distributed among the rescued.

Captain Paco went to the North Sea himself, to see his boat and bring it back to the port of Barcelona, the logistical hub of the operation. Because it was *his* boat. The captain unquestionably wanted to help; his goal was to rescue as many people as possible, but for him, the most important thing was the boat. For any captain, the most important thing is the boat. It was forbidden to speak ill of the *Dignity I* in his presence. One day, as we were sailing, I went up on the bridge, the dome from which the captain steers the ship, and criticized what I considered the boat's excessive movement.

"How can this wreck be rocking around so much when there aren't any waves?" I complained, my stomach churning, cursing myself for having embarked on that mission.

"The boat is perfect," said the captain, shooting me a look with his small gray eyes. This time, I truly saw flames.

There were successive cases of seasickness during the first few days of the voyage, as we left the coastlines behind us like shadows: Menorca, Tunisia . . . soon we drew nearer the rescue zone, off the coast of Libya. That journey was torture. The design of the boat's hull, the underwater section, was round, and without a keel or bridge wings to steady the rocking, the *Dignity I* pitched from side to side even in good weather, lurching around and causing those of us not used to being at sea to throw up. That was the technical explanation provided, but I'm convinced that Captain Paco sailed the *Dignity I* in such a way as to make the swell pound the boat especially hard during those first few days. Those of us who'd never been at sea before would have to get used to it. That's what Captain Paco was like: authoritarian, proud, fond of dramatic effects and of setting examples, always ready to teach a lesson to anyone who needed it.

Paco had set out to accomplish a mission. He was not going to fail. He was eager to get there, and for the action to begin. As we approached Libya and the time for the rescue drew near, he spent an entire afternoon perched high on one of the masts, installing a security camera. Always dressed tidily, the captain briefly took off his jeans, belt, and tucked-in Doctors Without Borders T-shirt, donned a red coverall, and performed a series of almost acrobatic maneuvers up on the mast. Without a harness.

His personality isn't merely an anecdote—it had a direct impact on the first rescue operation. And he wasn't the only one who knew how to give orders.

"I THINK THIS IS D-DAY. The conditions are ripe for a rescue. We need to get ready."

It was the first non-harsh comment made in several days by Francesca Mangia, the Italian aid coordinator on board the *Dignity I*. Always accompanied by a packet of Marlboros, this volatile Doctors Without Borders worker had spent the previous few months finalizing the logistics, organizing the team—preparing for this operation.

It was the moment of truth, and she recognized it immediately, something the rest of us failed to do. We had arrived twenty-four hours earlier in the critical zone, the rescue zone, less than thirty nautical miles from the Libyan coast—sometimes much closer—where the waters are no longer international and rescue boats can intercept vessels departing from Libya. The previous day, the sea had been rough and the Libyan coast had been lashed head on by strong winds. Now the whitecaps had disappeared and the sea was an immense, smooth, blue canvas. Ramadan had just begun, and a strange torpor had taken hold of the entire mission. I paid no attention to Francesca's admonishments and sat back down on the top deck to record my audio journal, in which I predicted, swayed by my own skepticism and weariness, that there would be no rescue that day.

We Are Not Refugees

A few minutes later, the message arrived. And Francesca was transformed. She took the lead and directed the entire operation. This is how it works: refugees usually have a satellite telephone on their boat that allows them to send out a distress call. The Coordination Center in Rome detects this signal and contacts the nearest ship so it can proceed with the rescue. Francesca was in charge of talking to Rome. That day, the sirens sounded at full volume. Eighty-eight people were crowded into a white, inflatable dinghy. The lifeboat was lowered, following the orders given by the intrepid Captain Paco. All the improvisation was transformed into professionalism: the approach was calm and efficient, and soon the rescued refugees climbed aboard the lifeboat, one by one, and were transferred in groups of ten to the mother ship, the *Dignity I*. Inside, Francesca was organizing the stations through which those who'd been rescued would pass when they came on board. Sometimes she shouted, but it was nearly always enough for her to appear suddenly, with her disheveled, shoulder-length hair, for everyone to know exactly what to do.

The boat was buzzing with energy. It had a strong leadership. People with an endless capacity for work. Enthusiasm, dedication. When night fell, an improvised crisis cabinet was set up on the bridge. The Coordination Center in Rome had sent word of a fishing boat at sea carrying four hundred fifty refugees. This represented a challenge for the *Dignity I*, which had capacity for only four hundred people—although in other operations, it would carry many more. Until that point, it had only rescued dinghies—rubber boats with a hundred or so people on board. An operation of this kind, at night, could end in tragedy. On the bridge were Captain Paco, who was in favor of taking action, Francesca, who was somewhat more cautious, and Samir, the cultural mediator, who called the fishing boat several times by satellite phone, initially without success. Because it was assumed that the first contact made with the boats might be with Syrians, the *Dignity I* had several Arabic speakers on board to act as cultural mediators. The two I met were as gentle as they were burly: Samir Sayyad, a Spaniard of Palestinian origin, and Salah Dasouqi, a Syrian also of Palestinian origin, whom we will meet later.

A Syrian finally answered Samir's calls but gave incorrect coordinates. The minutes kept passing, and we still didn't know whether the operation would take place or not.

"You can't see anything from the lifeboat at night," said Samir, who was a key figure in the rescue.

"We don't have the capacity, we'd have to call in reinforcements," said Francesca.

"We have to go," said the captain.

"Of course we have to go," said Francesca, "but to do what? Tell me, what? To save a few people, and leave the others to drown?"

The captain was determined to sail until we were almost in Libyan waters, to proceed with the rescue. It was a slow, ephemeral dawn, with cigarettes and coffee, on the bridge of a small rescue boat full of maps, thoughts, navigational triangles, sighs, screens, doubts, radars, phone calls, tiny blinking lights. We soon realized that something wasn't right about the coordinates we'd been given by the fishing boat loaded with refugees. We had thought they were near the Libyan coast, but they turned out to be dozens of nautical miles farther north, and moving full steam ahead. They were located near a freighter with the enigmatic name of *Melody V*, which, despite not being a rescue boat, had the obligation—as per the Law of the Sea—to save the fishing boat if it found itself in an emergency. Rome tried to call, but the *Melody V* ignored the notifications. So Francesca decided to call the freighter, bound for Libya with who knows what kind of cargo, herself.

"Melody V, Melody V."

They didn't respond.

"Melody V, Melody V, Melody V."

No answer.

"Melody V, Melody V, Melody V, Melody V, Melody V," Francesca shouted, furious.

"This is *Melody V*," answered a Slavic voice.

"We've just received information from the Coordination Center in Rome, there's a boat carrying four hundred fifty migrants near your coordinates, you need to contact Rome immediately to receive instructions. Do you hear me?"

"And who's going to pay for the satellite call?"

"That's not our problem. You have to call."

"I have to check with my safety supervisor."

"Negative. Call Rome."

Silence.

There were more calls, more confusion, more desperation. We were up all night, until four in the morning. In the end, neither the selfish *Melody V* nor the sympathetic *Dignity I* rescued that fishing boat loaded with Syrians. It was a German ship, farther out at sea, that saved the migrants, according to what we heard later from Rome. But the *Melody V* did end up calling Rome, as Francesca had insisted.

"We saved hundreds of lives. It was just like in the movies, with actors and everything. The guy in a turban, the rifle, the boat, the dinghies . . . we almost got shot, but we made it out unscathed."

The best chronicler of what happened out on the high seas wasn't me, despite the fact that I was the one getting paid for it, but Kike Riera, the Majorcan sailor. Gifted with a rare instinct, Kike had the ability to guess what was going through the minds of people whose culture he was unfamiliar with, decipher the will of the sea, and describe the workings of an operation—this rescue—before it happened. Always clean-shaven, Kike was thin and had eyes like a cat, full lips, and bulging veins on his featherweight sailor's arms.

At nine in the morning, Kike climbed the mast of the *Dignity I* with a pair of binoculars and saw a dinghy adrift at sea. It was the boat we were looking for. He was always the first to spot such boats. The mechanism was set in motion: the lifeboat was lowered from the mother ship—they had only done it a few times, but seemed to have been doing it all their lives—and Kike climbed on board. He was in charge of the lifeboat, which he sailed so naturally that it was as if it were part of his own body. He took orders from Captain Paco, and from Francesca, the coordinator.

In the rocking inflatable boat, there were 101 people, with two babies and two children among them. There was also a dead body, and one person who'd been wounded. The passengers said they'd been attacked by armed men. The babies and children were the first to be evacuated. They were handed into the lifeboat with Kike, some now crying at the top of their lungs, and transferred to the mother ship. Everyone was alarmed and frightened to see the children passed from one pair of hands to another, in the middle of the sea, like balls.

While the dinghy was being emptied of its passengers, a second vessel appeared, identical to the first. A double rescue operation was needed. To complicate the situation even more, in a few minutes, a dot on the horizon with a trail of white foam in its wake—it was moving at full throttle—turned out to be a high-speed rigid-inflatable boat with two 400-horsepower engines and three armed men on board, with a machine gun and an AK-47 at the ready. This is how Kike, who saw it all from the lifeboat, remembers the scene:

"It was like a full-blooded animal crossing the sea. When we saw how close they were, we put our hands up, but they told us to put them down and greeted us in Arabic. They didn't say who they were. They asked us what we were doing, prowled around the mother ship, the *Dignity I*, and then left."

The refugees being rescued at that moment were gripped by terror. When they saw the Libyans, one man threw himself into the sea, shouting that he would rather die than return to Libya, but he was soon pulled from the water and back into the lifeboat. It was those men—smugglers? The coast guard? A militia? All of the above?—who had shot at the boat at dawn. There was no doubt about it.

Half an hour after that first encounter, when the evacuation of the two dinghies was almost over, the rigid-inflatable boat reappeared, apparently annoyed at the *Dignity I*'s continued presence, and ordered us to leave. Immediately.

"Full speed ahead!" the captain ordered. Which isn't saying much with such a slow boat: barely ten knots per hour.

As we left the danger behind, Kike and I shared a cigarette. Kike seemed to glimpse in my eyes everything I'd seen on my travels through Africa and Asia, the lives of the victims of war I'd interviewed, the pain I'd witnessed when covering an Ebola epidemic . . . he knew what it all meant to me, could intuit the connection I was making to my past and recognize the symbolic field—wider than the Mediterranean—where for me, this was all unfolding: the violence all over the world from which people were fleeing; the exoduses. Before each rescue, he would say to me: tomorrow, tomorrow we're going to save lives. A look was enough. He spoke of the refugees with fondness and familiarity, feelings I'd developed only after many years of listening to them. He didn't seem to have needed that long. He'd understood it all from the beginning.

"I'm having a bit of a comedown, but I feel good about the result," said Kike as he finished the cigarette. "It was a success. Nobody we rescued got hurt. The effort, the tension, the sweat . . . wow. We rescued hundreds of souls. Children, pregnant women, young people. Everyone's on board."

THE FIRST PERSON TO BE RESCUED was a plump, three-month-old Nigerian baby called Praise. I began this story of the Mediterranean by talking about three Europeans and exploring their psychology, but if there's one person I often remember from the time I spent at sea, it's this little African boy, about whom I know almost nothing.

Praise was on that ill-fated boat, the one that spent hours adrift after being attacked by the men with the AK-47. After it was spotted, the lifeboat with Kike at its helm approached the dinghy and collected the babies and children, including Praise. As the lifeboat was brought alongside the *Dignity I*, the baby was lifted on board and Alberta Calderelli, the doctor, lifted him in her arms. I took a picture of that very moment.

"When I held him in my arms, I thought, he's safe now. No one can take him away from me," said the doctor. The little boy was healthy; he didn't have hypothermia, and you could tell he'd been nursing from his mother all along. His gaze was intense, and he was even smiling.

Praise was immediately taken to the clinic for a checkup, along with the other children. I followed the doctor with the baby in her arms and observed everything through the lens of my camera. Praise looked around with wide eyes like beacons drifting between innocence and wonder, trying to illuminate the strange scene going on around him. It was as if the little boy knew that something was going on, could tell that this was a crucial moment. He didn't cry even once, as if overwhelmed by the situation, as if anxious for someone to explain what was happening on this boat. In the background, you could hear the disconsolate cries of the other children, especially those of an eighteen-month-old who'd arrived with Praise, and who, like most of the children there, seemed possessed: crying at the top of his lungs, shaking the water off himself, calling for his mother.

They were alive. It was a miracle.

Miracle is a word of which the Nigerian baby's father, Kelvin, who gave his son the religious name Praise, would definitely approve. Kelvin arrived on the *Dignity I* soon after his son. He dried himself off, put on a navy-blue T-shirt with red, gray, and maroon stripes, and thanked God for having saved them. We were on the crowded stern, on a large wooden board where the refugees would sleep. I showed him the pictures I'd taken of his son and asked him if he'd like to talk.

We went up to the top deck, where it was more comfortable. He told me he was from Nigeria, from the state of Abia, in the polluted Niger Delta. He hadn't fled from violence. He'd migrated to Libya in search of a better life, but once there, he'd been robbed and beaten, and he decided that his only choice was to try his luck at crossing the Mediterranean, since south of Libya, his other way out, lay another sea—one of sand—that was just as terrifying, if not more so: the Sahara Desert. He paid the smugglers two thousand dollars for three passengers—for his wife, his son, and himself.

"I didn't want to go to Europe," he said. "In Libya, they locked me in jail for a month when I hadn't done anything. They ripped my passport to shreds right in front of me. In Libya, we were treated like animals. My wife didn't even get any care when she gave birth."

"How does it feel to have risked your baby's life by making this journey?" I asked him.

Libyan Waves

That was what I thought people wanted to know. People: the audience I write for, the limited audience that can be reached by writing about (non) refugees. I put that abstraction, my audience, before the person right in front of me, who had just survived an armed attack on a dinghy. Kelvin felt cornered. He looked for a way to justify something that he didn't know how to justify.

"I'm sorry, believe me, I never wanted to put my baby through that, but I think this is the end of my problems. I want to get to Europe, people know about life there, they know how to treat human beings, they know about human rights."

He wasn't annoyed. There was no reproach in his words, only hope for what was to come. He appealed time and again to God: He made this possible, He saved my son, He's here. This was true of many people: the appearance of a rescue boat in the middle of the sea seemed as though it could only be attributed to a miracle. Each person rescued had a story of violence, desert, torture, slavery, and poverty to tell, which I was always ready to question, not because I didn't believe them, but rather because the truth there was something unfathomable.

Often people seemed friendly, but my impressions sometimes soured as their stories came out—is he a smuggler? How does he treat his family? How does he treat women? Others wouldn't even look at me at first, but later revealed their full humanity, began to trust me. They had been silent for so long, and now they wanted to talk.

In any movement of population, there's a game of masks: you never know who you're talking to, you never know who is the victim, the smuggler, the pimp. It's a delicate network of silences and secrets, which as a journalist you want to break into, but as a human being, you prefer not to touch.

There, out at sea, the only truth was the look in Praise's eyes.

We Are Not Refugees

IN THE SAME INFLATABLE BOAT as Praise sat another of the leading characters of that day: a thirty-one-year-old Gambian DJ with dreadlocks, whose name was Lamin Jahcure. At least, that's what he said, but I later discovered that in fact, that was the name of a Jamaican reggae musician. After he was rescued, the doctor and nurses had hidden him underneath a bed, fearing that the armed men prowling around on the water were looking for him. The dawn attack had left one person dead and one wounded. The body of the DJ's friend was lying on the upper deck, wrapped in a sheet of plastic. And the DJ had been shot in the leg.

The medical team rallied to his aid. He was wearing an Inter Milan soccer T-shirt, which they changed for a navy-blue shirt with white embroidery. Now lying on the bed in the clinic, he cried, his dreadlocks shifting like snakes on the pillow. He charmed everyone with his kindness, his warm words, his resignation in the face of an injury that might have killed him, but which would now be cured. It was the price he'd paid for his freedom.

After a dose of morphine, Lamin was taken out to the starboard side on a stretcher. There, under a gray blanket, with a tear in his right eye that never fell, I found a man willing to tell me everything, to bare his soul, to let out all the suffering built up inside him.

"They treat us like slaves. In Libya, they don't treat you like a human being," said the DJ. "They rob you, kidnap you, arrest you. If you don't have any money, they put you in jail. I had no freedom. I was a slave. I saw things there that I've never seen in my life before. I feel terrible for the sub-Saharans in Libya. Going back there would be the worst thing that could happen to anyone. The smugglers put us in a container. You couldn't see anything. They locked us inside, it smelled of gas. They took us to the beach. Then they told us we had to run to the boat, they boarded us, and we left."

Lamin gradually grew weaker. The morphine was taking effect. He was bleeding and needed to be evacuated. A few hours later, after a call between the *Dignity I* and the Italian navy, a helicopter appeared in the sky above us to collect him. As the moment approached when he would be lifted and loaded into the aircraft like a package, I tried to continue our conversation.

"Did you DJ in the bars in Gambia? What did you play?"

"Yeah. Reggae, hip-hop."

After a few maneuvers, an athletic Italian soldier lowered himself onto the boat's upper deck, hooked a cord to the stretcher, and took the Gambian DJ away forever.

I never heard from him again. He gave me his name on Facebook, which didn't exist, and an email address, which wasn't valid. Who was he? A smuggler, as it was rumored? Just another victim? Would I see him again one day, spinning reggae in an underground club in Barcelona? As the helicopter flew into the distance and the refugees looked on, astonished—in just one day, they had set sail from the African coast, been attacked at sea by men with assault rifles, been rescued, and witnessed an evacuation by helicopter—I thought of the disparity in the resources that we employ for saving lives. Being in a dinghy meant being forgotten, still in Africa. At that point, the life of the DJ and those of the hundred people traveling with him had no value. Being on the boat of an international organization meant that they were now in Europe. Now that he was here, the single life of the wounded DJ was worth more than all the others combined a few hours earlier, when they had sailed from Africa in a small rubber boat.

PART V

Destinations
When Do They Arrive?

The word shame is pronounced emphatically and often in the European Parliament.

JUAN FERNANDO LÓPEZ AGUILAR
former Spanish minister and socialist
Member of the European Parliament

THIS BOOK IS LIKE AN ARROW drawn on a map: there are origins (war), flights (exodus), routes (journey), and destinations (arrival). We have already discarded a number of preconceived ideas about the first four stages of the refugee experience.

But perhaps the most deceptive is the last: arrival.

Does *arrival* mean finding shelter from Syrian bombs in Turkey, and then being exploited in a textile factory?

Does *arrival* mean being granted asylum in Germany? It does, right?

Is it possible not to have arrived when everyone believes you have?

Does *arrival* mean being a victim of racist attacks in Hamburg?

Can you arrive without arriving? Stay in Jordan, and still have arrived?

Here, there are three different destinations: one Asian, one African, and one Arab-European. Three answers to the same question.

When do they arrive?

We Are Not Refugees

When do the four hundred thousand internally displaced persons (IDPs) in the Central African Republic arrive at their destination? The usual answer in Africa is almost never.

When do the one hundred forty-five thousand Tibetans in exile arrive at their destination? Most have been living in India for half a century, but their destiny—to return to Tibet—still hasn't arrived.

When do the Syrians fleeing from war—particularly those headed for Europe—get to their destination? Many of them will never make it. But sometimes they do arrive, so I'll tell some of their stories.

I'm at the European Parliament in Brussels, where I've been invited to a seminar on migration and asylum, from which most of the Euroskeptic parties, and the British Tories, are conspicuously absent. I try to listen to the MEPs without prejudice, curious to understand what's going on in this Europe that, grudgingly, and faced with the indignation of its citizens at the images coming from the Aegean Sea, finally has decided to relocate only one hundred sixty thousand potential refugees, who, as I write these lines, continue to arrive in dribs and drabs.

One hundred sixty thousand people account for 0.032 percent of the population of the European Union (EU; which includes the United Kingdom—at least for now), estimated at around five hundred million. In Lebanon, which has over four million inhabitants, there are more than a million Syrian refugees: a quarter of the total population. And at least eight in ten people displaced by violence live in developing countries.

What's the matter with Europe?

In her statement during the seminar, the German MEP Ska Keller, from the European Green Party, gives her answer.

"The problem isn't the European Union, it isn't the European

Parliament, and it isn't the European Commission. For once, there are actually proposals on the table. The problem is the member states, who keep pointing the finger at one another, and refusing to comply with those measures. There is a profound crisis of solidarity."

Keller—short hair, combative rhetoric, a restrained vigor in her words—criticizes those wanting to divide refugees by nationality to decide whether they can enter, criticizes the fact that the burden of refugees is falling mostly on Italy and Greece, and criticizes the fact that access to asylum is limited.

And then she says that the best tool Europe has at its disposal is the system of quotas that it will use in the relocation of one hundred sixty thousand people, announced by the European Commission in September 2015. She is now speaking two months later, when those relocated number barely two hundred.

Keller raises her arms for a moment in celebration.

The first two hundred have arrived!

For anyone on the outside of that enormous bureaucratic apparatus that represents five hundred million Europeans, two hundred is a ridiculous figure. An insult. For someone on the inside, and whose commitment to refugees can hardly be doubted, two hundred seems like a great achievement.

Keller surely knows that this figure is ridiculous, but thinks, *feels*—probably because she's experienced the difficulty of relocating refugees firsthand—that this is a great achievement. The look on her face betrays this sense of having at least accomplished something.

Two hundred people as a lifeline, two hundred actual people, two hundred people as the beginning of something.

Keller's desperate celebration helped me to understand what's going on in Brussels far better than any of the other MEP's speeches.

This machine is impossible to set in motion.

We Are Not Refugees

"IT'S SHAMEFUL FOR THE European Union to claim to be overwhelmed by an allegedly unsustainable burden of asylum-seekers."

I've found the office of the Spanish socialist MEP Juan Fernando López Aguilar. He only has a few minutes to spare—there are other journalists waiting. I had everything prepared for a complete offensive, straight to the jugular: quotas, deaths in the Mediterranean, data on intake in other countries and on other continents.

But he said it all himself.

"Spain decided to be part of the solidarity mechanism, but at this pace, it won't take us two years to complete the relocation [of the refugees], but seventy-five."

The former Minister of Justice in José Luis Rodríguez Zapatero's government is a whirlwind. He interrupts me constantly. He doesn't let me finish my questions, answering them with indignation, sometimes raising his voice almost histrionically.

"The free movement of persons was the first casualty. The thing we most wanted!" says Aguilar, alluding to the border controls that were established in response to the great exodus, beginning in July and August 2015.

"The fundamental problem in Spain is that we keep distorting and overstating the pattern and scale of migration and the demand for asylum, as if it were a threat to our safety. Immigrants and refugees are being seen as a threat to our safety. It's a disgrace."

This may be the case, but the fact that refugees aren't coming to Europe doesn't seem so much a problem of logistics or of its citizens, as a problem of political will . . .

"Of a lack of political will and a lack of commitment to European values! The word *shame* is pronounced emphatically and often in the European Parliament, because that's what it is. Shameful."

Stunned by the force of Aguilar's arguments, I leave his office and head to the café. There, I meet with some other Spanish journalists, and we have an off-the-record conversation with David Chico Zamanillo, from the secretariat of the Committee on Civil Liberties, Justice, and Home Affairs of the European Parliament. In other words, the committee that deals with matters of asylum. Friendly and eager to explain, Zamanillo guides us through the ins and outs of European politics of asylum, and the changes it has undergone. A year later, I call to interview him again, this time via Skype, and with the understanding that any of his words may be published.

He said more things on the record than off.

Among them was the statement, "Asylum is for the minority."

In 2015, 1.25 million people sought asylum in EU member states: more than twice the number in the previous year. Half of these applications were made by Syrians, Afghans, and Iraqis. It's impossible to know now how many were accepted and how many weren't, since many were still under consideration after 2015, but in that year, the European Union offered some form of legal protection to 333,350 asylum seekers. Half of those were thanks to Germany.

The acceptance rate—the number of applications accepted at the end of the process in relation to those presented—was 14 percent.

"We need to approach this problem globally, rather than just focusing on asylum. Mass movements need to be managed, too."

Zamanillo explains the flaws in this system in need of change: potential refugees are required on paper to request asylum in the first EU member state they arrive in, and many attempt to go to the countries where they think they'll have a better chance—the acceptance rate differs greatly from country to country, and people aren't stupid.

"It's a system designed for fair weather. Once the storm arrived, these rules didn't work anymore," says Zamanillo.

We go over the European reform of the asylum system again and again. But in the end, it all comes down to the same thing: Brussels versus the member states. "The push and pull between the center and the periphery." A center, the European Commission, that gives the order to relocate one hundred sixty thousand people. A periphery, the member states, that refuses to do so, or that does so only while dragging its feet.

The same is true of many other things, such as austerity policies.

Refugees aren't considered a special problem in the European Union—they're just another file, another dossier, another political weapon. Another issue for parties and countries to position themselves for or against—for or against a ridiculous relocation policy that insults the intelligence of anyone who looks at the global numbers.

And why should refugees be any different?

I wonder as I leave the European Parliament.

A Ticket to Limbo in Refugee Class

Central African Republic

> The rainforest had always been a way out, and now,
> with the country falling into the abyss, it became
> a way out once more.
>
> Xavier Aldekoa, Africa Ocean

SOME CHILDREN CLIMB UP a wooden tower in the airport in Bangui, the capital of the Central African Republic. They play, pull on each other's T-shirts, raise their hands to their foreheads to shield their eyes from the sun. The image would be touching if it weren't for the fact that what they see isn't a Boeing 787 about to take off, a bus transporting passengers to their international flight, or the airport ground crew marshaling planes on the runway. What they see is a vast expanse of tents with tattered plastic sheets that stretches through aircraft hangars and along a rugged terrain of cultivated areas and shrubland; a camp hemmed in by rain forest to the east and by a Russian Tupolev and a tiny terminal to the west. This is their home: a camp for internally displaced persons (IDPs) in the Bangui airport.

We Are Not Refugees

More than twenty thousand people are living here, who have fled from war. Almost all are Christians who escaped from the December 2013 attacks by the Islamic coalition Séléka. This stretch of land adjacent to the airport has hosted up to one hundred thousand people. Many have returned home, or to what was left of their homes, but those who lived in the most troubled neighborhoods refuse to go back. Time passes, and the international community is indifferent; time passes, and the government of the Central African Republic fails to lift a finger; time passes, and thousands of IDPs remain trapped in this limbo, where they plant crops, seek shade beneath the wings of small, abandoned airplanes, and cover their ears every time an aircraft lands.

The most surreal corner of this camp is occupied by the hangars, where the IDPs have stayed since the beginning of the conflict. I wander through one of them, and it's like visiting an antique shop that's been seized by the masses: upside-down stools and tables; dilapidated small planes with their wing flaps raised, covered in a layer of dust; towels hanging from the wings; flip-flops stuffed into the holes made in these metal birds by the destruction; cabinets left over from another century; mosquito nets; straw brooms; buckets of water; cushions; baskets of clothing.

This is an open-air, decommissioned airport, inhabited by people who fled their homes in terror, in search of safety. Why here? A visitor arriving in Bangui might think that all these people crowded together are waiting for a plane to take them away from this city, or this country. But no, they took refuge in the airport because there was a French military contingent deployed here, and they thought it was the only safe place to be—much like in South Sudan. The French have now left and been replaced by a United Nations (UN) peacekeeping mission.

The United Nations isn't guaranteeing us total protection, say the IDPs, but they don't dare go back to their homes.

A Ticket to Limbo in Refugee Class

On leaving the hangar, I find two other aircrafts: a red biplane whose propeller children can't resist playing with, and a small white plane that has no chance of ever being repaired. Seriously, none. In the shade of one of its wings, a woman is stripping bundles of cassava leaves. I go over to speak to her and she immediately invites me to sit down. Her name is Mboudou.

"The Muslims burned our house down. We took refuge here. We lost everything. My husband couldn't stand it; he died of sorrow here in this camp. I'm a widow with seven children."

Oblivious to their mother's sad words, the children corner us under the wing of the small plane, run around, observe the foreigner; some neighbors join us.

"None of them are in school because I don't have any money to pay the tuition. We don't have anything. I get up in the morning, we don't have breakfast because we don't have any food; if I have any cassava leaves, I spend the morning here stripping them, then I grind them up, and cook them to feed the children. We don't even have any money to season them."

The whole family lives in a tent pitched just outside the door to the hangar. In this camp, as well as the usual kind of suffering, there is another source of discomfort: the deafening noise of the airport.

"I have problems with stress. I can't sleep well because of the noise. The big planes are the worst, when they're about to take off."

Mboudou says that she's alone. That she's afraid to go home until the weapons disappear from the neighborhood where she lives. She begs, "The international community needs to support us. It needs to disarm our neighborhoods and help us get out of here."

Mboudou wants to leave. Whatever it takes. Who can blame her—she's surrounded by poverty and decay. Most of the tents lack the classic tarps from the UN Refugee Agency and are instead covered with ordinary plastic sheets. Some have gaps patched up with trash bags. There is now no longer the same level of over-crowding, but at first, the IDPs were even living inside the air-planes. After saying goodbye to Mboudou, I continue my visit to the camp in the company of Luis Arias, coordinator of Doctors Without Borders in M'Poko, who explains some of the contradic-tions of this unusual place.

"The government here is nonexistent. It doesn't have the means to expel the IDPs from the camp. The police can't come in. Yes-terday three people were wounded when a Muslim tried to rob a motorcycle taxi whose driver turned out to be a Central African [Republic] soldier. The driver threw a grenade at him in response."

We walk through the camp, toward the terminal. The blue-striped wing of a white Tupolev cargo plane preparing to take off appears between the tents. The whine of the jet engine, the quiv-ering of the horizon: the height of chaos.

"I have to hold onto something so I don't fall every time a plane takes off. This is terrible for the babies," says Marcel, a leader of one of the camp's neighborhoods, as he grips one of the sticks holding up his tent.

Behind the Tupolev, there's a commercial jet and some light aircraft from the United Nations and some nongovernmental organizations (NGOs). We've reached the edge of the camp: now there's nothing but weeds, ears of sorghum, and a stream of water between the planes and the people. We leave the terminal behind and head toward the runway.

"You come here and pretend to be taking notes!" shouts a woman who sees me scribbling these impressions down in my note-book. "And then you leave us here, without food or anything!"

I don't say anything. I bite my tongue.

She's right, and I'm ashamed of my privilege.

A Ticket to Limbo in Refugee Class

I come across a yellow line connecting the camp to the paved runway. There are motorcycles and even cars driving around, a man carrying a bundle of straw, children running errands. Yes, the airport runway—the only paved area—is now a huge avenue, brimming with life, and the traffic is unusually orderly for Africa: it feels like a Sunday. Suddenly, Cameroonian peacekeepers start patrolling up and down the runway in a military vehicle. They've activated the takeoff protocol: they need to clear the airstrip so the plane can leave. Gradually, the traffic thins. The last people to cross the runway start to hurry, as if it were a pedestrian crossing and the light was blinking. A man passes with a cart, and a Cameroonian soldier lets him through, as if saying, "You're the last, though."

The Tupolev that we'd seen by the terminal reappears. Some gaze as if seeing it for the first time. Others are used to it by now. The plane turns around to take off, clouds of dust rise, a powerful wind begins to blow: from where I'm standing—about fifteen hundred feet away—it looks like the camp's inhabitants are underneath the jet engines; a blade is turning nearby, the Cameroonian soldiers, wearing orange bibs, hold their rifles and wait for the plane to take off, but anyone might walk out onto the runway and spark chaos. The grass moves like waves—Libyan waves, Mediterranean waves, I think to myself—the plane starts moving, picks up speed, children shout, brown and white exhaust fumes, the noise lasts just a few seconds, and now it takes flight above the largest camp for IDPs in the Central African Republic.

After the takeoff, we leave the runway and go back to the hangars. The two are joined by a kind of avenue: music stores, women frying fish heads, more motorcycles. The yellow line is here for a reason: although it may no longer seem like it, this street used to be the landing strip for light aircraft. Another woman rebukes us—not usually a common occurrence in the camps.

"Everything is more or less calm now," says Luis, "but remember a grenade only costs one hundred fifty francs here [about thirty-five cents in U.S. dollars]. Some people bury grenades and AK-47s under their tents."

On my way, I meet Augustine, a sixty-three-year-old man. We begin to talk, and he covers his ears with his hands.

"It's so loud here. When a plane lands, it wakes everyone up."

He speaks to me in one tent, but his family of thirty-seven occupies several in the area.

"I don't like this camp, I want to leave and go back to my neighborhood, with my family. If it's safe, and there's a disarmament process, I want to go back."

Augustine—wearing an imitation soccer shirt with the Spanish flag, a sparse beard, and a distant gaze—says that it's strange living in an airport, that the children don't go to school, that it's a disaster when it rains; that the living conditions are wretched, that they want to go home. And then, the same anger as Mboudou, the woman I spoke to beneath the wing of a plane.

"We can't go home now, everything's destroyed. We can't live surrounded by weapons. The government isn't doing anything. I beg the international community to find a solution and get us out of this camp."

In the terminal—so far away, so near—a UN helicopter is preparing to take off.

FRANCE'S LEAST STRATEGIC COLONY, the empire's Cinderella, the *colonie poubelle*—trash can colony—could be in only one place: the middle of Africa. In the beginning, the Central African Republic had a name that highlighted its dual identity. It was called Ubangi-Shari, after the two rivers dominating its geography. The Ubangi River flows south from Bangui, the capital, into the Congo River, of which it is the largest tributary. The source of the Shari lies in the middle of the country, and this river flows north into Lake Chad. The country's vague mode of existence, its lack of a distinct character, its territorial imbalance, are inscribed in that duality. There is no center here, all is periphery: part of the country—that of the Ubangi—is connected exclusively to sub-Saharan Africa: exuberance, rain forest, the Great Lakes region, the ongoing wars of the Democratic Republic of the Congo, the Kivus, Rwanda. The other part of the country—that of the Shari—looks toward the Sahel, toward the Arab desert, toward Chad and the Sudan, and the network of trade connections that its people have been weaving for decades. The peripheral areas of this country have far more contact with other regions—the Great Lakes, the Sahel—than with their own center. This country is a periphery of the periphery.

In the center of Africa there is nothing.

The Central African Republic. Even its name lacks personality. And if we refer to it by its customary initials, CAR, this is even more the case. For a long period of its history, the country was an area of transit and refuge for large population movements: first, those caused by the African slave trade, and then by the wars that crippled the region. In the center: nobody. The Central African Republic is almost as big as Texas, with a population of only 4.5 million people.

The Central African Republic gained formal independence from France in 1960, but the country remained under virtual French control, as if it were still a colony. When the time came to go it alone, the country had only one hospital, and the territory had for decades been leased to colonial companies that contributed to the establishment of a culture of crony capitalism in the new country. The state became its own predator, an inert organization living off the diamond and gold trades, bribery, and its French masters.

The most important political figure in independent Central African Republic is Jean-Bédel Bokassa, who later converted to Islam and renamed himself Salah Eddine Ahmed Bokassa. The Central African Republic's identity crisis can also be read in its most significant leader. He called himself Emperor Bokassa I. In the West, this extravagant figure, peppered with a generous dose of racism and sensationalism, was associated with every conceivable cliché regarding African elites: his sumptuous imperial coronation, his alleged cannibalism, his insatiable sexual appetite. When the character became a caricature, and, above all, when he distanced himself from the desires of the old metropolis, he was toppled in a coup in 1979.

The country is constantly subject to foreign intervention. During the last two decades, there have been countless peace-keeping missions, both regional and international: unilateral interventions by France and Chad, the European Union, the African Union, and, of course, the United Nations. Missions with long names, impossible to memorize, with absurd acronyms lacking all meaning, but which end up meaning everything. The most recent of these is MINUSCA (United Nations Multidimensional Integrated Stabilization Mission in the Central African Republic—the initials are from the French translation of this name), which has deployed twelve thousand soldiers to the country. The news most often heard about MINUSCA speaks not of the peace or stability it has brought to the country, but of the alleged rape of at least eight women by its soldiers.

The Central African Republic is a multinational protectorate. The state is a complete vacuum. Before the current crisis broke out, 70 percent of the population lived below the poverty line. The rate of HIV prevalence was 9 percent among people from fifteen to forty-nine years old. When aid arrives, it comes as part of a program, backed by France and other regional powers. But the irony is that here, the international attention received by other parts of Africa is considered disproportionate. The brutal wars in the Great Lakes region, involving the Congo and Rwanda; South Sudan and its dramatic genesis; Darfur and the human-rights campaigns led by George Clooney; Lake Chad and the violence of Boko Haram. Foreigners—not just white but also African—seek mirrors in the Central African Republic in which to contemplate other conflicts, those that matter.

To explain the war here, it's necessary to refer to others, since by itself it has no explanation. One of the biggest challenges faced by international aid organizations is defining the crisis in the Central African Republic: is the country in an emergency phase, requiring urgent deployment of humanitarian aid, or just a phase of development, therefore needing support to build schools and infrastructure? Between these two visions—two rivers—the country flounders.

WHAT HAPPENS BEYOND BANGUI? To travel anywhere in the Central African Republic, you have to fly: fly out of that airport teeming with IDPs, fly over a vast expanse of vegetation without paved roads or infrastructure. To reach the remotest places, journalists depend almost completely on the United Nations and NGOs, just as they do in South Sudan, in parts of the Congo, and in other countries in the region. From the small plane, just before takeoff, I see the hangars and the rain forest in the distance: women carrying firewood on their heads, children running, the strange bustle of the M'Poko airport. I'm accompanied on board by several aid workers and one patient: a five-year-old girl who can't walk, and who is on her way home with her father.

Once we're up in the air—there's a break in the turbulence, but my religious self still encourages me to pray—patches of dazzling green, a combination of the landscapes of South Sudan and the Congo, are visible through the clouds. Again, I'm comparing this country with others; again I'm seeing it through the prism of its surrounding countries; again I'm guilty of the very thing I criticize: our inability to construct a discourse about the Central African Republic itself, to see all this not just in its relation to something else, but for what it is.

But what is it?

I arrive in Kabo, in the north of all this, of this country. I'm traveling north in a four-by-four toward the border with Chad to find out what life is like on the periphery. On the road, there are several checkpoints: this territory, predominantly Muslim, is controlled by the Séléka. At one of the checkpoints, the Doctors Without Borders workers get out of the vehicle to greet the local leader. His face reminds me of Avon Barksdale, the drug kingpin in the TV series *The Wire*. He sits in a circle with several companions in front of some tents, and it's as if he's gone down to that orange couch in Baltimore where the dealers meet to do business. This Avon wears a long white tunic: an ethereal gauze, a celebration of the minimal.

Okay, you can come through, keep going.

It hasn't rained in the last few days, but the road is muddy and we have to negotiate puddles, sink into them, skirt countless millet plantations, cross the savannah, navigate these tropical lowlands until we reach the border with Chad. After three hours on the road, I glimpse an ocean of houses, modest but perfectly built for this location, ready to be lived in, as if the construction company were preparing to inaugurate a new complex. It's the Qatar Charity camp for IDPs. When thousands of Muslims arrived here—those fleeing the Christian militia Anti-balaka, from the conflict between Christians and Muslims, from the crisis of December 2013—the Qatar Charity arrived, built these houses hastily, and then left. Most now stand empty because the essential elements are still missing: water, food, aid. A metaphor for every-thing that doesn't work in the humanitarian field: large-scale construction, enormous shipments, containers full of clothing. For what?

Attending to the needs of people fleeing from war takes listen-ing and understanding.

I receive a text message. "Welcome to Chad." I am not in Chad, but in Moyenne-Sido, still in the Central African Republic, a couple of miles from the border. I visit more IDP camps scat-tered throughout the area, occupied as if unwillingly. The situa-tion is desperate, and one of the reasons, I discover, is the proximity of the border. When those throngs of thousands of Muslims arrived in the area, some remained in the Central African Repub-lic, but others decided to cross into Chad, become refugees, and leave their country behind forever.

Refugee: here, the word seems even more arbitrary, flimsy, deceptive. And, despite this, the world's great population move-ments can be understood better on this border than on the one between Greece and Macedonia. Because those who fled, the Central Africans who sought refuge in Chad, soon found that there was no aid distribution there, no water, no food. They soon found that the war in their country was cooling off, or at least so it seemed. So they decided to return, or attempt to return. And what did they find? A closed border and Chadian soldiers who shot at them and denied them access to their own country, demanding a bribe—fifteen thousand francs, twenty-seven U.S. dollars—to let them back into this place of limbo. And worst of all, once they return, they have no right to receive aid distribution because they no longer qualify as IDPs. They are not refugees, and they are not IDPs. They call them "returnees," just to call them something.

Kakopande—smooth skin, gaunt face, a green striped floral headscarf—tells me all this beneath the shade of a mango tree outside the only health clinic serving the people of Moyenne-Sido. She's wearing a T-shirt from MINUSCA, the UN mission accused of raping young women.

"In 2014, there was fighting between the Anti-balaka and the Séléka. They started killing Muslims, and we had to flee to the rain forest. The Anti-balaka militias pursued us there. We managed to join a convoy that took us directly to Chad, but there was no food or aid distribution there. We were sleeping under trees, so we decided to come back, me and my nine children. I couldn't cross at the official border, so I crossed illegally, through the brush."

Kakopande says that she doesn't dare to go back home to Dékoa, 155 miles south. She has returned to her country, to the Central African Republic, but now she scrapes out a living in one of these camps in the north, far from her home. Her story is the same as those of the thousands of people crowded together at the border, who either bribed or dodged army soldiers to get back into their own country. At first, on the other side of the border, in Chad, a camp had been set up to help the refugees, but after a few months, the authorities decided that it was time for them to leave, and they cut off food distribution.

On the other side, there is nothing: states all over the world see refugees as a burden.

APPROXIMATELY 15 PERCENT of the population of the Central African Republic is Muslim. The rest is Christian or animist. History tells us that the country has not been troubled by faith-based conflict, that peaceful coexistence has been the norm, and that religion isn't the key to understanding its current problems. Yet despite this, a diagonal line across the center of the map separates the areas predominantly inhabited by Christians and Muslims. Once again, the center-periphery binary: traditionally, the reins of power have been held by Christians who controlled Bangui with support from Paris; Muslims have survived at the periphery—mostly in the northeast—trading for a living, and their center is not Bangui, but rather the surrounding Arab countries.

December 2012 saw the birth of Séléka—which means "coalition" in Sango—an association of Islamic militias, an army made up of aggrieved young men, poachers, and mercenaries from Chad and Sudan, that aimed to topple the country's president, François Bozizé. In the context of the weakness of the national army, and the passivity of the foreign troops deployed there (Bozizé was unpopular with everyone), Séléka arrived in Bangui and took power in March 2013. Michel Djotodia, the leader of the Islamic coalition, proclaimed himself the new head of state. During those months, an antigovernment movement took shape: the Anti-balaka Christian self-defense militias, who took up arms—mostly hunting weapons and knives—and reacted with unusual violence to what they saw as an Islamic conquest. The Anti-balaka attacked the capital in December 2013, and then came the reprisals from Séléka. Chaos was unleashed in this African limbo. The result: countless deaths, and a million and a half IDPs.

One circumstance gives an idea of the extent to which the Central African Republic occupies a peripheral space in the global system. The country is invisible to most of the world, even when it's at war. Although it was a caricature of what was actually happening, international media coverage described the fighting as a faith-based conflict: Christians versus Muslims. Was there any reason for this? That same period, in other latitudes, saw the birth of the Islamic State and its rivalry with Al Qaeda for global hegemony. Here, in a majority-Christian country where Islamic militias had taken power, there was no echo of this.

Not even jihadist groups are interested in the Central African Republic.

We Are Not Refugees

I LEAVE THE BORDER BEHIND and retrace my steps southward: again, millet plantations, puddles, Séléka commanders. This time, they're not wearing white tunics but rather Ray-Bans and tactical vests, and have let their hair grow out. In one of the villages, the Doctors Without Borders team stops to talk to a young man who shakes our hands almost without looking at us as he assembles his homemade hookah: he removes the aluminum foil, adds the tobacco, takes a new piece of foil, pierces it; the aroma rises from the pipe in the scorching heat; I think it's peach-flavored and feel tempted to ask him, but I don't. He says no problem, we can do whatever we think best in the area.

We stop at a camp for IDPs that makes two things clear: First, those fleeing from war all too often find themselves forced to compete, to defend their rights, in religious or ethnic communities. Second, the best help available to refugees is often the help that they organize for themselves. Refugees are not passive subjects; they aren't (just) communities in need of help, but communities that can, and often do, formulate their own responses to their situation.

This is the peace camp—there are several camps bearing that ironic name in the area. In fact, it is two camps that border each other: one for the IDPs—for those who haven't left the country—and another for returnees, for the nameless, for those who were refugees in Chad, but who now don't know what they are. I visit this one first. About a hundred families are surviving in precariously pitched tents, beneath the suffocating heat. It's better to stay outside. I join in an improvised soccer match. Since I'm white, everyone passes me the ball and then tries to tackle me, amid laughter. It's the highlight of the day.

In the camp, people say there's a conflict with the neighbors.

A Ticket to Limbo in Refugee Class

The reason isn't precisely known, although rumor has it that a fire was started by a displaced woman setting fires inside the tents; someone in the other camp reprimanded her for it, and then someone else, from the other side, told them not to interfere. The basis of the dispute is clear: two destitute communities, one in an even worse situation than the other, are forced to compete for humanitarian aid. After the soccer match, I keep walking through the returnee camp, and someone in charge of the other camp, the IDP camp, comes toward me. With sunglasses and a serious expression, he looks like a hitman coming to get me.

"Are you going to visit the other camp or not?"

"Yes, of course! Let's go."

After ten minutes, we arrive at a kind of concrete stable—a space that's been set up for meetings. I'm greeted by an extensive welcoming party. I think—journalists always think the same thing—that I need to wade through the bureaucracy as soon as possible, that I should talk to the person in charge of the camp to explain what I want to do—talk to people, that's all. I get nervous because it's already late—how long will we be here? As journalists, we aren't easily convinced, we don't allow ourselves to be carried away by the moment, we think we know what's most interesting, we want to impose our own truths.

But the story was right there before my eyes. When I finish explaining what I want to do, I ask if they have any thoughts to share, any opinions about what's going on in the country. Nobody says a thing. I'm surprised because there are numerous people here, and somebody always has something to say. Just as I'm about to get up, an elderly man with a piercing gaze, wearing a brown tunic and a cream embroidered *taqiyah,* or Muslim skullcap, introduces himself as secretary general of the IDP camp committee at Kabo. His name is Hissene Moktard, and he's sixty years old. He does have something to say. He takes a letter out of his pocket, written on a sheet of lined paper in French, and begins to read. Here are some of the most notable fragments:

"We thank you sincerely for the courage deployed in getting to our camp, referred to as a peace camp. In the current context, CAR is affected by a range of tensions causing a wide variety of social problems. In the total absence of protection, the rural population is in a very difficult situation. Despite interventions by aid organizations, the displaced persons of the peace camp are all victims of forced displacement, theft, and destruction of their property. As a result, the displaced are vulnerable people who find themselves in extreme poverty."

Then we talk. The thousands of people in this camp form part of the Muslim community that fled from the Anti-balaka in December 2013 and the months that followed. They lived in a neighborhood in Bangui that was attacked by the Christian militias. At first, they were protected by the UN mission, the MINUSCA; then they fled north from the capital in a caravan of twenty vehicles, organized by the International Organization for Migration. More than two years later, they complain of feeling excluded and insist on their status as citizens—an affirmation that shows that the state insists the opposite—and say that they want to leave this camp and go home.

"The solution is peace. We're Muslims, but this is our homeland. We are Central Africans. We had never been displaced, until now. The government has forgotten about us."

It's late. After our conversation, there's no time left to talk to the people in the camp, but I visit the open-air office of this amiable secretary general: a humble structure built from sticks with a grass roof, full of papers, a stuffed toy belonging to his granddaughter hanging from the ceiling, and a kettle, a brass cup, and a logbook on the table. This is the headquarters of the IDP camp committee at Kabo: from here, an office with a beam of light and dust particles passing through it, the committee undertakes the defense of the rights of these nonrefugees.

WE HAD LEFT THE Central African Republic in the hands of the Islamic coalition Séléka and its leader, Djotodia. But the massacres of December 2013 in Bangui at the hands of the Christian Anti-balaka militias, an immediate military deployment by France, and international pressure on Djotodia forced him to resign. A new political process began: Catherine Samba-Panza, the mayor of Bangui, was named interim president. MINUSCA, the UN peacekeeping mission, arrived months later. Aid organizations launched humanitarian interventions. Once again, the state was nonexistent; once again, the Central African Republic had become an international protectorate, if indeed it had ever ceased to be one.

Positions began to stabilize, with the Séléka in de facto control of the Muslim areas in the north and northeast, and the government administering, with international aid, the capital and the few other places where its reach is felt. As violence was reduced in the communities, other unsuspected cracks began to appear. The Séléka coalition splintered, and groups began to fight among themselves, particularly the faction of the nomadic Fula. When fighting occurs between Christian, Islamic, or Fula militias, those who end up suffering most, those left defenseless, are the civilians. Occasionally, they become military targets: a strategy for demoralizing the enemy.

What happens when nomads become refugees? What happens when they no longer move voluntarily, but rather are displaced by war?

They come to a standstill. They don't know what to do.

Zara Abu Bakr—dark blue headscarf, a smile that doesn't fade—has been displaced in the north of the country.

"I managed to join a convoy heading north to get away from the fighting. On the way, the Anti-balaka launched a grenade at us, killing four people. There were other nomads who weren't in vehicles like me, but by themselves, because they were trying to escape with their livestock. But they were killed on the road."

Normally, Zara would have moved with the seasons, to the rhythm of the livestock and the grass sought by the oxen. This time, though, she had to move to the rhythm of the violence, and then she found herself trapped in the north.

Fadimatou sits in a remote camp on a bundle of firewood, speaking with other women resting on similar stools, who form a circle. Fadimatou is forty-eight. Her husband died before the war, and she has eight children to care for. When I ask why she doesn't leave the camp, her argument is irrefutable.

"I'm not going anywhere because I don't have the means. We used to live well, with our livestock. Now we don't know what to do. There's a huge difference between our lives then and now. We're nomads, but we're stuck here. We're not used to this."

Hamadou, another nomad stranded in a camp, wears a pale, threadbare, checked shirt, maroon pants, and a defeated expression.

"The Anti-balaka detained and killed many nomads," she says. "We took refuge in Cameroon and then in Chad. Then we came back, but now we have no livestock, and we've been stuck in a camp for a year and a half. We used to be able to sell oxen, but now we don't know how to get anything to eat. We go into the rain forest to collect branches, and not much else."

Refugees are not nomads: they aren't accustomed to constant movement. Nomads are not sedentary: they aren't accustomed to staying put.

A Ticket to Limbo in Refugee Class

Our departure from Kabo is delayed. It was planned for seven-thirty in the morning, but the Séléka—or whoever the Séléka happen to be at the moment, because it's a mess—have mounted a protest against the country's disarmament agreement. Once things calm down, we head south, toward Batangafo. We pass through villages of IDPs. They're here because of the most recent fighting between the different factions of Séléka: the nomadic faction, and the others. In one of the camps, built only a few weeks ago, the dwellings are made of palm leaves. The IDPs are quarreling with the locals because they have to use their well to collect water.

A few more miles to the south is Batangafo.

All wars have one city that suffers more than the rest, or suffers equally, but always sees every kind of conflict; that's in the thick of things, that bears witness to history. That name that is repeated over and over. That place that's strategic, or that has no real value but is transformed into a decisive location by the elements in conflict. In the Central African Republic, that place is called Batangafo, and it hosts a camp for over twenty-five thousand IDPs.

In Batangafo, there are Anti-balaka, Séléka, and UN peacekeepers—the protagonists of this war. All the rebellions coming from the north have passed through here on their way to Bangui, farther south. Batangafo lies on that imaginary line that divides the Christian southwest from the Muslim northeast. There have been clashes here between the Christian and Islamic militias. In June 2014, the fighting drove twenty thousand people, most of them Christians, to crowd into the Batangafo hospital in search of safety. Then they didn't dare go home, so they moved from the hospital to a camp established in the city, partially protected by UN peacekeepers.

The camp is divided into five sections. The neighborhoods of the nonrefugees: Catholic, Baga, Young, Alternative, and MINUSCA. I begin in this last one, which bears the name of the UN peacekeeping mission in the Central African Republic. I meet Patrick, forty-five years old, who says he has eight children and two wives, despite being a Christian.

"We were attacked by the Fula faction of the Séléka. The offensive lasted three hours, three people were killed and several were injured. They burned all eighty of the houses in the village."

Patrick gazes at the slopes of the camp spread out before us. From here, we can't see the end of the rows of tents: this is a large camp, unlike the remote, majority Muslim settlements farther north. Patrick tells me that a bullet pierced his side as he was trying to escape, but he survived. One of his sons was also shot and had to be evacuated to Bangui. This son also survived, but he has nothing good to say about either the Fula who attacked them or the Muslims in general.

"Life is impossible here, you can't grow crops, or work. We want to go home. If the disarmament process gets going, we'll go back. Right now, we're coexisting with the Muslims, but that's all. These people are dishonest: one day they tell you there's no problem, and the next day they give you a nasty surprise."

Patrick stays silent for a few seconds. A woman passes us, carrying cassava leaves.

I want to know if that hatred is still intact in other neighborhoods, so I go to the Catholic camp: its name is unequivocal. I'm welcomed by Joseph, the amiable secretary general of the camp's elderly residents, to whom I'll end up giving my cap from the 2013 Formentera marathon in Spain's Balearic Islands, which he took a fancy to as soon as we met. He's accompanied by Emmanuel, another neighborhood representative. The Muslims aren't the only ones organizing themselves into committees in the camps.

Emmanuel is from Batangafo and fled the city in August 2014.

"In 2014, Séléka arrived and destroyed our houses, and we took refuge here. There was looting, torture, murders . . . many people were killed. It was a brutal offensive. We're thinking about going home, but we're concerned for our safety, and our houses have been destroyed. An elderly woman died here because she had nothing to eat. Right here, next door."

But Emmanuel isn't only talking about the Islamic militias. He's talking about the Christian self-defense groups, too.

"In our community, the Anti-balaka buried many women alive. If a woman ever died of an illness after a dispute, they accused the other woman of witchcraft and killed her."

Alongside cannibalism and tribal violence, witchcraft is among the phenomena most exploited by certain sectors of the media. Witchcraft: primitive, exotic, African beliefs, unimaginable—or so they say—in the West. In the Central African Republic, social advancement is often attributed to obscure forces that conspire to ennoble some and humiliate others. Attributing the phenomenon to a so-called cultural backwardness—What does that even mean? How long will our positivist vision of culture, rooted in a naive idea of progress, survive?—clashes with the reality: Central Africans have always been open to change, as well as to practices brought from other countries that affected their social and cultural customs.

Ned Dalby provides the diamond example. According to him, people who work in diamond mining suffer a higher psychological impact than those working in other extractive industries such as timber, gold, or uranium. In Boda (in the southeast), miners sacrifice an animal in the quarry (usually a chicken) so that the spirits will be on their side. Elsewhere, diamonds are known as "stones of the devil," as if possessing them could determine the course of a person's life. Why? Because that is often the case. For the miners, the value of diamonds is inscrutable. So are the reasons why they might suddenly stop getting paid or end up making what for them amounts to a fortune. The miners believe that this lottery—behind which lies a complex maze of agents, markets, foreign companies, and corrupt ministers—must obey some obscure logic. It belongs to another world: to this world, the capitalist world. The relationship established by the miner with the diamond is magical, but in fact it demonstrates the impact of external influence on local beliefs and ways of life.

IT'S MY LAST DAY IN BATANGAFO: October 13. I can't believe they've given Bob Dylan the Nobel Prize in Literature. Goddamn it. I'm climbing the walls, but the feeling—its effect on my mood—soon makes me feel ridiculous, at odds with myself and my reasons for being here. On my way back, in a four-by-four, I visit a village on the outskirts of Batangafo, where some of the IDPs are returning after having fled. We pass through a checkpoint installed by some civilians, who've placed a branch across the road to prevent cars from passing. It's a shoddy but effective solution: everyone stops, and they charge a toll to get through.

We keep driving, pass the airfield, and start seeing destroyed adobe houses by the side of the road, alongside tents with thatched roofs. A strange but unequivocal sign: the people living there have just returned home and haven't yet been able to rebuild their houses. We park in a bend in the road. I get out of the car, and Florence, a thirty-year-old Central African, tells me we're in the village of Bogidi. He says his family was attacked "by the nomads" in August 2014, and he fled to somewhere dozens of miles from here. Then there was fighting between the Anti-balaka and the Séléka, and he fled again. Now he has come home. If this can be called a home.

"When we came back, we saw the house had collapsed, and we had to rebuild it. The nomads burned it down. They killed someone in this village. We're not afraid anymore, the situation has more or less calmed down, even though the Fula still bother us every now and then."

The ground is littered with charred firewood, rocks, a grimy pot. His children scamper around. The temporary dwelling is made of palm leaves. Of the previous one, a small adobe house, only a perforated wall remains. It isn't a dwelling so much as a ruin, an archaeological discovery.

Just a few miles away, there's another handful of similar-looking houses. Paulin, who has six children, tells me he fled in 2013, when an armed group burned down all the houses in the village. He kept fleeing, this time from fighting between French troops and the Séléka. In the end, he decided to come back. He had several small houses, built with salvaged bricks: one is in ruins, but there's another still standing, which he's covered with palm leaves. It looks like it's in construction. I ask him if this is the case. The logic of his answer is devastating:

"I'm rebuilding it myself. I want to completely fix it up. If things stay calm, like they have so far, I'll do it little by little. But if not, I'll stop. It isn't worth it."

In other words, it's better not to rebuild the house in a hurry because it might be destroyed again. I feel as if someone has answered a question of which I am ignorant. I dive into my memories. My mind travels beyond this nonexistent country, this country that doesn't appear in the headlines or on TV, but that explains better than any other what this world in movement, this world of exoduses, is really like, and hands me the question I was searching for.

"Why don't they go home?" say the xenophobes.

"Are they trying to take advantage of us?" say those who are "against" refugees (Is it possible to be "against" refugees, just like that, in the abstract?).

"Why do they come here?" say those who are suspicious of people fleeing from war, even though the overwhelming majority will never arrive in the West, or even cross a single border.

"Why don't they go home, if there's no war there anymore?"

I gaze at the grimy walls of Paulin's "house" and find the answer to all the questions we ask ourselves from the safety of our own homes.

In December 2016, the Bangui airport camp was finally closed by the Central African Republic government.

The Refugee Parliament

Tibetans in Exile

> "And what about the Dalai Lama?" he [Mao] is said
> to have asked.
> When told that I had escaped, he replied,
> "In that case, we have lost the battle."
>
> *Freedom in Exile: The Autobiography*
> *of the Dalai Lama of Tibet*

T HERE ARE SOME REFUGEES who will never be refugees, and
there are some refugees who have been refugees for decades,
but who don't see themselves as refugees.

Like the Tibetans.

I'm at the tiny headquarters of the Tibetan Parliament in
Exile, a Buddhist structure in the foothills of the Himalayas. This
is the town of Dharamsala, in the north of India.

"There is one difference. Of half an inch."

"What?"

In the drab foyer on the ground floor hangs a gallery of photos
of the successive Tibetan Parliaments in Exile: the first, in 1960,
had only twelve members; the current parliament, forty-five.

Ahead is the chamber that houses the legislature, if you could call this political experiment by one of the longest-exiled communities in the world by such a name. The room—clean and white—is presided over by a slender orange throne belonging to the Dalai Lama, who never attends the Parliament. Well, he did attend the inauguration of the chamber, clarifies the protocol officer who's showing me around.

Behind the throne hangs a portrait of the Dalai Lama; on either side, to complete the Tibetan political universe, is a photo of Norbulingka—the summer palace where His Holiness lived in Tibet—surrounded by snow-capped mountains; and a magnificent map of Tibet that looks like a map of the entire Asian continent. Behind the new-looking wooden tables are ergonomic chairs as in a modern bar, instead of the more formal seats traditionally reserved for honorable members.

"They're the same color," I say.

"There's no opposition here," says the protocol officer in a satisfied tone. "Members are elected as individuals, independent of any political party."

"There's no difference between any of the chairs," I say.

"There is one difference. Of half an inch," she says.

"What?"

The official points at the two chairs closest to the throne of His Holiness, to the left and right. It's almost unnoticeable, but she's right: they're half an inch higher than the rest. They belong to the prime minister and the president of the parliament.

Everything in the Tibetan Parliament in Exile is made up of tiny details.

HOW DOES A REFUGEE PARLIAMENT WORK? I'm obsessed with this question as I wander through the building. A legislative chamber is where the sovereignty of the people is placed and rule proclaimed over a territory. *Sovereignty* relates to concepts such as state or power—not to refugees. *Territory* relates to belonging or rights—not to refugees. The Tibetans, who have lived for so many decades in exile, have found a tool with which to become something more than a refugee population.

I seek answers in the same building that houses the Tibetan Parliament, downstairs, along a corridor that looks like it belongs in a university: white office doors, signs with long titles and numbers. In one of those offices, I'm welcomed by Acharya Yeshi Phuntsok, the deputy speaker of the Parliament, who, as soon as I walk in, places a white *kata*—a silk scarf—around my neck, a traditional way of honoring guests. He's already winning 1–0: I feel as if he's hung a medal around my neck just for getting this far, as if he is buying my favor—thank you for your interest in the Tibetans, thank you for being here—as if he already knows my supposed sympathy for the Tibetan cause. It's an awkward situation, given the neutrality required in an interview. Taking it off is a bad idea, since that would be impolite. Keeping it on is also a bad idea, since as you write, you see how the white scarf you've been honored with as a gift hangs down over your notebook.

I don't take it off.

We sit down, and he hands me his card, which lists not only his position as deputy speaker of the Parliament, but also—all this fits onto that magical card—adviser to the Central Council of Tibetan Medicine, board member of the Central University for Tibetan Studies in Varanasi, and board member of the Tibetan Cultural and Religious Publication Center.

Something strange happened to me in this interview. Throughout my career, I've interviewed a wide range of people: Albert Rivera, when the new Spanish political party Citizens had just been founded—he wasn't important yet, that's why they sent the intern—the Pakistani minister of minorities who was assassinated by the Taliban, Shahbaz Bhatti, members of the Pakistani secret services, the leader of the Election Commission of India, the Mexican poet Octavio Paz's Indian secretary, an Afghan former Taliban minister, Sufi leaders, South Asian poets and painters, and a great many refugees. Usually, after transcribing the conversation, my impression of the interview's subject might alter slightly—a clever phrase that I hadn't noticed, a well-ordered thought that enlightens me, a single metaphor that surprises me—but it remains essentially the same. With Phuntsok, for the first time in my life, this wasn't the case. When I left, I felt as if this had been a dull, insipid interview; but when I looked over my notes, I realized that in fact, we had been wrestling over some important points.

It went something like this:

"How does the Tibetan Parliament in Exile work?"

"In exile, we use a charter, rather than a constitution like independent countries. Under this charter, we have twenty-seven rules and regulations relating to living spaces, pensions . . . we have rules about parliamentary procedures that . . ."

"But they aren't laws, are they? They can't be, since there isn't a territory."

"They aren't exactly laws. They're rules and regulations for the whole community in exile, which consists of some one hundred forty-five thousand people, though the population still in Tibet is six million."

"The way members are chosen is different from other parliaments."

"Don't confuse the refugees with the parliament. You requested an interview to find out more about refugees, right?"

"Ah, would you like to talk about the situation of Tibetan refugees in India first?"

"Refugee status is different in India from in other countries, because India hasn't signed the UN Convention. They offer us refugee status according to the constitution and laws of India. We're not under the protection of the UN Refugee Agency, we don't receive any kind of help from them. India has helped Tibetans a great deal: the Government in Exile is here, twelve Indian states have Tibetan settlements, and many schools for Tibetans have been founded with Indian funding."

And the deputy speaker of the Parliament plunges into a monologue: there are schools run by the Indian government, by international organizations, and by the Tibetan authorities . . .

I want to end the conversation. I don't understand why he's talking so much about education, but I'll find out later. Details matter at the headquarters of the Tibetan Government in Exile.

"So, how are the elections run here? Are they democratic?" I ask.

"In the sixties, we established an electoral system. We don't just have a parliament, we also have local assemblies in each Tibetan community, where they hold their own elections. It's a grassroots democracy. And, of course, His Holiness is always there; it's he who symbolizes Tibetan unity: he's respected in Europe, the United States, and Asia."

"But how does the voting happen?"

"Only Tibetans in exile over the age of eighteen can vote. There are forty-five members of parliament. Thirty of them correspond to the three historical provinces of Tibet. The ministers don't have to be members of parliament: they're chosen by the political leader, but the parliament must approve them."

Someone brings in a document for him to sign.

"Religion is very important for you."

"Tibetans in exile still feel tied to Tibet through family, society, and school. There's a commitment to the Tibetan lifestyle. That's important for the community."

"Do you hope to go back to Tibet someday? Although in fact you were born in India, not Tibet."

"We've been in exile for over fifty years. In some ways, compared with a century or a person's lifetime, fifty years seems like a long time, but for a movement or a cause, it's nothing."

Silence.

"Even in the twentieth century, with so much technology and development, competition and conflict, we managed to fight to keep the Tibetan movement alive. I think we're very courageous. Everyone else goes after money, strength, and military power, like China, but we're focusing on nonviolence."

"Do you feel any solidarity with the refugees who are suffering most in recent years? I'm thinking of the Syrian community."

"But refugees from Syria and other countries are very different. Unlike us, they're in conflict with their own country, their own government. So the comparison is irrelevant. The Afghans are also in conflict with their own government. Our conflict is with the Chinese communist government, which isn't our own government, and which is occupying our country. In the case of other refugees, their homeland hasn't been occupied."

"And the Palestinians?"

"But the Palestinian conflict is different. And I don't think Tibetans can be compared to Syrian refugees. There's always sympathy and dialogue, but every scenario is different."

"Every scenario is different, but I mentioned it because in the end, we're seeing civilians all over the world who live in one place and who, for whatever reason, whether it's a civil war or a military invasion, are being forced to abandon their homes and live somewhere else."

"You mean like Israel?"

"All over the world. The U.S. invasion of Afghanistan, for example."

"Those are problems with governments, systems. It's too bad. And I also think the UN is useless. If they can't find a solution to that, what's the point of their existence?"

"Should the UN be more active in the question of Tibet?"

"Tibet is always present in the subcommittees."

"But not in the resolutions."

"Until 1992, there were resolutions on human rights violations in Tibet, but there are more important issues, like sovereignty, self-government . . . we still haven't achieved that. There are twenty-two autonomous regions in the world that have relationships with their governing countries. Did you know that? We have relationships with them. Greenland, San Marino . . . I think there's one in Spain, too . . . the Basques."

"And Catalonia, I suppose."

"The Basque country," he says, taking out a dossier.

"And Catalonia, no?"

"Maybe it's here . . . yes, here it is. Catalonia! Haha. We are doing fantastic work," he says, handing me the dossier. "You can keep it. Everything you've learned here, you can explain to people over there, not only through your work in journalism, but in lectures, seminars . . . the survival of the Tibetan cause depends on it."

The white scarf drapes over my notebook.

"And do you hear any news from Tibet?"

"Before social media, we hardly heard anything, only from people able to visit Tibet. But since 2008, we've been hearing more. Look, this is the Chinese communist occupation of Tibet," he says, showing me photos of protests and acts of repression, taken on cell phones. "This is Tibet today. Students protesting the Chinese army. This is Tibet today, a dumping ground for nuclear waste. This is Tibet today, under the Chinese communist occupation."

We Are Not Refugees

WHEN DID THINGS GO WRONG FOR TIBET?

One of the twentieth century's most significant cases of exile began with a Chinese dance company on its way to Lhasa. The Chinese government had invited the Tibetan spiritual leader, the Dalai Lama, to a traditional dance performance. It was March 1959, and Tibet had already been under Chinese control for eight years. Tibetan guerrillas supported by the U.S. Central Intelligence Agency (CIA) were fighting Chinese troops in the east of the region, with little success. During those years, Tenzin Gyatso—the name of the fourteenth and current Dalai Lama—had attempted to negotiate with Mao Zedong to achieve autonomy and respect for the rights of the Tibetans, but the dialogue was about to be derailed.

The invitation to the performance included a special condition: the Dalai Lama, who at the time was twenty-three years old, would have to visit the Chinese military barracks in the Tibetan capital of Lhasa alone, without his armed bodyguards. His Holiness, aware of the importance of not slighting the Chinese, accepted the proposal. The performance date was set for March 10. Word spread, and the people assumed what to them seemed obvious: China was planning to kidnap the Dalai Lama. Up to thirty thousand people, according to the Dalai Lama's memoir, thronged around the gates of Norbulingka, his summer palace, to protect him. There were barricades. There was chaos. Tibetans accused of colluding with the Chinese were murdered. Messages of calm from the Dalai Lama fell on deaf ears. Obviously, the Tibetan spiritual leader decided to cancel his attendance of the performance, but the Chinese government even invited him again, reaching the heights of sarcasm, this time on the pretext that if he liked, he could take refuge from the unrest at the Chinese military barracks in Lhasa.

The Refugee Parliament

The Chinese military intervention was only a matter of time. How many days of protests would there be before all hell broke loose? The Dalai Lama asked the oracle three times whether he should flee. The first two times, a clairvoyant monk possessed by the spirit of Dorje Drakden, the Dalai Lama's protective spirit, said no, the Dalai Lama should stay. The third time, on March 17, 1959, the Dalai Lama's guardian angel changed his mind.

"Leave! Leave! Tonight!" the monk said in a trance, and before losing consciousness, he wrote down on a piece of paper the route that His Holiness should take. As if to reinforce his divine counsel, two suggestive blasts of Chinese mortar rang out near the palace.

This, at least, is how Tenzin Gyatso tells the story in his autobiography, where he offers skeptics a lesson on the oracle and how it works: "I am certain Dorje Drakden had known all along that I would have to leave on the 17th, but he did not say so for fear of word getting out. If no plans were made [to flee], nobody could find out about them."

(Revisiting these details represents neither an attempt to defend nor to ridicule the religion, but rather to illustrate something essential to understanding a refugee community with one of the longest histories in the world. It's impossible to delve into those decades in exile without considering the expansive figure of the Dalai Lama and the Tibetan religious worldview, which permeates every aspect of Tibetan history and culture. Details, like the half-inch that separates the prime minister's chair from those of the other members of parliament, are important.)

With the acquiescence of the gods, Tenzin Gyatso shed his monk's tunic, took off his glasses, put on some ordinary trousers and a black coat, and slung a rifle over his shoulder. He left the palace escorted by two soldiers and managed to pass through the crowds unnoticed.

Exodus.

With his entourage, the Dalai Lama had to outwit the Chinese troops deployed in Tibet and cross the Lhasa River on stepping stones, his vision blurred without the help of his glasses. He traveled through remote areas, escorted at a distance by soldiers and Tibetan guerrillas who'd been advised of his route.

Flight.

Tenzin Gyatso arrived in the district of Lhuntse Dzong on the Indian border, repudiated the Seventeen Point Agreement for the Peaceful Liberation of Tibet enshrining the Chinese presence in his country, and proclaimed his own parallel government. His entourage, however, was soon notified that the Chinese army was on its way, so without losing any time, he continued across the Himalayas. They heard the hum of airplanes overhead.

Exile.

"Whatever the identity of the aircraft, it was a forceful reminder that I was not safe anywhere in Tibet. Any misgivings I had about going into exile vanished with this realization: India was our only hope."

These are the words of an illustrious Tibetan refugee in 1959, but they could easily have been uttered today by a Syrian, a South-Sudanese, a Congolese, or an Afghan. For His Holiness, afflicted by dysentery, the last miles seemed to go on forever. He was so sick that he couldn't even ride a horse. He had to be carried on the back of a dzo, a cross between a cow and a yak.

"And it was on this humble form of transport that I left my native land."

ONE OF THE FIRST THINGS the Dalai Lama did in exile was to create a roving musical ensemble that used its concerts to proselytize in India.

"When His Holiness arrived in India as a political refugee in 1959, he felt a need to have a cultural group to explain Tibetan

culture to Indians," says Tenzin Lhaksam Wangdue, secretary
of the Tibetan Institute of Performing Arts. In time, that roving
group became a cultural institute located near the Tibetan Government in Exile, a few miles up the road, where the traffic begins
to disappear.

I arrive at the institute on foot, observing a geometric forma-
tion of pines and fir trees that pierce the fog and look from above
like a row of cauliflowers whose dense florets obscure their trunks.
Pastel- and cream-colored houses cling to the mountainside,
dilapidated buses climb the road; satellite dishes, electric cables,
and frayed strings of Tibetan prayer flags blink and flutter in
the snow, weaving a maze over entire villages: McLeod Ganj,
Dharamsala.

Absorbed in contemplation, I stumble upon an enormous
sign telling me that sixty feet away is the institute. Sure enough,
there it is: a colorful Buddhist archway opening onto what looks
like a school lost in the vastness of the mountains, with a courtyard occupied by an indoor soccer pitch with small goalposts that
look almost like water-polo goals. The children are playing a game
of trust with their German teacher, running around with their
eyes closed until the teacher grabs them by the waist before they
can crash into a doorway, or worse. One boy forges such a mean-
dering path that everyone starts laughing hysterically.

"He's only thirteen! He's very young. Let's give him some
applause."

It echoes across the entire mountain range.

"This institute was founded soon after the Tibetan exile," says
the center's secretary as he smokes and observes the scene from
the office balcony. "At first, it went on tour, educating the Indians
about Tibetan politics and music. This was urgent because China
introduced the Cultural Revolution and began destroying Tibetan
monasteries and educational institutions . . . it was important to

preserve Tibet's cultural legacy. So we went from being a cultural bridge to being a place where our cultural identity could be preserved. We began to recruit Tibetan students from various Indian settlements, for them to come here and learn Tibetan music and folkloric dance. Also *achi lamo*—Tibetan opera."

Soon afterward, in 1962, this institute was built and became part of the political-cultural complex of the Tibetan Government in Exile. As the secretary keeps talking—students of the diaspora in Europe, music workshops, dancers and singers, names of exotic musical instruments: *pewang, dranyen*—I remember how insistently the deputy speaker spoke of education.

Against military force: identity, culture, religion.

The secretary accompanies us to the institute's museum, in whose foyer we're greeted by the figure of a yogi: the yogi who presides over all Tibetan operas. At the end of our tour, I notice a diorama: a miniature opera scene that helps visualize what the staging would be like. Tenzin explains that the figures' yellow masks represent compassion, red represents power, and green, maternity. After the masked men dance, the narrator comes forward. This is one of the institute's activities that requires the most preparation by the students.

We return to the courtyard where the children were playing. It's almost midday, and they've gone for lunch. We go into a classroom, and see not students, but women working, making necklaces and garments for the musical performances. It's a kind of small workshop. One of the women working tells me that it takes her a whole day to make three necklaces.

"They're here every day," says the secretary.

"Every day, every day," repeats the Tibetan woman, as if making fun of him, or of herself and her destiny. When I observe up close the painstaking skill required to make the necklace, I think of how little we appreciate the labor that goes into an object: a necklace isn't just a necklace, but also an exhausted Tibetan woman threading beads onto a string for hours on end, stretching her arms, going to lunch, coming back to the workshop, threading beads again.

I HEAD DOWN THE ROAD and arrive in McLeod Ganj, home of the Dalai Lama. I have lunch in a simple, cozy tavern: spinach and cheese *momos*—South Asian dumplings—and crispy noodle soup with mushrooms and onions. I take a taxi farther down the road, leaving the dirt paths behind, the dense fog enveloping everything. The rain keeps falling. I pass a physical therapy center, a hotel with only one room—the large sign states unequivocally: ONLY ONE ROOM—a mechanical shop that repairs Royal Enfield motorcycles, blankets with a diagonal pattern of trees and nettles, houses arranged in a chasm like rocks about to tumble into the ravine. The taxi drops me off at the headquarters of the Tibetan Government in Exile. Everything is under construction: bulldozers and fencing and equipment and cement—I don't know how to get in, and it's pouring rain; I make a run for my destination, toward the place that will explain what Tibetan exile is made of: the Tibetan library in exile.

Because culture is a refugee, too.

Murals of the Wheel of Life preside over the entrance to the library, whose gate stands ajar today, with the indolence of a rainy day that dampens the spirit. I've arranged to meet the librarian, the quintessentially Tibetan Sonam Topgya, unceasingly smiling and cheerful, on the first floor. He wears a blue shirt with perfectly turned-up sleeves as if it had come folded like that from the factory, dark pants and shoes, short hair, and stubble just beginning to show. After greeting me, he places his thumb on a fingerprint scanner—no joke—and opens the secret door to the archive. It's a plain, functional room, an extension of the temperament of the librarian himself. Hundreds of manuscripts wrapped in cloth of different colors are arranged on shelves lining three aisles.

Sonam takes out a table and sets it up in one of the aisles. We sit down and start talking.

"There are one hundred thousand documents in this library; 40 percent are original, and 60 percent are facsimiles. Most of the valuable objects were left behind after the Lhasa Uprising, but a few books, statues, and manuscripts were recovered. There was an order for monks and disciples to do everything they could to get manuscripts out of Tibet. It's very hard to gather these documents and keep them safe in exile. People donated the manuscripts to the Dalai Lama, who decided to build this library along with the government in exile. It's unique, because it isn't a monastic library. There are all kinds of things here—the teachings of the Buddha, and the commentaries of the Indian and Tibetan masters. Manuscripts on Buddhist philosophy and rituals. Books of poetry, grammar. Tantric texts."

The librarian proudly takes out a manuscript of a book by an Indian Buddhist master. It's somewhat larger than the manuscripts of the previous Tibetan masters, but somewhat smaller than the teachings of the Buddha—in the city of the Tibetan Government in Exile, details are important. The manuscript—a thick bundle of two hundred eighty-five pages with writing on each side and filling the margins, since paper was a precious commodity in the seventeenth century—is wrapped in a mustard-colored cloth, a kind of Indian scarf. The book's title is hidden by a hard cover.

"This is an Indian master's commentary on the Tantra. The paper is handmade. The ink has run on some of the pages. Remember, they were brought here into exile from Tibet."

Sonam takes out another manuscript and begins to say some more mantras. He looks serious and is concentrating hard.

"I don't know what it says. It's very old calligraphy."

Sometimes his laughter is contagious; at others, it's disarming.

The librarian tells me that he was born in exile in Dharamsala. His father was a servant to the Tibetan education minister—one of the most important—second today only to the prime minister, the one with a chair a half-inch higher than the others, and of course, the Dalai Lama. He cared for the minister's horses. They came into exile in India together.

"Before, he used to be with [the minister] all day. That was no longer the case here. Everything changed. The minister told my father that he had to be free—well, it's not that he wasn't free, but he told him to make his own life. Everything is different in exile!"

His father remained faithful until the minister's death, in 1967. He worked in the official print shop of the Tibetan Government in Exile, where Sonam acquired his interest in books and paper as a little boy.

Sonam then begins to talk about identity. Not about being a refugee, but about being Tibetan. The Indian government grants Tibetans permission to stay in the country, but they have to renew it every year. He shows me the document, much like a passport: an identity card issued by the Indian authorities. Sonam's nationality: Tibetan.

"We still want to be Tibetan. A few people have tried to become Indian nationals, but most of us haven't. We don't vote in Indian elections; we have our own. We pay our taxes, which we call donations, to the Tibetan Government in Exile. For us, the last elections for prime minister were like the Clinton–Trump election."

"Religion seems to play an important role in the community."

"When His Holiness was young and had no experience in government, he met with Mao Zedong. He thought it was going to be a friendly meeting, but Mao told him that religion is poison. Imagine! Poison!"

I SPEND MY LAST FEW DAYS in Dharamsala finishing the Dalai Lama's autobiography. Little by little, I find in its pages everything that the deputy speaker of the parliament, the secretary of the cultural institute, and the librarian told me.

This is the Dalai Lama's version of what the deputy speaker told me: ". . . the present situation could not last forever, even if it did last our lifetimes."

This is the Dalai Lama's version of what the secretary of the cultural institute told me: "I told them the future of Tibet depended on us refugees. If we want to preserve our way of life, the only way to do so was by building strong communities."

This is the Dalai Lama's version of the statement by Mao Zedong mentioned by the deputy speaker: "Your attitude is good, you know. Religion is poison. Firstly it reduces the population, because monks and nuns must stay celibate, and secondly it neglects material progress."

I wander through the temple and the residence of the Dalai Lama, bewildered by my encounter with a people in exile—not for a decade, but for more than a half-century—that struggles onward, that's convinced it will win, though it doesn't know when. The monks walk clockwise around the temple facing His Holiness's residency. They pass me with prayer beads in their hands, and they seem to be leaving a trail of reflections, ideas, and meditations behind them, which they're eager to shed and which I can't escape. They turn their golden prayer wheels, which correspond to mantras, mantras, and more mantras. The complex is austere, almost industrial; the silence is overwhelming, a silence impossible in India, a silence only the Tibetans could have brought. From here, you can see Dharamsala spread over the hills, the dense fog whose thick paintbrush obscures the landscape; in the distance, if you listen carefully, buses and cars and motorcycles and horns—the Indian chaos that strives to drown out the Buddhist silence; it doesn't succeed.

A white tented walkway connects the temple to the Dalai Lama's residence. On the right, there's a garden with some stones and a lawn for walking, some green benches—always green—monks with school backpacks or shoulder bags, monks wearing plastic-framed glasses, monks checking their cell phones.

The monsoon is dying down. There are trees with moss growing on their bark. The banister leading to the residence of His Holiness is brown, with an abstract gold design. The building has a green roof, three floors, a reception area, a gatehouse. Behind a black fence, an Indian policeman stands guard with a rifle over his shoulder and a khaki jacket with the word POLICE written on the back in English, in yellow letters. The entrance is like a temple-garage held up by two large white columns. Some bedrooms can be glimpsed through half-drawn curtains.

Two women—two shadows—wander through the house. I approach the gatehouse, where a protocol officer keeps watch. As I walk toward the home of the most famous refugee in the world, I think of Muhammad, the surgeon who was murdered in Syria; of Ronyo, the teacher who survived the war in South Sudan; of Ulet, the Somalian who died after being rescued in the Mediterranean; I think of Afghanistan, Pakistan, the Congo, the Central African Republic, Mexico, South Sudan, Jordan, Turkey, Greece, Serbia, Croatia, Tibet, and this world of unrelenting exoduses, of nonrefugees, that can only begin to be understood by looking beyond the West.

We Are Not Refugees

When I get to the Dalai Lama's house, I ask the same question I asked when arriving at Osama bin Laden's house.

"Is this the Dalai Lama's residence?"

"Yes."

"Is he at home?"

"No."

"And where is he?"

Silence.

"Out of station."

The Last Border

Syrians in Europe

> The pilgrim reaches the wall
> breathless, resting his hands,
> his brow there, seeking relief:
>
> but soon he draws them back, since some hands
> and a burning brow
> ·sustain him from the other side.
>
> ÁNGEL CRESPO, The Wall

THE SONG "WORK" by Rihanna is playing in a large warehouse with a high ceiling, red industrial pipes, and light streaming through its windows. *Work, work, work, work, work, work.* It's Saturday, but work is getting done here: people of all ages, as if in an assembly line, place scarves, colored hats, bootees, and even a flamenco dress in boxes about to be loaded onto a ship destined for Lebanon. *You see me I be work, work, work, work, work, work.* Jeans, sweaters, scarves, blankets with bear patterns. A girl climbs into one of the boxes so that others can pass her the clothing; a boy stationed at a refreshment stand with pieces of Spanish omelette and cured sausage distributes bottled water to the volunteers.

"You! You never stop eating!" shouts a man who is cheerleading the volunteer effort.

The ship belongs to the Schenker transportation company in the Logistics Activities Area of the Port of Barcelona, technically in El Prat de Llobregat territory. Several members of the assembly line wear eye-catching orange T-shirts from the association El Poble Ajuda al Poble (which means "The People Help the People" in Catalan). The operation is managed by Jad, a handsome, blue-eyed Syrian, whom everyone is asking questions. The other orange T-shirts are worn by his family members—his siblings and his mother, who all live in Catalonia. Jad wants his family's integration to go as quickly as his own. This is one of the first things they've done since arriving: help to pack food, clothing, and toiletries into boxes for Syrian refugees in Lebanon.

"Come on, come on, let's not slow down," shouts the cheerleader.

Now the music has switched to reggaeton. Jad writes numbers on the boxes with a black marker. I follow him around the facility as he folds jeans and sweaters, and meanwhile—when he has a chance—he tells me about the work being done by the association.

"We're sending all this to Lebanon, to places where there are a lot of refugee families. We have a partner organization there. Now we're trying to open a health center in Beirut."

The pallets that will be loaded onto a cargo ship bound for Lebanon are being stacked. The boxes proclaim: "Baby food 2000," "Adult soap 70," "liquid soap/lotion," "Vegetables 444 kgs," "Baby bottles," and "Syria" with a heart drawn next to it.

"Right now, I think more help is needed in Lebanon than in Greece. There are over a million Syrian refugees in Lebanon: a fourth of the total population. And I've worked in Greece. I was there in December 2015, in Lesbos, on the coast where the dinghies were arriving full of refugees. I was a volunteer, and worked closely with Proactiva Open Arms. You were working twenty-four hours a day, you slept for an hour, then at three in the morning the volunteer group started getting WhatsApp messages, and you jumped in the car and headed down to the coast."

"Come on, we're slowing down, and we have to go have a beer!" says the cheerleader.

They're almost done. Jad's fair-haired brother, Amir, who's now of university age, climbs onto a pallet jack, raises the forks, and takes a picture of all the participants with his phone.

People are delighted to be here.

"Whenever you need anything, just put some music on for us and we'll get it done. Next time we'll go to Vic [a town in the province of Barcelona] and eat at your restaurant," one of the volunteers tells Jad as they recover from their efforts and get ready to leave.

Jad agrees, and keeps labeling boxes: methodical, maniacal, obsessive. I follow him around, notebook in hand, but it's impossible to take any notes. He never stops. I wonder where he gets all his energy. I wonder how, in his situation, he can manage a restaurant—two restaurants, he corrects me: he recently opened a second. I wonder where he finds the time to run an aid association for refugees that's now planning to open a health center in Lebanon. And above all, I wonder how he can do all this at once when his mother, two brothers and two sisters have just arrived from Syria.

When Salah Dasouqui touched down in Oslo, still carrying the chocolate bars and cigarettes that he'd bought to blend in with the other passengers, an immigration official asked to see his passport, to let him into the country. He handed it over, and she began asking him questions in Norwegian.

"I don't speak Swedish or Norwegian."

"And how is that possible, if you have a Swedish passport?"

"I live in Malmö, in Sweden, and I'm surrounded by Arabs there, I work in an Arab restaurant, and never speak any Swedish."

"Aah."

The official fed the passport into the machine. The expression on her face changed: the system was telling her something.

"Is this your passport?"

"No, it isn't mine. I'm Syrian, and I want to request asylum."

A Norwegian policewoman accompanied Salah to the airport police station. They gave him some cookies and searched his luggage. Then they took him to the immigration office: on the way, he spoke Arabic with the driver of the police car, whose wife was Lebanese.

Salah spent a month in a center for migrants, waiting for the interview where they would decide whether to grant him asylum. Born in the Palestinian refugee camp of Yarmouk, on the outskirts of Damascus, he had his papers in order and knew what he needed to explain about his past. The interview took place on April 24, 2013. A day later, the answer arrived: asylum granted.

He began taking Norwegian classes and looked for a job. On TV, he saw how his countrymen were risking their lives at sea. He had already worked on aid projects in Syria, so it was obvious: he needed to help the people who hadn't arrived yet. One day, he saw a job advertised with Doctors Without Borders. They were looking for a cultural mediator, someone who spoke Arabic, for their rescue mission in the Mediterranean.

Salah sent in his résumé.

———

The Last Border

"I TOLD YOU, AFTER FIVE O'CLOCK!"

"What?"

"At five!"

Jad refuses to speak Arabic with his siblings. Only Spanish and Catalan. He runs into one of them—Amir, his fair-haired, nineteen-year-old brother—walking the streets of Vic one Saturday at three in the afternoon, with the innocent goal of finding an optician to fix his glasses.

"I've told him a thousand times that everything's closed. That he should try after five. That's how things go around here."

I'm in Jad's car; he's just picked me up from the train station in Vic. We head toward his restaurant, the one that's been open longest, the original. At first glance, the logo of El Tast is a jumble of famous tourist attractions: the Statue of Liberty, the pyramids of Egypt, the Eiffel Tower, the Sagrada Familia . . . but then I see something I don't recognize. I don't even know if it's a representation of a monument.

"That's the sword of Umayyad Square in Damascus," says Jad.

We go into the restaurant-bar: two TV screens for soccer, a Heineken poster with a picture of a green brain, a bar with few customers at this time of day. I'm hungry: I look at the menu, and choose spinach and cuttlefish cannelloni with meatballs. We share two plates of hummus.

"One day we were in *El 9*," says Jad, referring to a local newspaper. "People come here to watch Barcelona play. Once when they won, I sprayed everyone with champagne. We had a big party, and it was in the newspaper."

Jad's wife, Susana, is at the table, along with his eighteen-year-old sister, Aseel, who's already made friends and seems to have been here for years, and his twenty-eight-year-old sister, Jehan, who can now fumble her way through Spanish.

"We've hardly been to the beach at all this year."

"I don't like it. I don't know, I have mixed feelings about it. A lot of people die there," says Susana.

It's only been a month since Jad's family arrived in Vic. Aseel—with blue eyes like her mother and brother—is the one who is integrating most rapidly.

"Aseel wants to study in Germany," says Jad. "We're going to apply. She does the same thing I did: she goes around writing things down in her notebook all the time. She knows more than any of us."

"For me, this is an opportunity to start over," says Assel. "It's a new system."

When dessert and coffee arrive, Amir reappears, euphoric. He's managed to get his glasses repaired—although, obviously, not before five o'clock. He says the saleswoman tried to speak English with him, but that he refused, explaining that he needed to practice his Spanish. He's feeling very proud of himself.

"They're lucky," says Jad. "Being here with someone who knows the city, and on top of that, has a restaurant, is nothing like arriving as a family of refugees who don't know anyone. People have given them a big welcome."

Meanwhile, another conversation is taking place at the bar between the family and some customers. Today, they went to gather *bolets*—mushrooms—an ultra-Catalan tradition, and something that Jad's sisters tried within a month of arriving, but which I've never done in my entire life.

Jad says, "I went to Lebanon six years ago and had trouble getting out with a Spanish passport. You don't feel safe. When you get back here, to Barcelona, you feel at home. I speak Spanish with my wife because I still didn't know Catalan when we met. You never forget your own culture, but I want to make my life here."

Jad's sister Jehan speaks up. She hasn't fully understood what Jad said, but she knows that we're talking about integration. She's quickly adopted the common Catalan question tag, *saps?* (You know?).

"People know you've come from a war zone, and sometimes the sympathy feels good, but sometimes it makes me feel sad. *Saps?*"

The family is toying with the idea of opening an Arabic school, which would surely be a success, but Jad isn't so interested.

"I don't watch TV in Arabic. Just Spanish and Catalan. I try not to translate anything for them. If I have time, I explain the words to them little by little, with gestures."

"Jad is impossible. He always wants to do things his own way," says his wife, Susana. "He won't tell you what his plans are, then you find out later what he's been up to."

A regular customer invites Jad's siblings to play pool at another establishment. Jad gets annoyed—they promised me they were going to study now, he says—but in the end, he lets them go. We stay behind with his mother.

"My mother has health problems. You should have seen all the bags she brought from Syria. Three packets of those medications cost sixty euros here; they're much less back there. I told her not to bring anything, but she paid no attention. Luckily, because Social Security doesn't cover those medications."

His mother looks at him as if thinking, what is this man talking about? I try to speak to her. Right then, she realizes who I am—we first saw each other at the food and clothing collection in the warehouse at the port. She gives me a hug—how are you? I didn't recognize you, it's great to see you. We stumble through a conversation in Spanish and Arabic. Our knowledge of each other's languages goes just far enough for us to make a deal: she'll teach me Arabic if I teach her Spanish.

Jad smiles. His family has reached their destination: a sports bar for Barcelona fans in the Catalan town of Vic.

IN THIS CREW, THERE IS SOMEONE UNIQUE. An overgrown boy with a mischievous face, who likes to bake chocolate cakes for the sailors and aid workers. Someone especially sensitive to what happens here, on the *Dignity I* rescue boat. Someone whose job is to climb into the lifeboats to reassure the refugees, but who does so with an additional sense of foreboding: the fear that he might recognize someone among those trying to escape.

This is Salah Dasouqui, the Palestinian Syrian who left his country and flew to Norway. He managed to get the job with Doctors Without Borders. Sitting in a chair on the top deck of the *Dignity I*, Salah tells me that his parents and his brother and sister also managed to get out of the Palestinian refugee camp in Yarmouk, but they took the route through Turkey, Greece, and the Balkans: the route of shame. They risked their lives at sea on a dinghy, crossed Europe, arrived in Germany, and were granted asylum. As he looks out at the Mediterranean, an electric blue canvas on this sweltering July morning, Salah can't stop thinking about his family. Perhaps there will be Syrian refugees on the next inflatable boat rescued by the *Dignity I*; perhaps there will be refugees from Yarmouk, the camp where he used to live.

"Each time there's a rescue and I go out in a lifeboat, all I can think on the way is that maybe I'll see someone I know. It's a stressful thought. The fact that my family crossed by sea gives me stronger feelings about working here. I feel what they feel. They don't know anything! We know, and we can help them, but they don't even know where they are, they have no idea, all they know is that they're in the middle of the sea. When I get there and I see them . . . it's a fantastic feeling, because you see the happiness in their eyes when they realize there's someone there to help them."

The Last Border

On this mission, any mistake, any sign of panic, can cause the boat to capsize. The psychological exhaustion takes its toll: Salah will stay on the *Dignity I* five months, with a few short breaks. His personal life will also take a new turn while he's there: he'll meet his new partner, a Scottish woman called Hayley, who is also an aid worker on the *Dignity I*.

THE VILLAGE OF SAHNAYA lies on the outskirts of Damascus. It's part of Ghouta, a rural area whose name shot to fame in August 2013 when a chemical attack killed between two hundred and fourteen hundred people—that's how wide the range of figures can be when two opposing factions spread propaganda about a historic event. The "red line" that President Barack Obama had drawn for intervention had been crossed, but in the end, Russia proposed a plan for chemical disarmament in Syria, which the United States accepted. Bashar al-Assad breathed a sigh of relief.

Jad is from Sahnaya, but he never saw what Damascus and its surroundings became like after the civil war broke out. He left earlier, much earlier. At seventeen, he was already working, and he was convinced that he didn't want to stay in Syria. The word he most hated: *mushkil*. Problems, problems, nothing but problems. Where others saw *mushkil*, he saw only solutions. Though Syria wasn't yet at war, Jad didn't want to do military service, so when he turned twenty, he left and never went back. That was in 2005. His destination: Barcelona.

Jad wanted to study medicine, but to be accepted, he had to take the university entrance exams. That meant first, he had to learn Spanish and Catalan. He managed this within two years, but by that time, his mind was on other things. He moved to Vic and met Susana, whom he would later marry. He opened a restaurant, El Tast, that became a success. He sometimes talked to Arabic-speakers if necessary, but his method was pure immersion;

he didn't want to meet anyone from his own country or region. Within a few years, his Spanish and Catalan were perfect. His customers were charmed.

War broke out, and the problems began. Jad's family had stayed behind in Sahnaya: his mother, a diabetic, had also survived cancer and two heart attacks. Apart from his older sister, who was twenty-three at the time, the rest of his siblings were younger. Sahnaya was a government-protected enclave: the bombs were falling only five minutes away, but the family never directly experienced a bombing. At first, like many Syrians, they thought — hoped — that the conflict would pass, the war would soon be over, and the violence wouldn't reach them.

They planned to keep hanging on.

Because Jad had obtained Spanish citizenship, his mother could join him in Barcelona, but this permission did not extend to his siblings. His mother refused to leave without her children. As the fighting progressed, the family's morale declined. They were worried that one of Jad's brothers, the fair-haired Amir, would soon have to do his mandatory military service and go to war. They spent hours on end in darkness, with the thrum of helicopters flying overhead. Food was scarce, and more and more displaced people were arriving in the area. They had to leave.

Jad is stubborn, hard-working, and uncompromising: his goal was for his family to come to Spain legally. He tried everything he could, without success. Desperate, he even considered his family leaving through Turkey, and then picking them up in a rented yacht so they wouldn't have to risk their lives traveling in inflatable dinghies. In the end, he didn't. Those months put a strain on the family. Jad's mother pressured him constantly, asking him what he was doing to get them out of there. He was the one who could make it happen because he was in Europe. Sometimes they went for days without speaking, and his mother talked to Susana,

Jad's wife, via WhatsApp. They had no shared language, so they sent each other emoticons: an airplane, a smile.

Ultimately, it wasn't necessary for them to travel illegally. After several years of negotiation, Jad managed to persuade the Spanish embassy in Lebanon to issue his family a visa. They'd been granted a nonwork residence permit. Before the war, Jad's family had been able to travel to Spain on vacation. Now they were making the same journey to leave the war behind.

A month before leaving, Jad's mother knew that the visa had been granted. Later, his older sister also found out. But the other three—Mario, Aseel, and Amir—weren't informed; they could only suspect. They packed light when they left Sahnaya: they were told that they were going to try their luck in Lebanon. Jad traveled to Beirut to collect them, and together they took the flight of their lives, to Barcelona.

"I was finally happy. I had a tough few years, but on the plane, on the way back to Barcelona with my family, I had no more worries. I didn't have to think about anything."

"I'm tired," Salah says.

Four months after we last saw each other on the *Dignity I*, on the Mediterranean rescue mission, I arrange to meet Salah in a teahouse in Barcelona. He's a thirty-one-year-old overgrown boy who still has a childlike innocence: a look on his face as if butter wouldn't melt in his mouth, mischievous comments, a nervous giggle. Despite all the chocolate cakes that he baked on board the ship, he's lost a few pounds. He isn't alone—his girlfriend, Hayley, is with him.

"It was an incredible experience," says Salah. "I took part in a rescue where we brought over nine hundred people onto the *Dignity I*, which has a capacity for far fewer. It was a crazy day. But I'm not going back. Five months is a long time to be at sea, and I'm done. Right now, all I can think about is resting. I get up at eleven every day. And you know what the best part is? Not hearing the rescue alert siren every morning."

Hayley puts her hands on his left knee. The couple is trying to decide between Barcelona and Oslo, where Salah still has a home. He has been granted Norwegian citizenship. He's not interested in going to Africa or the Middle East. For the moment.

His family lives twenty minutes outside Berlin, and he often visits them. They have already met Hayley. Salah and his family know they've been lucky: he was granted asylum only a day after he applied—something almost unheard of—and his family obtained it in only three months.

Salah has gone from being a member of the Palestinian diaspora—stateless—to forming part of the global minority of people who enjoy freedom of movement. He now has a passport that will take him practically anywhere he should wish to go. He is free of financial worries. Finally, he can do something he's wanted to do for a long time: visit Palestine, the land of his ancestors.

"Are you going?"

"Yes, of course!"

"I met another Palestinian from Yarmouk on the refuge trail. His dream is also to go to Palestine."

"You told me on the boat. Don't you miss Pakistan and India?"

The question surprises me. Salah knows that I spent more than five years living in South Asia. I must have told him about it in a moment of melancholy out on the Mediterranean.

"Yes, I miss them both."

"I'm not going there, but I'll send you a postcard from Jerusalem."

Salah has reached his destination. He's no longer a refugee. His next trip will be for pleasure.

As we drink another cup of tea, he tells me about his whole journey.

Salah's grandfather was sixteen when he arrived in Syria. In 1948, after the first Arab-Israeli war, more than seven hundred thousand people lost their homes. Some sixty thousand took refuge in Syria, particularly in the Yarmouk camp on the outskirts of Damascus. It's called a camp because it's inhabited by refugees, but really it's a city.

That was the family's home for decades. Salah was born in 1985: he belonged to the third generation of Palestinians exiled in Syria. A generation that grew up in peace, with living conditions perhaps better than those of many of the Palestinians surviving in the West Bank, and especially in the Gaza Strip. A generation that wanted to hold onto its Palestinian identity, that had a special sense of belonging to its community, but which at the same time often also felt tied to Syria. A generation of people who, though they weren't on the move, still had a document saying that they were refugees.

Salah's childhood—a childhood without war—was the happiest time of his life. He then enrolled at the University of Damascus to study business. In his second year of college, he began to work for the United Nations Relief and Works Agency (UNRWA), the United Nations (UN) agency supporting Palestinian refugees. His first project was an interesting one: digitalizing the documents—archives, papers, birth certificates, writings—of Palestinian refugees in Lebanon, something that was essential for them to be able to reclaim their property, to prove that the land belongs to them. The project was carried out in Damascus because the process had already been successfully completed in Syria.

He was promoted to administrative assistant, a job that was appropriate for his course of study. But the job he most enjoyed in his youth was the one that came afterward. At the time, another group was also arriving in Syria in search of refuge: Iraqis fleeing the war in their country. The U.S. Agency for International Development financed a project to help them. While Washington waged war, Washington also assisted refugees, paying for rentals and providing health care and education. Salah worked closely with the project's director, a Norwegian woman now working for the UN Refugee Agency in Colombia. They established a system to determine the degree of poverty of the refugees, and find out the real needs of each Iraqi family.

In the spring of 2011, the protests began that would later develop into the Syrian civil war. The aid program that Salah was participating in continued; he often had to travel all over the country, in vehicles carrying a fortune in the trunk. They went to Latakia, Homs, and Aleppo to distribute money for the recipients to use to pay for rent and food. It was reckless to travel like that through some of the country's hot spots: security forces were conducting checks everywhere, and checkpoints operated by the rebels and by the various Islamist militias were also beginning to appear.

Salah was detained by Assad's forces because he had taken photos of a Yarmouk destroyed by the war. To take photographs is to spy, to oppose, to denounce. He spent some time in prison. In the end, he was released, but some of his friends weren't so fortunate: they were arrested, and disappeared. Soon he would have to enlist to complete his military service. These were reasons enough to flee Yarmouk, which was no longer the prosperous camp of his childhood.

In November 2012, Salah boarded a bus to make the first leg of his journey, from Damascus to the Turkish border, through Hama, Idlib, and Aleppo. From one checkpoint to another: crossing battle front lines, watching as the flags changed. The Syrian government, armed opposition groups. Salah couldn't contain his nerves. At each checkpoint, the ritual was repeated: Where are you from, where are you going, what do you want to do? At one of those government checkpoints, the soldiers were using computers to verify the passengers' identities, one by one. Nothing could guarantee safety, not even a lack of presence on social media, which had been a key tool for the opposition. An hour passed, then two. Salah gazed out of the window, undaunted, trying to find the perfect facial expression, the inscrutable look. This might be the last time I see daylight, he thought.

They let them through.

Salah arrived at the border in Bab al-Hawa. On one side of the highway, there was a metal barrier that you could go around to get into Turkey. The Turkish soldiers let him through, after a payment to help grease the wheels. The first Turkish city where Salah stayed was Nisrin—now called Görentas—in the south, near the border. He contacted a Turkish smuggler, who sold him a Swedish passport. The plan was to board a plane to Oslo, and once there, request asylum. He paid three thousand dollars for that passport, in addition to the plane ticket. They decided that it would be best to try to leave from the smaller Adana airport instead of from Istanbul. Salah was arrested and held in a detention center for six days before being returned to Syria, right on the border, in no-man's-land. This time they wouldn't let him through.

He switched borders: he managed to get to Azaz, and from there to Bab al-Salam, the busiest border crossing, the one crossed by many of the Syrians in this book. Again, Salah tried to cross illegally, this time through the olive groves. The Turkish soldiers started shooting, puncturing the backpack of one of the refugees traveling in his group. Panic broke out; they ran and ran and ran, and disappeared among the trees. They waited an hour, and then tried again. They crossed.

Salah repeated the operation. He went back to Nisrin, but used a different smuggler: this time, a Syrian from Aleppo. He paid seven thousand dollars—more than twice the previous fee—for another Swedish passport. This time, the chosen airport was Istanbul. The smuggler told him to go through window 25, that there was a customs agent there who had supposedly been bribed, that he was going to let him through without any trouble. But when he arrived, there was no one at window 25. Salah turned around—what do I do now? The smuggler gestured at him: keep going, don't worry, go to the next window. It was a lottery. Salah showed the agent his passport. He looked like the document's original owner. They let him through.

He still couldn't declare victory. The authorities study those who arrive with a magnifying glass, not those who leave. But the airline knows that if anyone travels illegally on one of its flights, it will have to pay a hefty fine. Salah wasn't alone: on that flight from Istanbul to Oslo, several Syrians were relying on that way of getting to Europe. When he arrived at the gate, he saw men dressed as civilians observing the passengers. He went to a duty-free store and bought some chocolate bars, some toys, and a box of cigarettes, even though he doesn't smoke. "Illegal immigrants don't buy Marlboros, right?" he thought to himself. He went back to the gate: at no time did he pay any attention to the observer. He struck up a conversation in English with a Swedish family and gave the children some chocolates. This helped him dispel his nerves. He watched as two visibly nervous men and a woman were called from the line—Syrians with fake travel documents, like him.

The passengers walked through the gate. Salah's turn came. He showed his fake passport.

"Mmmhmmm. Go ahead! Welcome!"

My life has changed forever, thought Salah.

———

The Last Border

BOTH SALAH'S AND JAD'S FAMILIES arrived at their destination. In many ways, they are privileged, if that word can be applied to people fleeing countries at war. But it's important to remember that they are the exception. For this book, I interviewed dozens of Syrians; I couldn't keep track of every one of them, but the majority probably not only didn't make it to Europe—which isn't always their goal—but also are surviving somewhere in limbo.

Many names echo constantly in my head.

I don't know what happened to Nermin, the girl whose diary fascinated me. The cell phone number they gave me never worked again. Some Syrians who knew the family told me that they had managed to make it to Turkey. Others said they hadn't, that they were still in Syria.

I don't know whether Hassan Nasser, the young victim of a bombing whom I met in the Zaatari camp in Jordan, went back to Syria to join his family, as he had planned.

Fatima, the young photographer I met in that same camp, published some of her work in the first print edition of the magazine that I edit, 5W.

Peshang Alo, the activist-journalist who was attacked by a sniper in Aleppo, is in Turkey, and he always likes the photos that I post on Instagram when I travel in Africa.

Hassan, the man whose two sons were so unlike each other, held on in Turkey and didn't dare cross the Aegean Sea to get to Europe. His daughter born in exile looks prettier every day—at least in the photos that he posts on Facebook.

Deek, the young Kurd I accompanied on his journey across Europe and who was stopped by Frontex, is now in the United Kingdom, has married a Canadian, and wants to cross the Atlantic so they can live in Canada together.

Adham, the young mathematician with bent glasses whom I met on the route of shame, made it to Germany. He has had a son, just as he was planning. After the Paris terrorist attacks in November 2015, he wrote me this message:

"People look at me with hatred. They've shouted at me, go back to Syria. But I'm here because I've fled from the crimes of the Syrian regime and from Islamic terrorism. They don't get it."

I lost touch with Salwah, the young woman with pale eyes who was left in a wheelchair by a Syrian sniper. I'm told her older sister married a Turk, but that he began to threaten the whole family, and they fled somewhere far away.

Her phone has been disconnected.

Acknowledgments

THANKS TO EVERYONE who allowed me to interview them, who made this book possible. I wouldn't have done it. Most of all, I remember Ulet, Salwah, Muhammad, Deek, Jad, and Salah. And thanks also to those I interviewed who don't appear in these pages.

Thanks to my wonderful literary agent, Ella Sher, and to Mary Ann Sabia, publisher of Imagine (Charlesbridge), for giving me the chance to publish this book in English. To Charlotte Whittle, for her beautiful translation, and to Don Weise, for his thoughtful editing.

Thanks to my Spanish editor, Eva Serrano, for believing in my writing. And to Círculo de Tiza, for being such a great publisher.

Thanks to the fixers, translators, and friends I've had in all the countries I've worked in. Especially to Waqas Khan, the most loyal of them all.

Thanks to Julia R. Arévalo, my uncompromising journalism teacher. To Martín Caparrós, teacher from a distance and master of long-form reporting: you're present in almost every one of these pages.

Thanks to the founders of 5W: this book has grown alongside our global dream.

Thanks to the Agencia EFE team, because with them, I learned how to be a journalist. And to my Doctors Without Borders family, because with them, I learned how to be a person.

Thanks to all those who have helped improve these pages. To Rebeca, who inspired my first—unpublished—book, and who inspires my way of telling stories. To Garmor, my eternal nemesis, a worker in whom I see myself reflected. To Igor G. Barbero, for allowing himself to be fooled so many times. To Maribel Izcue, for reading my work over and over and over, and for being so generous. To Judith—if we talk about literature, we agree. To Joan Pau, author of a secret trilogy.

Thanks to Xavier Aldekoa for his passion and friendship, for writing *Africa Ocean*, and for reading the African sections of this book. To Mikel Ayestaran: OK. Thanks to Andrés Mourenza, Alberto Arce, and Nicolás Castellano, journalists I admire. And to Quim Zudaire, the web man.

Thanks to Juan Carlos Tomasi, one of the best photographers I know. A genius.

Thanks to Carlos Francisco, the mellow cowboy.

Thanks to José Antonio Bastos, who taught me what little I know about the world of humanitarian aid. To Muhammad Mahmoud Ibrahim, Arabic teacher at the Instituto AlQantara.

Acknowledgments

Thanks to Carolina Nanclares (next destination?), Maribel Garcia, Samir, Francesca, Manoj, Dimitri, Alfonso, Samuel Makuach, Gemma Pinyol, Mónica G. Prieto, Xavi Casero, Albert Viñas, Pedro Domínguez (a great reader), Amaia Esparza, Mar Padilla, Núria Miranda, Paula Farias, Lali Cambra, Silvia Fernández, Javier Sancho, Edu Ponces, Guillermo Algar, Raquel González, Reyes Varella, Carmen Vicente, Verónica Fara, Olimpia de la Rosa, Teresa Sancristóval, Mónica Pérez, Susana López, Pablo Marco, Alberto Cristina, Juanma Rodilla, Julia Kourafa, Marc Bosch, Shinjiro, María, Luis, and Obayed.

The European Union is strongly criticized in this book. Thanks to the European Parliament for sharing its views.

Thanks to the journalism students who keep my faith in the future alive, and who always ask me where I'm going next. Thanks to Santiago Tejedor for his patience, and the great Alfonso Alegre for his poetry.

And thanks to my friends in my neighborhood and in India, who had little to do with this book, but who will help me to write the next one.